Little Red Riding Hood Uncloaked

Little Red Riding Hood Uncloaked

SEX, MORALITY, AND THE EVOLUTION OF A FAIRY TALE

Catherine Orenstein

BASIC BOOKS

A MEMBER OF THE PERSEUS BOOKS GROUP

Published by Basic Books,

A Member of the Perseus Books Group

Designed by Jennifer Dossin

Library of Congress Cataloging-in-Publication Data

Orenstein, Catherine, 1968–

Little Red Riding Hood uncloaked : ten moral tales from the forest / Catherine Orenstein.

   p. cm.

Includes bibliographical references and index.

ISBN 0-465-04125-6

1. Little Red Riding Hood (Tale)   I. Title.

GR75.L56 O74 2002

398.2'0943'02—dc21   2002004240

02 03 04 / 10 9 8 7 6 5 4 3 2

To my mother and father,
with love and respect

Little Red Riding Hood was my first Love. I felt that if I could have married Little Red Riding Hood, I should have known perfect bliss.

—CHARLES DICKENS

CONTENTS

List of Illustrations   XI

Introduction: Cloaking the Heroine   I

I   *Little Red Riding Hood*: To Be Chaste—or Chased?   17

II   *Little Red Cap*: To Walk the Straight Path   39

III   *The Grandmother's Tale*: To Come of Age   63

IV   *Stubbe Peeter, Werewolf*: A True Story   85

V   *Red Hot Riding Hood*: A Babe in the Woods   107

VI   *The Waiting Wolf*: In the Belly of the Beast   131

VII   *The Company of Wolves*: She-Wolf or Bitch?   155

VIII   *Red Riding Hood Redux*: The Cross-Dressing Wolf   177

IX   *The Punishment of Red Riding Hood*:
Fairy-Tale Fetish   205

X   *Freeway*: A Ride in the Hood   219

Epilogue: Under the Cloak   239

Notes   247

Bibliography   263

Sources   271

Acknowledgments   275

Index   279

LIST OF ILLUSTRATIONS

ii   Max Factor "Riding Hood Red" lipstick ad, *Vogue* magazine 1953.

1   Estella Warren as Red Riding Hood in Chanel No. 5's 1998 television commercial.

17   Red Riding Hood and Wolf, engraved by Gustave Doré, 1862.

23   Blushing heroine on the cover of Bruno Bettelheim's *The Uses of Enchantment*, 1976.

26   Perrault's *Le Petit Chaperon Rouge*, 1697.

27   Mother Goose, from Perrault's manuscript, 1695.

39   In Walter Crane's color print the heroine meets a wolf in sheepskin, 1862.

47   Walter Crane's hunter rescues the heroine from her folly, 1862.

52   Lydia L. Very's "toy book" cut in the shape of a standing Red Riding Hood, 1863.

57   The heroine gets a red cap from granny on the frontispiece of the Grimm's 1847 collection, *Kinder und Hausmärchen*.

58   Francis Wheatley's "A Woodman Returning Home, Evening," 1795.

63 Wood cut of an old woman walking, from *Divers Proverbs* by Nathan Bailey, 1721.

85 Wolf or werewolf attacking men, from Johannes Geiler von Kaiserberg's *Die Emeis*, 1516.

92 The crimes, trial and torture of the werewolf Stubbe Peeter, from an original 1590 pamphlet.

99 Werewolf attacking a girl, 18th century engraving.

104 Wolf disemboweling granny, from *Tales of Terror,* 1808.

107 "On my way to grandma's in my little red Hertz," ad from *The New Yorker* 1962.

115 Tex Avery's *Red Hot Riding Hood* – an animated stripper, 1943.

118 Tex Avery's tuxedoed wolf woos Miss *Riding Hood* at the Sunset Strip, 1943.

120 "The Girl and the Wolf," by James Thurber, 1939.

121 Identical Prince Charmings, from Hudson Talbott's book adaptation of the musical *Into the Woods*, 1988.

124–125 Max Factor's "Riding Hood Red" lipstick ad from *Vogue* magazine, 1953.

131 The heroine and her grandmother best the wolf, illustration by Trevor Skempton for "Little Red Riding Hood" by the Merseyside Women's Liberation Movement, 1972.

155 "Daughter," sculpted by Kiki Smith, 1999.

165 Heroine in a wolf fur coat, illustrated by Quentin Blake in *Roald Dahl's Revolting Rhymes*, 1982.

165 Heroine in wolf fur stole and hat, from Hudson Talbott's book adaptation of the musical *Into The Woods*, 1988.

169 Actress Kim Cattrall plays Red Riding Hood *and* the wolf in Pepsi One's television ad, 2001.

177 "Every food tastes supreme with Heinz salad cream" ad appearing in Britain's *Empire* magazine, 2001.

188 Lon Chaney, Jr. hunches over his swooning "date" in *The Wolf Man*, 1941.

191 A leather-clad motorcyclist fingers Red's dress, in an ad for eLuxury.com photographed by Ellen von Unwerth, 2000.

195 The "expecting" wolf, drawing by Barbara Swann from Anne Sexton's *Transformations*, 1971.

195 Inside the wolf's belly, illustration by Beni Montresor, 1989.

205 "The Punishment of Red Riding Hood," cover of porn video, 1996.

217 "Little Red Riding Crop," postcard by Carlos Aponte.

219 Reese Witherspoon and Bokeem Woodbine star in the urban fairy tale *Freeway*, 1996.

234 Our heroine (Reese Witherspoon) holds her attacker (Kiefer Sutherland) at gunpoint in *Freeway*, 1996.

239 Three-in-one Red Riding Hood doll, photographed by Adriana Miranda.

Introduction:
Cloaking the Heroine

A GIRL, A WOLF, a meeting in the woods. Who doesn't know the story of Little Red Riding Hood? She is the age-old star of bedtime drama, a symbol of childhood innocence. She is every Girl Next Door, every Damsel in Distress. She debuted in Walt Disney's first animated cartoon in 1922, six years before Mickey Mouse. She was Charles Dickens's first love. "I felt that if I could have married Little Red Riding Hood," he once declared, "I should have known perfect bliss." "Little Red Riding Hood" is told on every continent, in every major language. Barnes and Noble sells more than one hundred different editions, including one diagrammed in American Sign Language. It is one of the first stories that many adults ever heard, and odds are it is the first or among the first they read to their own children. But most people don't know the tale as well as they think.

Once upon a time, hundreds of years ago, "Little Red Riding Hood" was a bawdy morality tale for adults, quite different from the story we know today. Over the centuries it has undergone a series of changes and disguises. New stories have been made out of the old, and its original meanings are now buried. Only recently has it become a children's tale. Today "Little Red Riding

Hood" is rife with symbols and glaring peculiarities left over from its colorful past lives, but most of us overlook them. Parents and children alike think the story simple. We pass it down from one generation to the next, unaware of its history and its power.

Over the years, scholars have piled an entire cosmos of meanings on this small girl's shoulders. Some call her tale a seasonal myth, an allegory of the sun swallowed by night, or the personification of Good triumphing over Evil. Her basket of wine and cakes, it's said, represents Christian Communion; her red cape stands for menstrual blood. Some see the tale in Freudian terms as the Ego overcome by the Id; others see it as symbolic of the relationship between Man and Woman. And inevitably the tale has been a vehicle for imparting sexual ethics in keeping with the social fabric of the times. Tellers have consciously and subconsciously manipulated the plot to portray a seduction by a temptress, the rape of a virgin or the passage of a young girl into womanhood. From a structural perspective, the plot is powerfully simple. Opposites collide—good and evil, beast and human, male and female. How the heroine negotiates this clash determines her fate. Thus over time "Little Red Riding Hood" has become the quintessential moral primer.

But what morals does the story teach? Many, it turns out—and not always the ones we remember. The heroine encounters a wolf (or a werewolf, depending on the version you're reading) who hides himself in Grandmother's bed. In the earliest written version of the tale, the girl strips off her clothes, joins the beast under the covers—and dies. A rhyming moral at the end warns young women to watch out, because a man can be a "wolf," popularizing the use of that term, still common today, to mean a seducer. In later versions of the story a hunter or woodsman comes to the rescue, imparting the revised moral that a good man—a father, or perhaps a husband—can save a woman from her folly. With his knife, or sometimes scissors, he cuts her free, lifting her out from the belly of the beast as if from a bad dream and giving her a second chance to walk the straight path through life. In modern versions of the story, which echo themes of the earliest known oral folktale, the girl escapes on her own, teaching that women can save themselves. She carries her own pair of scissors, or tricks the wolf with a clever ruse, or sometimes fights. The plucky red-leather-jacketed heroine of the 1996 movie *Freeway*, based on the "Red Riding Hood" plot, wrestles her wolf-like stalker to the floor and kills him. Alternatively, in some modern revisions of the tale Red kills the hunter-woodsman or is killed by him. (The tellers are evidently less bothered by the lascivious wolf than by the patronizing savior and the high-maintenance heroine, respectively.)

As for the story's main characters, far from simple, their roles and meanings subtly shift over time, and even dramatically flip-flop. Traditionally, the wolf represents Evil: "That is why we need prisons and policemen," says a version of the tale published in New York in 1916. Peasants who told the story in France's Old Regime called it a *bzou*, a sort of demon or were-wolf. British illustrator Walter Crane drew the wolf in sheepskin—a biblical reference to the Devil. But surprisingly often it is Red who is in the moral wrong. The tale as told at Versailles suggests that an unchaste woman is as good as dead. In Victorian versions of the tale, the girl's mother forbids her to stray from the path, and later the tearfully contrite heroine promises that she will never again be disobedient. Some even blame Little Red Riding Hood for perpetuating the fear of wolves that has led to their persecution and near extinction in the continental United States. "Get your hands off of that endangered species!" yells the woodsman to Red Riding Hood in a version of the tale circulating on the Internet.

The storybook heroine, drawn with rosy cheeks and dimpled kneecaps, embodies childish innocence and naïveté. Her lesson, the age-old parental adage: Don't talk to strangers. But in popular culture sweet Little Red Riding Hood has grown up and become an ode to Lust. In the wartime cartoons of Tex Avery, she performs a lurid nightclub striptease for a very excited wolf. On Madison Avenue she is a femme fatale, with a knowing Mona Lisa smile. And about those strangers? Ripe young "riding hood red" lipstick will "bring the wolves out," Max Factor promises in a double-page, poster-sized ad appearing in *Vogue* magazine in 1953.

Sometimes our heroine is a helpless prude in dire need of a man. But today she is also the namesake of a lesbian dominatrix porn star—who cracks her whip and obviates the centuries-old need for either seducer or savior. Sometimes our wolf is just a man being a man, as Sam the Sham and the Pharaohs sang it circa 1966—*Hey there Little Red Riding Hood, you sure are lookin' good! You're everything a Big Bad Wolf could want! Owoooo!* Or, sometimes the wolf is just a man being a woman—as cartoons of the cross-dressing villain point out.

Little Red Riding Hood's perennial popularity is due in part to her ability to adapt to the times. Every year, reincarnations of the story pop up in print, on television, on billboards and advertisements, in children's games and adult jokes. In the 1997 movie *The Ice Storm,* young Wendy Hood (Christina Ricci) traipses through the woods in a red cloak on her way to raid the neighbor's liquor cabinet and lingerie drawers and to fondle the boy next door. Three years later in *Big Momma's House,* an FBI agent (Martin Lawrence) dresses up in Granny's nightgown and climbs into Granny's bed to get the girl. And a 2001 Pepsi One television commercial cast sexy celeb Kim Cattrall in a little red dress and cape searching for the perfect man and the perfect soft drink.

Yet for all Little Red Riding Hood's ubiquity, most people today remain remarkably, and sometimes even comically, oblivious to the tale's origins and underlying meanings. In 1990 two California school districts banned the story, because of an illustration showing Red's basket with a bottle of wine as well as fresh bread and butter. The story line of Red disrobing and climbing into bed with the wolf passed muster. But the *wine,* they said, might be seen as condoning the use of alcohol.

The lessons that children learn from fairy tales are important to adults. Yet the lessons adults themselves learned from "Little Red Riding Hood," a tale that to many is symbolic of childhood itself, remain somewhat of a mystery.

THIS BOOK is about a fairy tale: the story behind the story, or more accurately, the ideas behind the story. What makes Little Red Riding Hood so interesting to folklorists, feminists, psychoanalysts, poets, advertisers, and for that matter, me? The answer, and the premise of this book, is that beneath her simple appearance—beneath her cloak—Little Red Riding Hood embodies complex and fundamental human concerns. Her tale speaks to enduring themes of family, morality, growing up, growing old, of lighting out into the world, and of the relationship between the sexes. It brings together archetypal opposites, through which it explores the boundaries of culture, class, and, especially, what it means to be a man or a woman. The girl and the wolf inhabit a place, call it the forest or call it the human psyche, where the spectrum of human sagas converge and where their social and cultural meanings play out.

Today we approach fairy tales with a false sense of their simplicity. Unlike myth or legend, which concern the sacred, the miraculous and the heroic, fairy tales are devoted to the mundane: the drama of domestic life, of children and courtship and coming of age. They are not "true"; indeed, to "tell a tale" also means to lie. Thus they seem inconsequential. We believe we outgrow them. Nonetheless, fairy tales provide a unique window into our most central concerns, our sense of social and cultural identity, who we think we are (or should be)—and how we change.

What exactly is a fairy tale? Technically, the term is no older than the late seventeenth century, when the nobility of the French Court and the ladies of the Parisian literary salons told the first *contes de fées*, and when Charles Perrault published his now famous collection of tales ascribed to *ma mere l'Oye*—"my Mother Goose." But the sources of our most popular fairy tales go back much farther. Peasants in Europe's Old Regime told tales around the fire at nighttime gatherings and to pass time while spinning or working in the fields. Perrault and his contemporaries borrowed from them, as well as from literary sources:

classical mythology, Boccaccio, the "Venetian babbler" Giovanni Francesco Straparola, and the Neapolitan fabulist Giambattista Basile. Straparola's *Piacevoli notti* (Pleasant Nights) of 1550 and Basile's posthumously published collection of fifty tales, *Lo cunto de li cunti* (The Tale of Tales), penned between 1634 and 1636, include prototypes of many of our best-loved classics (though not "Little Red Riding Hood"). Other sources are more elusive; the story patterns that we find in fairy tales go so far back that it is hard to tell where they begin, or indeed if they have a beginning at all.

In folklorists' terms, the fairy tale is simply a genre of stories—distinct from myth, legend, or nursery rhyme—that share certain common elements. Fairy tales are told as flights of fancy. They occur outside of history, in an unquantifiably distant past: "Once upon a time." They do not always have fairies, but as a rule there is magic: enchantments, talking animals, impossible beasts. Objects fly; rivers speak; men live as beasts, and beasts are often, secretly, women. Folklorists who stress the oral roots of fairy tales classify them as a subset of the folktale genre and identify them according to plot: In the Aarne-Thompson Tale Type Index, a classic folklore reference book, they are the "Tales of Magic," numbered 300–749.

But in folklore as in life, definitions are sometimes blurry. Tales slip in and out of genre. Terms are used differently in popular practice than in theory. By "fairy tale" most people today mean those tales that come down to us through the best-known children's authors Hans Christian Andersen, whose popular fairy tales are really modern literary creations, and the German brothers Wilhelm and Jacob Grimm. The Grimms' collection of

Children's and Household Tales, first published in 1812, has become one of the most popular and widest-circulating books of all time. In Germany, it is second only to the Bible.

Far more important than how we define the fairy tale, however, is how the fairy tale defines *us.* Beneath the nursery veneer, or perhaps because of it, fairy tales are among our most powerful socializing narratives. They contain enduring rules for understanding who we are and how we should behave. In the pages of fairy tales, as scholars point out, we find ourselves as princes and princesses, our parents as kings and queens (or ogres and wicked stepmothers), and our siblings as villainous rivals who are punished in the end, to our great delight. There are giants (as grown-ups seem to children) and dwarfs (as children may see themselves in relation to adults). The goals—kingdoms for boys, marriage for girls, at least in the popular canon—put social expectations in blunter terms than we may ever hear again. The stock ending—"happily ever after"—makes short shrift of lingering doubt. Fairy tales are the first words read to us before we know the meaning of words, and the first models of society we encounter before we ever leave home. They teach us how to read and write; they teach us Right from Wrong. Under the guise of make-believe, they prepare us to join the real world and provide us with lessons that last a lifetime.

Think you haven't read a fairy tale lately? Look around. Fairy tales are in the pages of *People* magazine, profiling Hollywood princesses; on the labels of beauty products that promise "snow white skin"; in our movies. The subconscious knew that Julia Roberts in *Pretty Woman* was rags-to-riches Cinderella all over again, even before one of the characters gave it away. And on television: In an episode of the hit HBO drama "Sex and the City," which repeatedly recycles fairy-tale themes, thirty-something, man-hunting sex columnist Carrie (Sarah Jessica Parker) runs to catch a midnight boat, losing her glittering Jimmy Choo designer slipper along the way. (Fashions come and fashions go, but the sexual symbolism of costly, uncomfortable shoes is apparently forever.)

Fairy tales take wing in our habits of speech, revealing our dreams for a "fairy-tale wedding," our disappointments when "life is no fairy tale," and our very way of thinking. They shape our ideas about love and sex—right down to our understanding of conception itself, which science books often describe as if it were a fairy-tale romance, with Sperm Charming charging up the perilous oviduct, beating out other suitors to awaken the Sleeping Egg with his magic kiss. (This popular fertility narrative continues to dominate textbooks, despite new research that shows it to be, well, just a fairy tale. Sperm, it turns out, are actually quite weak, while the egg exerts a powerful "tethering" force.) From cold creams to textbooks, from our first crush to our first born, fairy tales permeate reality and resonate across generations. They determine how we will perceive our mates, our children and ourselves—all years in advance. In the journey through the fairy-tale forest, princes and princesses (and boys and girls) learn the social and psychological lessons that must be absorbed to reach adulthood. We think we outgrow them. In fact, we internalize them.

The idea that fairy tales contain important messages is of course not a surprise. Nearly thirty years have passed since the psychoanalyst Bruno Bettelheim brought the deep psychological power of fairy tales into popular focus and almost single-handedly catapulted the genre into modern vogue. According to the late doctor, fairy tales provided a safe place for children to tackle their inner demons (not to mention their oral aggression and penis envy). Bettelheim's 1976 bestseller *The Uses of Enchantment* became a classic, providing a revelation of the deeper meanings in these seemingly simple tales. Years later, Bettelheim's professional reputation would come under fire, but by then his work had already inspired a generation of readers. Even the surprisingly bloodthirsty brothers Grimm, who always loved a good decapitation, were forgiven their, well, *grimness*.

Yet while Bettelheim mined fairy tales for their timeless and universal truths, one important thing that he missed—and, indeed, that most scholars failed to acknowledge until recently—is that fairy tales *change*. In fact, fairy tales have remarkable mercurial properties. They adapt to the weather, to local fashions, and to the mindset of each new teller and audience. They record regional cuisines and local hairstyles—and, of course, more important things. They are not just psychological blueprints; they are also what the Princeton historian Robert Darnton calls "historical documents." That is, they catalog not only broad elements of human experience but also the particular details of each day and age. They express our collective truths, even as these truths change beneath our noses. And part of their magic lies in the fact that as they do they provide not only a glimpse into our present concerns but also a record of our past.

Folklore is collective, oral and ephemeral. It is a dance between tellers and listeners that includes jokes, tall tales, gossip at the kitchen table, and fairy tales as they were once told around the fire or in the fields—always changing and constantly adapting to new cultural landscapes. Yet as pen meets paper, characters freeze in time and space, like the chef caught in the act of slapping the kitchen boy in Sleeping Beauty's palace. There he stands, arm raised, mouth open in reproach, and a century-old grease stain on his apron. Text is forever locked in context. Storybook heroes and heroines acquire not only a period wardrobe but also a date, author, presumed audience and worldview. Whether in the homespun cloak of an old yarn, or powdered and perfumed for the French Court; whether bound and corseted in the fashion of Victorian Europe, or dolled up by twentieth-century drag queens, fairytale heroes and heroines record the mentality of their day—and none more impressively than Little Red Riding Hood. Of durable identity, unmistakable even when she changes nationality, age, appearance, name and (yes) even clothing, Little Red Riding Hood is instantly remembered and easily recognizable amongst thousands of tales and tens of thousands of characters. And over the years she has been cloaked, according to social and ethical fashion, in countless meanings and morals, warnings and winks.

THIS BOOK is an exploration of society's "vested" interest in Little Red Riding Hood—in the messages she wears, and those she covers up. In particular it is an exploration of how her tale speaks to enduring themes about men and women, of gender roles and how they change. Its approach is narrow, with only ten featured texts (or costumes, so to speak), chosen mainly from Europe and America either because of their historical importance, their great popularity or their clear and interesting lessons. The selections are obviously personal, inevitably some-what arbitrary, but nonetheless the result of careful and difficult decisions. It is with great regret, for example, that I leave out the very entertaining but less pertinent "Ladle Rat Rotten Hut," written in 1940 by the French teacher H. L. Chace, who substi-tuted each word with a near homonym so as to illustrate the importance of intonation in learning a foreign language. "Wants pawn term," it begins, "dare worsted ladle gull hoe lift wetter murder inner ladle cordage, honor itch offer lodge, dock, florist. . . . " Likewise it's a pity to pass on the quirky mathematic ren-dering of the tale that begins with the fraction "Once upon a time $(1/T)$. . . " and ends, "If you want to keep your expressions con-vergent, never allow them a single degree of freedom." Not to mention the legalese version in which the characters sue each other for breaking and entering, entrapment and wrongful death and the State advises the Occupational Safety and Health Administration that the Woodsman's ax is substandard and unsafe.

Red Riding Hood will never, of course, be fully uncloaked. The past is inevitably colored and shaped by the events and issues at the heart of our own historical moment and of our own personal experience. This book is a twenty-first-century Ameri-can woman's effort to unravel an old yarn, requiring translation not only of language, but of era and culture—and every act of unraveling also, inevitably, involves casting a new spin. What's more, the authors who first put the fairy tale to print were them-selves interpreters, spinning the yarn as they saw fit. Literate men who culled from wives' tales and from each other, the early tale-tellers translated stories from one class and age into another, transforming ideas and meaning and perhaps even fashion, too. Was Cinderella's slipper really made of "glass" *(verre)* or did someone mistake an older French word for "fur" *(vair),* as the *Encyclopedia Britannica* suggests? The layers are generations thick, and it is an irony of interpretation that each attempt to sift through them inherently engenders more opportunities for misunderstanding. That is, even my own reader must peer over my shoulder and through my worldview. In the spirit of at least minimizing this last double vision, I have preceded each of my chapters with the texts of the stories to which they refer, so that my reader can review the evidence—and possibly disagree with me.

Little Red Riding Hood does not, of course, represent every woman or even an average woman, if such a woman could ever be said to exist. Nor does her tale encapsulate the thinking of a society, be it seventeenth-century France or twenty-first-century America. It is not the whole truth. But it provides a way in. The endeavor of this book is to draw Little Red Riding Hood forth from her literary crypt, to unwrap the protective vellum that mummifies her in the rare book section of the library, and simultaneously to unravel the preconceptions that surround her in our minds: To revisit the fairy-tale canon with a more secular eye—and to explore some of her multitude of reincarnations, not in search of universal truths, but on the contrary, as evidence of how human truths change.

Little Red Riding Hood: To Be Chaste—or Chased?

Little Red Riding Hood
(Le petit chaperon rouge)

By Charles Perrault

Once upon a time there was a little village girl, the prettiest anyone ever saw. Her mother was crazy about her, and her grandmother even more. This good woman made her a small red hood which looked so fine on her that wherever she went she was called Little Red Riding Hood.

One day her mother baked some cakes and said to her: "Go see how your grandmother is doing, for I have heard that she is sick. Take her these cakes and this small pot of butter." Little Red Riding Hood went off at once to visit her grandmother, who lived in another village. Passing through the woods she met old neighbor wolf, who wanted very much to eat her but did not dare because of some woodcutters who were in the forest. He asked her where she was going. The poor child, who did not know that it is dangerous to stop and listen to a

Source: From *Histoires ou contes du temps passé* (Tales of times past with morals), also called *Contes de Ma Mere L'Oye* (Mother Goose tales), published by Claude Barbin, 1697. Rhyming moral translated by S. R. Littlewood, for *Perrault's Fairy Tales* (London: Herbert & Daniel, 1912).

wolf, said: "I am going to see my grandmother, and am bringing some cakes with a small pot of butter which my mother has sent her."

"Does she live far away?" asked the wolf.

"Oh, yes!" said Little Red Riding Hood. "Past the mill which you can see right over there. Hers is the first house in the village."

"Well, well," said the wolf. "I want go and see her, too. I'll take this path here, and you take that path there, and we'll see who'll get there first."

The wolf ran as fast as he could on the shorter path, and the little girl took the longer path, enjoying herself gathering nuts, running after butterflies, and making bouquets of small flowers. Before long the wolf arrived at the grandmother's house. He knocked: toc, toc.

"Who's there?"

"It's your granddaughter, Little Red Riding Hood," said the wolf, disguising his voice. "I brought you some cakes and a little pot of butter that my mother has sent you."

The good grandmother, who was in her bed because she was not feeling well, called out: "Pull the bobbin, and the latch will open."

The wolf pulled the bobbin, and the door opened. He pounced upon the good woman and devoured her in nothing flat, for he had not eaten in more than three days. After that he closed the door and lay down in the grandmother's bed to wait for Little Red Riding Hood, who after awhile knocked at the door. Toc, toc.

"Who's there?"

The gruff voice of the wolf scared Little Red Riding Hood at first, but, believing that her grandmother had a cold, she said: "It's your granddaughter, Little Red Riding Hood. I've brought you some cakes and a little pot of butter that my mother has sent you."

The wolf softened his voice and cried out to her: "Pull the bobbin, and the latch will open."

Little Red Riding Hood pulled the bobbin, and the door opened.

Upon seeing her enter, the wolf hid himself under the bedcovers and said to her: "Put the cakes and the pot of butter on the bin and climb into bed with me."

Little Red Riding Hood undressed and climbed into bed, where she was quite astonished to see the way the grandmother looked undressed. She said to her: "Why, Grandmother, what big arms you have!"

"The better to hug you with, my child."

"Grandmother, what big legs you have!"

"The better to run with, my child."

"Grandmother, what big ears you have!"

"The better to hear you with, my child."

"Grandmother, what big eyes you have!"

"The better to see you with, my child."

"Grandmother, what big teeth you have!"

"The better to eat you!"

And with that, the wicked wolf threw himself upon Little Red Riding Hood and ate her up.

MORAL:

Little girls, this seems to say,
Never stop upon your way,
Never trust a stranger-friend;
No one knows how it will end.
As you're pretty so be wise;
Wolves may lurk in every guise.
Handsome they may be, and kind,
Gay, or charming—nevermind!
Now, as then, 'tis simple truth—
Sweetest tongue has sharpest tooth!

—TRANSLATED BY CATHERINE ORENSTEIN

Wolf: a man given to seducing women

—Oxford English Dictionary

O NE OF THE MOST FAMOUS and frequently reproduced illustrations in all children's literature is an old wood engraving that shows a girl in bed with a wolf. Side by side, against a backdrop of voluptuous pillows and drapery, they make an interesting pair. The wolf, in a white bonnet, is dark and menacing and leans forward slightly. The girl, in a short-sleeved nightgown and cap, sits stiffly, slightly recoiling. The bed fills the picture frame, and the couple seems caught in an intimate cliché. It's as if we're peering through the keyhole into an old Parisian boudoir. The girl's loosened hair tumbles over her shoulders; she clutches the sheets to her breast. Saucer-eyed, she stares at the enormous snout emerging from the bedcovers a whisker away.

Most readers today never stop to ponder this image, or countless others like it. "Little Red Riding Hood" is so well known as a nursery tale that it seems innocent and unremarkable. This is probably why, on the cover of his 1976 bestseller *The Uses of Enchantment*, the Freudian analyst Bruno Bettelheim felt it necessary to touch up the otherwise black-and-white illustration with a telltale blush on the girl's cheek—

Bettlcheim's blushing covergirl

The better to suggest your subliminal desires, my Dear!

Rendered by the famous Strasbourg illustrator Gustave Doré in 1862, the original image was one of several he intended to accompany the fairy tale —but not the prude German fairy tale for children that appears in modern storybooks. Instead, Doré chose for his subject matter the first published version of the tale from France, over a century older and considerably racier. What Doré captured, and Bettelheim later enhanced, is the fairy tale's buried meaning as a sexual parable.

Charles Perrault first penned "Le petit chaperon rouge" in 1697 for the luxurious, indulgent French Court of the Sun King. Louis XIV had created an elaborate playpen for the aristocracy at his rural estates outside of Paris—a sort of Vegas at Versailles.

Wine, gaming and sexual intrigue distracted the nobles from their ennui and kept them from scheming against the monarchy. Ballets, billiards and boating excursions filled the days. Even as much of France was starving, Versailles was notorious for its excesses. The palace was in a state of perpetual expansion. Charles Lebrun frescoed the ceilings; the *Mona Lisa* hung on the wall. A Saturday evening banquet, served at the stroke of midnight, required no fewer than 498 servants. Courtiers took hours to dress in yards of fabric. Codpieces enhanced the nobleman's assets; tight-laced bodices exaggerated the female form; bosoms leaped to meet the eye. And sexual indiscretions were notoriously indulged.

It was the age of royal courtesans, high society prostitutes trained in the arts of seduction. Those who made it to the King's bed might earn the title *maîtresse-en-titre*—"official mistress." This, however, hardly guaranteed the King's fidelity. In 1675 his royal lechery grew so indiscreet that his current public mistress appealed to the Queen who replaced the Court's maids-of-honor with twelve elderly matrons. Monsieur Le Duc d'Orleans, the King's bisexual brother, was so promiscuous that, according to one author, every Roman Catholic royal family of Europe can claim him among its ancestors. Even the architecture of Versailles, which afforded wives separate apartments from their husbands, facilitated sexual indiscretions. Wives made husbands rich through their extramarital affairs—the obliging cuckold might get an appointment at Court in exchange for looking the other way. The Princess de Soubise, a courtier and brief favorite of the King, wore emerald earrings to signify her husband's absence and thus her availability for a royal rendezvous.

And Marie de Rabutin-Chantal, the Marquise de Sévigné, a darling of the Court and one of the great documentarians of courtly gossip, wrote dozens of pages to her daughter every day in which she described the mating rituals of the courtiers.

None of this was scandalous, or at least never more scandalous than amusing. Sévigné laughed, for example, at news of her son's conquests, and of his occasional bouts of impotence. "A favorable occasion had presented itself, and yet . . . dare I say it?" she joked to her daughter in a letter on April 8, 1671. "I told him I was delighted that he had been punished for his sins at the precise point of origin!"

Nonetheless, for a certain portion of the players at Versailles, such affairs could be dangerous—or even, as in the tale by Charles Perrault, fatal. Perrault's first published version of "Little Red Riding Hood" was accompanied by an engraving far more sexually suggestive than that which brought a blush to Bettelheim's cover girl. Copied after a watercolor vignette Perrault had provided with his manuscript two years earlier in 1695, it shows the wolf, without disguise, under the sheets with a girl. He lies on top of her, paws on either side. Red Riding Hood, considerably older than in Doré's portrait, reclines against a pillow and touches a hand to his snout. According to Perrault's plot, she has just undressed and slipped into bed with the wolf.

"What big arms you have," she says.

"The better to hug you with, my child," replies the wolf.

A moment later the tale comes to an untimely end when the beast bares his fangs and devours her. There is neither salvation nor redemption, as in later versions of the story that children know today.

Any courtier who read this tale or saw the accompanying image would have readily understood its meaning. In the common slang of the day, even in the scholarly works of Charles Perrault, when a girl lost her virginity it was said that *elle avoit vû le loup*—"she'd seen the wolf."

Perrault's *Le Petit Chaperon Rouge*, 1697

S UCH A HISTORY FOR "Little Red Riding Hood" seems shocking today, in an age when fairy tales are synonymous with children's literature. To see a copy of the book in which her famous adventure first appeared would do little to alter this belief.

Charles Perrault's *Tales of Times Past with Morals* is no larger than one's hand. Bound by hand, with delicate pages and gilded edges, it contains eight of the most enduring tales of all time: "Cinderella," "Sleeping Beauty," "Tom Thumb," "Ricky of the Tuft," "Puss 'n Boots," "The Fairies," "Bluebeard"—and the shortest among them, "Little Red Riding Hood." The frontispiece of the collection bears the words "Tales of My Mother Goose." Beneath them is an illustration of an old crone sitting before a fire, her finger raised to hold a strand of yarn, entertaining a gaggle of children.

Mother Goose, as she appeared in Perrault's 1695 manuscript.

This image and these tales have since become classics of the nursery and even the foundation of children's literature. The Mother Goose frontispiece has been reproduced or imitated in countless storybooks, her fame forever established by Charles Perrault. But contrary to appearances and modern presumptions, Perrault's collection was neither from nor for the nursery. These "children's classics" were in fact carefully crafted allegories. Between their plots, they captured the concerns of the Court and the social and sexual politics of the seventeenth-century French upper class.

As a genre, the French fairy tale, or *conte de fées,* flourished for a brief few decades at the end of the seventeenth century, when the tales were told amongst adults—at least, as the term *adult* was then understood. In the day of the Sun King it was not unheard of for a boy to be crowned at the age of thirteen, while "women" of twelve years of age were marriageable, if indeed they were not already married off. The first recorded reference to a fairy tale seems to occur in a letter Madame de Sévigné wrote to her daughter in 1677 describing one of "the stories they amuse the ladies with at Versailles." It concerned "a Green Island, where a princess was brought up, as bright as the day! The Fairies were her companions and the Prince of Pleasure was her lover, and they both came to the King's court one day in a ball of glass." Before long the fad caught on, and to "simmer," or *mitonner,* each other with tales became all the rage. By the end of the century the fashion had become almost a craze, so popular that people attended festivities at Court dressed up as their favorite fairy-tale characters.

Despite the cooking term *mitonner,* which lent them a fashionably folksy air, these tales were the elaborate and highly sophisticated creations of the most educated members of society. The genre had not so much trickled up from the nursery or from the lower classes as it had migrated to Court from the ladies' salons— the elegant drawing-room gatherings that were the feminine heart of seventeenth-century Parisian intellectual life. Madame de Rambouillet had launched the first salon early in the century, and her series of halls and corridors leading finally to her famous *chambre bleu,* a daring departure in color, became famous. By the second half of the century, the salon had become a vibrant and powerful center of learned discourse, under the auspices of such erudite hostesses as Marie-Catherine D'Aulnoy, Marie-Madeleine Pioche de la Vergne (known as the Comtesse de La Fayette), Madeleine de Scudéry and Sévigné herself. In contrast to the stiff formality of Versailles, these women entertained in a fabulously informal style, receiving their guests in bed and allowing their favorites access to *les ruelles,* the narrow corridors between bed and wall. They brought together men and women, bourgeois and aristocrat, with intellect the common denominator. Word games and artful verbal sparring prevailed. Wit and eloquence were highly prized, and a well-told tale was not only a means of entertainment but also a mark of distinction. Short fables and fairy tales, told and discussed in the span of an evening, became a vehicle for flattery, utopian musings, and on occasion sharp social criticism, frequently about marriage, love, education, and the roles of men and women.

Though the first published fairy tale is attributed to D'Aulnoy, who slipped "The Island of Happiness" discreetly into the pages of her 1690 novel, *History of Hippolite, Count of Douglas,* Charles

Perrault launched the craze that would establish the fairy tale as a literary genre. Perrault's *Tales of Times Past with Morals,* often called *Mother Goose Tales,* quickly became a best-seller by the standard of the day: Reprinted once in France and twice in Holland the same year that it was published, it inspired a fleet of copycat collections. A frequenter of the salons (his niece, Marie-Jean Lhéritier de Villandon, had inherited Scudéry's halls), Perrault wrote his tales in the fashionable "faux-naïve" style. In addition to the attribution to Mother Goose (a figure already understood to mean a storytelling crone), the collection contained a dedication issued by his teenaged son, Pierre D'armencourt, to the nineteen-year-old niece of the King, known as "Mademoiselle." Witty, short and lighthearted, these eight tales were obviously meant to entertain; but they also had a more serious purpose.

Perrault was a well-known intellectual who stood at the intersection between the worlds of art and politics: a distinguished administrator charged with promoting the monarch's absolute glory, but also an artist, essayist, member of the French Academy and frequenter of the sometimes rebellious salons. The seventh child of a middle-class lawyer, Perrault had joined the ranks of the expanding royal bureaucracy as Louis XIV marched his armies across the continent commissioning artists, poets and historians to sing his praise (and justify his military expenses). Under the wing of the King's powerful minister of finance, Jean Baptiste Colbert, Perrault rose to become administrator of the King's buildings and a talented royal sycophant whose duties included crafting flattering slogans for the royal family. (His suggestion for the personal motto of the King's baby son: *Et ipso terret in ortu*—"He terrifies even from birth.")

With Colbert's backing, Perrault entered the Academy—the old boys club that met in the Louvre, which had been established earlier in the century to debate the most important intellectual matters of the day in the official style. In 1672 Perrault became the Academy's president, and it was here, to the forty learned members—sometimes referred to as *les quarante*—that he presented his first tale, "The Patience of Griselda," in 1691. This parable of the rewards of female suffering and endurance, along with two other verse tales published in a popular journal (and later as a three-tale collection) and finally Perrault's *Mother Goose Tales,* were all clearly inspired by the salon vogue; but they were also part of a raging debate within the Academy, a culture war about the times, the Court, its men and its women—the so-called "Quarrel of the Ancients and the Moderns." Perrault himself had sparked the war with a controversial poem, "The Age of Louis the Great," which proclaimed civilization under the Sun King to have reached its zenith, a height superior even to the "golden age" of Augustus—heretofore the model of human accomplishment, imitated slavishly by almost all contemporary artists, architects and writers. Among other things, the Quarrel articulated contemporary concerns about gender.

Modern woman, it was argued by conservatives aligned with the "Ancients" of the French Academy, was destroying family life and social values. The debate on women was, of course, old hat: The questions—What is woman's purpose? Can she be educated?—had floated around for centuries. But they acquired new importance in the late seventeenth century when the Court provided women with unprecedented access to education. By the end of the century, literacy rates were higher among aristocratic women than men, and women had become producers of culture and arbiters of literary taste. Consider Sévigné, darling of both the Court and the salons, who learned to sing, dance and ride; took declamation lessons; studied Latin, Spanish, Italian; had access to an extensive library; and became one of the best-read aristocrats of her time. Her letters, filled with vivid descriptions of extravagant evenings, treacherous social scheming, and of course boudoir histories, helped launch a new literary genre—the epistolary novel that would bloom in the eighteenth century.

Salon life also provoked controversy. The salons fostered feminism, before the existence of that term. Some of the prominent bluestockings fought for legal reforms to give women the right to marry or remain single, to refuse to have children, and to look after their own affairs—and later in the century, their fairy tales, when eventually published, would express these struggles. The salon hostesses were also so powerful that the approval of certain among them was the unofficial prerequisite for election to the French Academy. But while they were centers of progress, the salons were also targets of derision and ridicule. Conservatives cast them as elegant brothels and decried the mixing of classes and sexes. The seventeenth-century French moralist Jean de la Bruyère compared an educated woman with a collector's special firearm, "which one shows to the curious, but which has no use at all, any more than a carousel horse." The playwright Molière mocked the salon hostesses' pretensions to culture in *Les précieuses ridicules* (The Ridiculous Women, 1659), but the term "précieuses," when used by the hostesses, implied a compliment. Others sought to restrict access to salon life by limiting girls' education. Literature, said the Abbé Fénélon, confessor to the King's second wife Madame de Maintenon and architect of the conservative curriculum for her girls school at Saint Cyr, would take a girl's attention away from domestic functions. These issues in particular occupied the Academy, and became part of Charles Perrault's personal and professional life, and ultimately part of his fairy tales.

As leader of the "Moderns," Perrault became a prolific defender of Court society. He penned volumes of cultural criticism, collected biographies of illustrious men, wrote comedies and poetry, and authored a four-volume, 1,160-page Modernist manifesto, *The Parallel of the Ancients and Modernes* (1688–1697). But today virtually all that is remembered of his work are the brief fairy tales he penned in the final years of his life. Though playful and ironic, these were also explicitly intended to illustrate courtly morals. Each ends with a rhyming verse that transforms the story into a lesson: morality through the lens of official culture. Collectively, the tales present a portrait of the duties and expectations governing the lives and relationships of the men and women of Versailles and of the central institution that united them: marriage. That portrait, far from romantic, is frank, and sometimes horrible.

A NYONE WHO HAS EVER wished for a "fairy-tale wedding" has surely never read Perrault, for the marriages of his fairy tales are about money, cruelty and deception. His husbands are murderous, his couples frequently meet on their wedding day, and his mothers-in-law sometimes try to eat the heroines. In "The Patience of Griselda," a poor young woman marries a king who distrusts her virtue. He subjects her to a series of Jobian trials that last for decades. After she gives birth to a daughter, he convinces her that the child has died and banishes her to poverty for fifteen years—during which time he announces his marriage to the daughter. The young bride of a wealthy widower in "Bluebeard" appears to have made a better match—until she discovers she has married a serial killer. One day he leaves her alone in the castle, with keys to all the rooms, including one which he forbids her to enter. She does, of course, and there she discovers the proverbial skeletons in his closet: the bloody remains of his former wives hanging neatly on the walls. In her panic, she drops the key, and a bloodstain that will not wash away later betrays her to Bluebeard, who condemns her to join his former wives in the bloody chamber. Only through the timely arrival of her brothers does she manage to escape. In "Donkey Skin," a princess flees her father's incestuous desires in the skin of an ass. And Sleeping Beauty is impregnated by a deceptive prince, who hides their relationship and their children from his family for four years until his father dies. When at last he brings Sleeping Beauty and their children home, his mother, an ogress whom the prince's father "had married strictly for her wealth," attempts to eat them *à la sausse robert*.

Perrault's audience would have readily recognized the setting of these tales. Sleeping Beauty passes through a hall of mirrors that is like the famous one at Court. Bluebeard woos his bride with picnics, hunting, dancing and banquets, all reminiscent of favorite court pastimes; the tapestries that decorate his palace might have adorned the walls at Versailles. Cinderella wears dresses that recall Madame de Sévigné's specific, detailed descriptions of the wardrobe of the King's official mistress, the

Marquise de Montespan. She rides a gilded "pumpkin" coach that bears a striking resemblance to that of Louis XIV as shown in contemporary paintings. Her stepsisters purchase beauty spots from the toniest dealers. Even the details of the plots—the weddings between strangers, the punishing parents, the sudden wealth or poverty—were familiar to all.

The seventeenth-century aristocratic marriage was the *mariage de raison,* an affair orchestrated by parents for social and economic advancement, often no more than a crass exchange of assets. The noble Grignon family, relatives of Sévigné, were heavily indebted when they went to the bargaining table. "Get, as I said, the most cash you can," Madame de Sévigné's nephew, Philippe-Emmanuel de Coulanges, counseled Madame de Grignon in a letter of June 28, 1694, "and console yourselves for a *mésalliance* . . . by the relief you will feel at no longer being harassed by creditors when you sojourn in your large, beautiful château." The Grignons traded their son to the daughter of a wealthy tax farmer for the sum of 400,000 francs. The young couple in question, not mentioned in the correspondence, did not meet until a week after the marriage contract was signed.

The importance of the mariage de raison can hardly be over-stated, and the institution was protected by a series of edicts that gave parents, or more accurately, fathers, the legal right to decide the lives and mates of their children. An edict of 1556 outlawed "clandestine" marriages, meaning secret unions between a con-senting couple without parental consent. Minority ages were raised from twenty to thirty years for males, and from seventeen to twenty-five years for females, and extended to include wid-ows in 1579. Finally the limits were abolished altogether in favor of total parental dominion. An ordinance of 1629 declared *all* off-spring, regardless of age, sex or marital status, to be minors. For those who disobeyed the patriarch, punishments were severe—disinheritance, banishment, or worse. Under seventeenth-century law a marriage without parental consent was considered a form of *rapt*—meaning seduction or abduction, which was punishable by death.

From this background comes Charles Perrault's tale of sexual suggestion and moral warning as well—the erotic paradox of his "Le petit chaperon rouge." Because virginity was a requirement of the *mariage de raison*, in the French Court a strange contradiction prevailed. The age of seduction was also an age of institutionalized chastity. Alongside the Court's notorious lechery, girls were raised in convents. Perrault's wife had entered one at the age of four and did not emerge until shortly before their wedding. He had seen her only once when he discussed his marriage plans with Colbert. A 1673 ordinance gave a father the right to confine his daughters until the age of twenty-five, or marriage. Any man could seek out a *lettre de cachet* from the King to sequester any female relative. And even the King's mistresses, once fallen from favor, frequently made the trek from castle to cloister. Louise de la Baume le Blanche, Duchess de la Valliere, the King's first public mistress, took the nun's vows shortly after her eight-year-old daughter by the King was presented at Court. Courtiers' handbooks stressed the importance—for both men and women—of guarding one's reputation. And education, along with Charles Perrault's "Little Red Riding Hood," warned of the dangers of female promiscuity.

Perrault cloaked his heroine in red, the color of harlots, scandal and blood, symbolizing her sin and foreshadowing her fate.

Her *chaperon,* or hood, suggested the double meaning of the tale and would later acquire its modern meaning in English as well: a matron who accompanies and protects single girls from men. Finally, for good measure, Perrault added an explicit verse moral at the end of his tale, warning *desmoiselles*—that is, young women of society—to remain chaste. The popular English version of this moral, translated to rhyme and reproduced with the text of "Little Red Riding Hood" that precedes this chapter, captures Perrault's sly rhythm; but a literal translation of his original verse better reveals his specific meaning.

On voit icy que de jeunes enfans	As one can see by this, children,
sur tout de jeunes filles	especially pretty young girls
belles, bien faites et gentilles	well bred and refined
font tres-mal d'écouter toute	would do well not to listen to
sorte de gens,	just anyone
et que ce n'est pas chose étrange	in which case it would be no
	strange thing
s'il en est tant que le loup mange.	if a wolf should eat them.
Je dis le loup, car tous les loups	I say wolf, because all wolves
ne sont pas de la mesme sorte:	are not of the same sort:
il en est d'une humeur accorte,	some of them are quite charming,
sans bruit, sans fiel et	not loud or rough at all,
sans couroux,	
qui, privez, complaisans et doux	cajoling sweet-talkers who
suivent les jeunes demoiselles	follow young ladies
jusque dans les maisons, jusque	right into their homes, right
dans les ruelles.	to their bedsides.
Mais, hélas! Qui ne sçait que ces	But alas! Everyone knows these
loups doucereux	smooth wolves

de tous les loups sont les   are the most dangerous of all!
   plus dangereux!

Perrault's "wolves" follow young women not only on the streets but into their homes, right up to the *ruelles*—their bedsides. This intimate space, where salon hostesses received their favorite guests and which sometimes concealed a private door leading into another room, was so central to the salon culture that *ruelle* had become shorthand for the salon itself. Perrault's "girls" are *bien faites* and *gentilles*: of the aristocracy. His warning is not simply to girls, but to the well-bred, educated women of high society who, in inviting men and women together in mixed company, set a dangerous precedent.

Perrault's wolf is the dapper charmer of Parisian high society, seducer of young women and a threat to the family patrimony—he is, as one folklorist has called him, the "unsuitable suitor," who insinuated his way into the best beds in town, deflowering young women and robbing their value as virgin pawns in the *mariage de raison*.

Later, Perrault's sexually suggestive moral would be cut from the tale and from the fairy-tale collections that modern readers know. But some of the villain's metaphorical power remains. Today we still use the term *wolf* to mean a womanizer.

Little Red Cap: To Walk the Straight Path

Out set Riding Hood, so obliging and sweet,
And she met a great Wolf in the wood,
Who began most politely the maiden to greet,
In as tender a voice as he could.

He asked to what house she was going, and why;
Red Riding Hood answered him all:
He said, "Give my love to your Gran; I will try
"At my earliest leisure to call."

Little Red Cap (Rotkappchen)

By Jacob and Wilhelm Grimm

Once upon a time there was a sweet little girl. Everybody loved her instantly on first sight, though it was her grandmother who loved her the most. She gladly fulfilled the girl's every wish. She once gave her a little red velvet cap, which looked so beautiful on the girl that she did not want to wear anything else. From then on, she was known as "Little Red Cap."

One day her mother said to her, "Please, Little Red Cap, take this piece of cake and this bottle of wine and bring them both to your grandmother, who is ill and weak. Be a good girl and give her my regards. Walk carefully and do not stray from the path, or you might fall and break the bottle. Then your grandmother will not have any food." Little Red Cap promised her mother that she would do as she was told.

Grandmother lived out in the forest, half an hour away from the village. No sooner had Little Red Cap entered the forest, than she met the wolf. She did not know that the wolf was an evil animal, and therefore she was not afraid of him.

Source: From *Kinder-und Hausmärchen* (Children's and household tales), First Edition, published by Realschulbuchhandlung, 1812.

"Good day, Little Red Cap," the wolf said.

"Thank you very much, wolf."

"Where to this early, Little Red Cap?"

"I'm on my way to my grandmother's."

"What are you carrying in your basket?"

"Cake and wine for my sick and weak grandmother, to strengthen her."

"Where does your grandmother live?"

"Another quarter of an hour into the forest, underneath the three big oak trees, down by the hazel bushes," Little Red Cap said.

The wolf thought to himself, "This young and tender thing is a perfect meal, even better than the old woman. I will need a cunning strategy to catch them both." So he walked alongside the girl for a while and then he said, "Little Red Cap, have you noticed the beautiful flowers growing here? Why don't you take a look around? Have you noticed how sweetly the birds are singing? You are marching along as if you were going to school, when it is so jolly out here in the forest."

Little Red Cap opened her eyes and saw how the sunlight broke through the trees and how everything was full of beautiful flowers. She thought, "Well, if I bring Grandmother a bouquet of fresh flowers, it will make her happy. It is so early in the day that I will still arrive on time." So she ran off the path into the forest to look for flowers. And every time she plucked one, she thought she saw a more beautiful one, deeper in the forest. The wolf meanwhile went straight to Grandmother's house and knocked on the door.

"Who's outside?"

"Little Red Cap, bringing you cake and wine. Open the door."

"Just push the handle down," Grandmother answered, "I'm too weak and can't get up."

The wolf pushed the handle, the door opened, and without a word he leaped upon the old woman in bed and devoured her. Then he put on her clothes and her nightcap, lay down in her bed and drew the curtains.

When Little Red Cap had as many flowers as she could carry, she remembered her grandmother and continued on her way. Upon arriving at her grandmother's house, she wondered why the door was open. As she entered the living room, something felt odd. She thought, "My goodness, how scared I feel today, though usually I like so much being at my grandmother's." She called, "Good morning!" but there was no answer. Then she went to the bed and drew back the curtains. Her grandmother was lying there with her cap drawn deeply into her face, looking rather peculiar.

"Oh, Grandmother, what big ears you have!"

"The better to hear you with."

"Oh, Grandmother, what big eyes you have!"

"The better to see you with."

"Oh, Grandmother, what big hands you have!"

"The better to grab you with."

"But, Grandmother, what a terribly big mouth you have!"

"The better to eat you with."

With that, the wolf jumped out of bed right onto poor Little Red Cap and ate her up.

After the wolf had satisfied his cravings, he went back to bed, fell asleep, and began to snore very, very loudly. A hunter happened to be passing by the house and thought, "How can the old woman snore so loudly? I had better see whether she is all right." He went inside, and as he approached the bed he saw the wolf lying in it. "So here you are, you old sinner," the hunter said. "I've been looking for you a long time." He drew his gun and was about to fire, when it occurred to him that the wolf might have eaten the grandmother and that she might still be saved. Instead of shooting, he took out his shears and began to cut open the belly of the sleeping wolf. As he made the first incision, he saw the little red cap shining through. A couple more snips and the little girl jumped out. "Oh, how frightened I was!" she cried. "How dark it was in the wolf's body." Then out came the old grandmother, alive as well, struggling to catch her breath. Little Red Cap quickly gathered some heavy stones, with which they filled the wolf's belly. When he awoke he tried to run off, but the stones were so heavy that he fell down dead.

All three were overjoyed. The hunter skinned the wolf and took the fur home. The grandmother ate the cake and drank the wine and recovered. Little Red Cap, however, thought to herself, "You will never again leave the path and run into the forest on your own as long as mother forbids it."

It is also told that once, as Little Red Cap was bringing baked goods to her grandmother, a second wolf tried to convince her to stray from the path. But this time Little Red Cap was careful and went straight ahead. She told her grandmother that she had met a wolf, who had greeted her nicely, but had an evil look in his eyes. "Had we not met on the open road, he would have gobbled me up."

"Come," her grandmother said, "let's bar the door, so he can't enter."

Soon, the wolf knocked on the door. "Open up, Grandmother, it is Little Red Cap, I am bringing you baked goods."

Both of them remained silent and they did not open the door. So he circled the house over and over and finally jumped up on the roof. He wanted to wait until Little Red Cap went home at night, so he could follow her and devour her in the darkness. But the grandmother realized what the wolf was up to. There was a big stone trough in front of the house, and she said to the child: "Fetch the bucket, Little Red Cap. Yesterday I boiled some sausages. Take the water they were boiled in and pour it into the trough." Little Red Cap carried water until the huge trough was completely filled. The smell of sausages reached the wolf's nose. He sniffed and looked down, and eventually he stretched his neck so far that he could no longer hold himself on the roof and began to slide. He slid from the roof right into the trough and drowned. Little Red Cap went home happily, and no one harmed her on her way.

—TRANSLATED BY RAINER BRAUN

A S SHE AGED FROM THE LIGHT of the Sun King to the shadow of Queen Victoria, Red Riding Hood grew more discreet. But still foolish and prone to err, now she needed a man to save her. In the first great revision of Perrault's tale, "Little Red Cap," published in 1812 by the brothers Jacob and Wilhelm Grimm, a fatherly hunter rescues Red from the beast's belly and gives her a second chance to walk the straight path through life. Popular Victorian illustrations of this tale show Red as an innocent. In one memorable series she grows smaller and smaller with each frame, until in the finale she sits on the hunter's shoulder, no bigger than a doll. Walter Crane's 1875 color print shows a variation of the happily-ever-after outcome that most people know today: The hunter has shot the wolf with his rifle. Red Riding Hood runs into his arms. Tearfully contrite, she promises never again to be disobedient.

The Grimms' "Little Red Cap" conveys the popular lessons now most often attributed to the fairy tale: Stick to the path; don't speak to strangers; be obedient. To many, these have become classic lessons for life—folk wisdom passed down through the generations. When they presented their first edition of *Children's and Household Tales* to the world, the Grimms claimed to have tapped the oral tradition of the German country-

Walter Crane's hunter rescues the heroine from her folly

side, recording exactly what peasants and other simple folk told them, with not a line or rhyme added or improved upon. They noted their sources, jotted down regions and dates of collection, at least partially, and for their efforts became known as the "fathers of folklore." But it seems that the brothers did not preserve the lore of common folk as faithfully as they claimed.

It used to be a common assumption that the Grimms made trips deep into the countryside to capture the living folk tradition. While not entirely wrong—the Grimms did take some of their tales from simple peasants—their more general methodology was quite different. Despite the Grimms' long-standing reputation, late twentieth-century scholarship has shown that they did much of their collecting in their own home. Their sources were not primarily wizened and wrinkled German country women, but more often their own mostly middle-class friends and family, who were familiar with a wide range of story traditions, including the fairy tales of France. The Grimms, who were voracious readers and commanded between them at least fifteen languages or dialects, were themselves well acquainted with Perrault's version of "Little Red Riding Hood," as almost certainly was the woman from whom they recorded their variation on it, "Little Red Cap." That woman, Marie Hassenpflug, was not the celebrated Märchenfrau of Niederzwehren—the folk storyteller of the German countryside that the Grimms had idealized and even provided illustrations of—but rather a neighbor and friend, young and educated, middle class and, to top it off, of French Huguenot blood. Since the Protestant Huguenots brought their culture and stories with them when they fled from the persecution of Louis XIV, Marie would surely have read the famous *contes* of Marie-Catherine D'Aulnoy, Marie-Jean Lhéritier and Perrault.

Furthermore, the Grimms were not very faithful to their original transcriptions. A comparison of the brothers' early manuscripts with later editions of the tales revealed that over the course of seven editions during their lifetime, they radically altered their collection. Led by Wilhelm, they embellished, redacted, combined the best elements of parallel tales, and eliminated some stories altogether. The Grimms' final collection of 1857, refined to the expectations of Victorian readers and critics, and especially parents, presented not the folklore of the past, but on the contrary, stories for a new age.

Their 210 tales are the grand culmination of a trend that had been growing since the latter half of the eighteenth century: fairy tales aimed, for the first time, at children. In their hands, and in numerous translations and adaptations by others, "Little Red Cap" came to embody both the new nineteenth-century child and the new Victorian woman—two concepts that, it turns out, were in some ways indistinguishable.

BEFORE THE AGE of the brothers Grimm, children's literature scarcely existed. Nor, for that matter, did children, at least not as we think of them today. Historians like Philippe Ariès have argued that the prolonged period of childhood and adolescence that is now commonplace is a fairly recent development in human history. Centuries ago, children often died very early, and so they were largely ignored until they had proven their ability to survive. Once they had, they quickly joined the ranks of adulthood. Dressed as miniature adults, aristocratic "children" wore waistcoats and powdered wigs and body-altering corsets—like those accurately depicted on the frontispiece of Charles Perrault's *Tales of Times Past with Morals*. They were married off as soon as possible, before untimely death might curtail a strategic alliance, and so that they could immediately get on with the duty of bearing as many children as possible in order to increase the odds of one surviving to carry on the bloodline. Young people of the middle and lower classes were even less durable than their wealthy cousins—a poor woman might bury as many children as she bore—and they went almost directly from swaddling clothes into the workforce, as young adults, at around the age of eleven or twelve. But in the nineteenth century, the vast economic and social impact of the industrial revolution struck Europe, forever altering the notion of maturity.

Factories spread, railroads stretched, and towns transformed into cities. Along with its technological impact, the industrial revolution brought demographic shifts. Masses of people moved from the country into great factory centers. An urban middle class and a new Victorian family emerged. Children became newly visible. Young people worked in factories instead of being apprenticed out, and so lived at home longer. Families tended to have fewer children, in part because those they had were more likely to survive. The sense of the nuclear family strengthened. Increasingly, a concept of childhood emerged as a distinct period of life with its own particular characteristics and needs—play, education and particularly moral instruction.

At the same time, the Industrial Revolution changed the book market in a way that would meet these needs. In the seventeenth century, when "Little Red Riding Hood" first appeared in print, books were a luxury. They were expensive—hence the small size of Perrault's collection of fairy tales—and were generally reserved for subjects tried and true: calendars, almanacs, prayer books, religious tracts and ABCs. By the early eighteenth century, inexpensive chapbooks began circulating widely. Perrault's fairy tales reentered popular culture through this "Bibliotèque bleue"—so called because of the chapbooks' blue paper covers. As the middle class grew, literacy rates rose. New industrial printing processes and economies of scale dramatically reduced the cost of books. Whereas women once "wove" or "spun" tales along with cloth, the Industrial Revolution brought inventions that carried cloth-making and the fairy tale alike from fireside to factory. The spinning wheel gave way to the spinning jenny, the electric loom and the spinning mule. Expensive handmade cloth books gave over to those turned out on sturdy iron frames and printed on wood pulp paper. By the nineteenth century, even artisan households could afford more than just a few small books. Above all, the growth of the reading public fertilized specialized markets, including children's books.

Edward Lear's first *Book of Nonsense* came out in 1846, with odd little line drawings and funny verses—precursors to his limericks. Aesop's fables had been in print for centuries, but they had been intended for adults. Now they appeared with illustrations clearly aimed at children. In England, an epicenter of the market, books for children featured black-and-white prints, and by the 1860s an innovative entrepreneur by the name of Edmund Evans, along with his star engraver Walter Crane, began experimenting with color. Within the decade, "toy books" in bright colors, cut in playful shapes or sometimes with pop-up figures, became all the rage. An 1863 book by Lydia L. Very, for example, was cut in the form of a standing Red Riding Hood, with the story told between her image on both the front and back covers.

Above all Walter Crane's immensely popular six-penny books of illustrated fairy tales, which are now collector's items, helped establish the Grimms' fairy tales as the standards that most people know today.

At first, however, the Grimms were not concerned with either children or children's books. They were linguists, scholars and folklorists intent on preserving their cultural heritage. Born in the central German province of Hesse, into a large, middle-class

"Toy book," by Lydia L. Very, 1863.

Protestant family, Wilhelm and Jacob Grimm grew up during the age when today's Germany was a patchwork of territories occupied by France. Scholars by profession, they were deeply tuned to a blossoming German cultural revival, led by such names as Schiller and Goethe. Jacob studied law and comparative linguistics; Wilhelm researched medieval literature and folklore. Over their lifetimes they also studied and collected German song, myth and legend, and they were in the process of compiling an etymological dictionary of the German language when Wilhelm died in 1859. (After almost twenty years of work, he had gotten as far as "Fruit.") In 1812, the year they published their first volume of *Children's and Household Tales*, Napoleon had been defeated and a rising sense of German national pride colored the day. Following in the footsteps of the German romantics, who rekindled interest in German culture, the brothers set out to study and collect the precious tradition of the German folk— what they called "natural poetry."

Heavily annotated and unillustrated, the Grimms' first edition of *Children's and Household Tales*, published in two volumes in 1812 and 1815, was hardly a light read. Their intention was not to entertain but rather to present a scholarly resource for those interested in German folk tradition and provide a basis for comparison with foreign tales. Indeed they sparked an interest in collecting and documenting folktales amongst scholars around the world who followed their lead (or at least, their professed lead) in faithfully documenting the sources of their tales.

But the Grimms were not well off. Hardship shaped their intellectual ambitions, and before long they shifted their emphasis from a scholarly audience to the potentially more lucrative children's market. While in the preface to their first edition of tales they had proudly claimed to be preserving peasant tradition, in their second edition of 1819 they equally boasted of improving upon it. They had completed fragment tales; admitted to retelling stories more simply and eloquently; and above all took pains to address the younger reader: "In this new edition, we have carefully eliminated every phrase not appropriate for children," wrote Wilhelm, who nonetheless also advised parental discretion in deciding which tales to read to children at all. An 1823 English translation of selected Grimm tales by Edgar Taylor launched the Grimms' popularity as children's authors. Finally, in 1825, the Grimms presented their own much shorter edition of selected tales, illustrated by their brother Ludwig. Issued at Christmastime, its aim was to turn a handsome profit.

Over the course of their lifetimes, the brothers (or mostly Wilhelm) continued to edit the collection for "childish" ears—and parental ones. The goal was "that the poetry living in it be effective and bring pleasure wherever it could, and also that the book serve as a manual of manners." To that end, they made a number of "improvements" on their beloved folk traditions.

References to sex, incest and what Wilhelm called "certain conditions"—that is, pregnancy—were purged. Take the story of Rapunzel, who sits in the window of a high tower and lets down her extraordinary lengths of hair like a ladder, so that the witch, her guardian, can climb up. Later, Prince Charming happens by and Rapunzel does the same for him. In the popular version of the tale that appears in the Grimms' final edition, there is no reference to any sexual impropriety: The prince chastely visits, and the witch learns of Rapunzel's visitor only when the girl absentmindedly comments one day that the weight of the witch on her hair is heavier than that of her sweetheart. But in the Grimms' version of the story appearing in their first edition, Rapunzel not only has a visitor, but one who is her lover: The witch learns of this betrayal when the girl naively asks why her clothes no longer fit her.

Violence, by contrast, the Grimms kept—and often embellished on. Indeed a few selections from the Grimms' editions over the years show how the standards of what is "appropriate" for children have changed. In their story "The Juniper Tree" a woman decapitates her stepson and attempts to conceal the crime. She ties the boy's head on his neck with a handkerchief, sits him on a chair in front of the door with an apple in his hand, and waits for her unsuspecting daughter to knock it off and take the blame. In "The Robber Bridegroom," a young woman witnesses her betrothed and his drinking buddies kill and eat a young woman. Cinderella's stepsisters mutilate themselves to fit into her tiny slipper—one succeeds after cutting off her heel but is found out when "the Prince looked at her foot and saw the blood flowing." And in "Fowler's Fowl," a variation of Perrault's "Bluebeard," the Grimms could not help but give a full description of the heroine's horrifying discovery in her husband's secret chamber: "There in the basin lay her two dear sisters, miserably murdered and hacked to pieces." The exaggerated violence, as scholars like Maria Tatar have suggested, dramatized Good and Evil, exaggerating the plight of victims and the wickedness of villains. It also served the Grimms' overarching aim—to clarify their lessons, teach morality to children, and promote their German middle-class values for the new Victorian family: discipline, piety, primacy of the father in the household and, above all, obedience.

In the context of this new fairy tale focus, Little Red Riding Hood developed a new identity. The Grimms purged the French implications of seduction from their version of "Little Red Cap," along with Perrault's earlier sexually suggestive moral. Instead, the heroine came to represent the Victorian child and the story gained the context of the new nuclear family: a more prominent mother who orders the heroine not to stray from the path (an extended warning not found in Perrault's earlier tale) and an authoritative father figure—a hunter—who arrives to save the day. In some Victorian variations of the Grimms' tale, such as one from "Father Tuck's Little Folk Series," the hunter-woodsman is not just father-like; he actually *is* her father. This is the version, mentioned earlier, that shows the doll-sized heroine riding on her father's shoulders at tale's end, shortly after he rescues her with his good old dog, "Trusty."

As the story morphed from sexual parable to family fable, and as it spread through Europe, it also increasingly emphasized Christian messages. Whereas the French tale warned of the perils of female promiscuity, the Grimms' "Little Red Cap" became an allegory of obedience necessitated by spiritual danger. In a famous print by Walter Crane, the heroine is cloaked in the garb of the Victorian middle class and the wolf is depicted in sheepskin. The thinking behind the biblical reference is clear: Our heroine must be on the alert lest she be fooled by the Devil. Women as much as children were the intended target of this warning—for if in the seventeenth-century Court of the Sun King a twelve-year-old girl was considered an adult, in Victorian times a very different sense of female maturity prevailed.

O NE NEED LOOK no farther than her clothes to see that the heroine of the nineteenth century is vastly different from her earlier courtly sister. The red *chaperon* or hood of Perrault's day was a small, stylish headdress of velvet or satin, worn by women of the aristocracy and middle classes in the sixteenth and seventeenth centuries. The Grimms' heroine wore not a hood but a small cap—like that depicted in an engraving accompanying their 1847 edition of tales.

But Little Red Riding Hood did not acquire the costume or the name by which English speakers know her today until she arrived in England, where the red riding habit was a staple, or even the *icon,* of rural women's dress. English country women

The heroine gets a small red cap from granny
on the frontispiece of the Grimms'
1847 collection.

wore this modest, tailored riding garment throughout the eighteenth and nineteenth centuries. They were made of wool for warmth and low cost (cotton was too expensive for the working class) and double milled for weather resistance. Scarlet cloth became so popular for rural wear that the red riding hood became one of the few English garments that can be called traditional. Indeed, it was so popular that legends arose around it during the Napoleonic wars: French soldiers approaching the English shores were said to have mistaken the scarlet-cloaked women assembled on the coasts for British soldiers in their red coats—and so called off invasions. Numerous artists immortalized the costume, among them George Morland, William Redmore Bigg, and Francis

Wheatley—whose oil painting *A Woodman Returning Home, Evening* (1795), shows a burly man walking alongside a young woman who drapes her red cloak over her arms. The image seems almost meant to illustrate the fairy tale, although the Grimms' collection would not be published (let alone reach England) for another seventeen years.

Francis Wheatley's "A Woodman Returning Home, Evening," (1795)

The red riding hood adorned a heroine not only of a different age, but of a different social class, with a different set of moral and social concerns. The life of the young country woman of the nineteenth-century middle class revolved around her social isolation and the universal imperative to marry. Since she would not be expected to work much, she could otherwise become a drain on family resources. Thus her education was minimal, designed only to win her a mate: A girl learned to cook and keep house, while boys began their trade with their fathers. As for the daughters of wealthier families, their schooling is well summed up by the description of the boarding school attended by one of the characters in Jane Austen's 1816 novel *Emma*: "a real, honest, old-fashioned Boarding-school," where a girl might acquire "a reasonable quantity of accomplishments at a reasonable price" and where "girls might be sent to be out of the way and to scramble themselves into a little education, without any danger of coming back a prodigy."

The limited position of the nineteenth-century Victorian woman is evident not only in Austen's novels but also in her life. A contemporary of the brothers Grimm, she published her novels anonymously. *Sense and Sensibility* (1811) was "By a Lady"; *Pride and Prejudice* (1813) was "By the author of *Sense and Sensibility*." The superfluousness of girls in the Victorian household so overwhelmingly shaped Austen's worldview that it overshadowed her own experience. One of eight children, all but two of them boys, Austen nonetheless wrote almost exclusively about families of girls, all struggling heartily to make a good match. The famous opening lines of *Pride and Prejudice* (whose female characters wear red riding cloaks in film adaptations) sum up the social mission of this Victorian woman, projected onto the shoulders of her unsuspecting target: "It is a truth universally acknowledged that a man in possession of a fortune must be in want of a wife." These ironic words, offered at the outset of a novel exploring the emotional, social and economic needs that drive the romantic (and in some cases decidedly unromantic) attachments of four sisters and their female friends and acquaintances, underscore the Victorian woman's plight. Without marriage, she was dependent upon her parents. When they died, she might find herself in dire straits; in *Pride and Prejudice*, the family estate will pass to the next male heir—a distant cousin. And so long as she remained unwed, she remained locked in a sheltered and deadly routine, and trapped in childhood.

In British author Anthony Trollope's 1873 novel *The Eustace Diamonds,* the spinster Augusta must be chaperoned and protected from unsavory socialites. Though she longs for independence, "as her position was that of a girl, she was bound to be obedient—though over thirty years old—and she obeyed." A single woman of the middle class might become a governess or a hired companion for a wealthy elderly woman. Wealthier young women were expected to sit at home and wait. Until they married, they were simply "the girls at home." Yet late marriage was a Victorian tradition, since men often had to build up the financial resources they would need to support a family. And, because of the low ratio of men to women due to migration to the United States, many women would face this limbo status indefinitely. A "spinster" well into middle age remained, conceptually, a child.

T HE GRIMMS' "LITTLE RED CAP," with its patriarchal lesson in female obedience, easily found purchase in the social landscape of Victorian Europe, and the heroic rescue by the hunter echoed the social protection that the nineteenth-century man—father, then husband—represented. The arrival of a hunter-woodsman who cuts the heroine from the beast's belly is a motif not found in the French tale of Charles Perrault: The Grimms may have borrowed the ending from a different folk tale, *The Wolf and the Kids.* As in that story, after his victims are rescued alive from his stomach, the wolf receives a Dante-esque punishment for his gluttony. Heavy stones are loaded into his belly and he is sewn up again. When the wolf awakens he tries to run off, but the heavy stones drag him down and kill him.

The Grimms also offered a second ending, far less known, in which Little Red Riding Hood meets a second wolf and proves that she has learned her lesson. Together, she and her grandmother set a trap and kill the wolf on their own without much trouble. This ending offers a picture of women that sharply contrasts with prevailing Victorian ideas of femininity—Red Riding Hood and her grandmother are more resourceful here, not helpless, childish, and in need of rescue. But more salient than the lesson itself is the fact that the Grimms' epilogue was omitted from popular translations of the tale and remains even today virtually unknown.

Because the Grimms restored a happy ending to the tale, scholars long considered their "Little Red Cap" to be the authentic version of the tale, more representative of folk tradition than that of Charles Perrault. So they thought, that is, until twentieth-century folklorists proved them wrong. As it turns out, the Grimms' story, and its lessons, could hardly differ more from the oral folk tradition that spawned it. Long ago, "Little Red Riding Hood" was a "wives' tale"—that is, a story told by women, before that term came to mean a lie.

III

The Grandmother's Tale:
To Come of Age

The Grandmother's Tale

There was once a woman who had some bread, and she said to her daughter: "Take this hot loaf and a bottle of milk to your granny." The little girl set off. At the crossroads she met a *bzou*.[1]

"Where are you going?"

"I'm taking a hot loaf of bread and a bottle of milk to my granny's."

"Which path are you taking," said the bzou, "the path of needles or the path of pins?"

"The path of needles," said the little girl.

"Well then, I'll take the path of pins."

The little girl amused herself picking up needles. Meanwhile the bzou arrived at her grandmother's, killed her, put some of her flesh in the pantry and a bottle of her blood on the shelf. The girl arrived and knocked at the door.

"Push the door," said the bzou. "It's closed with a wet straw."

"Hello, Granny; I'm bringing you a hot loaf and a bottle of milk."

Source: From an oral folktale collected around 1885. Translated from P. Delarue and M.-L. Tenèze, *Le conte populaire français* (The French popular tale), published by Erasme, 1957.

[1] A werewolf.

"Put them in the pantry. Eat the meat that's there, and drink the bottle of wine on the shelf."

As she ate, a little cat said: "She is slut who eats the flesh and drinks the blood of her granny!"

"Undress, my child," said the bzou, "and come to bed beside me."

"Where should I put my apron?"

"Throw it on the fire, my child; you won't be needing it anymore."

And she asked where to put the other garments, the bodice, the dress, the skirt, and the stockings, and each time the wolf replied:

"Throw them in the fire, my child. You won't be needing them anymore."

"Oh, Granny, how hairy you are!"

"It's to keep me warmer, my child."

"Oh, Granny, those long nails you have!"

"To scratch me better, my child."

"Oh, Granny, what big shoulders you have!"

"All the better to carry firewood, my child."

"Oh, Granny, what big ears you have!"

"All the better to hear with, my child."

"Oh, Granny, what a big mouth you have!"

"All the better to eat you with, my child!"

"Oh, Granny, I need to go badly! Let me go outside."

"Do it in the bed, my child."

"No, Granny, I want to go outside."

"All right, but don't stay long."

The bzou tied a woolen string to her foot and let her go out, and when the little girl was outside she tied the end of the string to a big plum tree in the yard. The bzou became impatient and said: "Are you making a load out there? Are you shitting a load?"

When he realized that no one answered him, he jumped out of bed and saw that the little girl had escaped. He followed her, but he arrived at her house just at the moment she was safely inside.

—Translated by Catherine Orenstein

CENTURIES AGO in the remote hills of France, a grotesque and peculiar tale circulated by word of mouth about a girl who eats her grandmother. The tale begins, familiarly enough, with a strange encounter in the woods. At a fork in the path to her grandmother's house, the girl meets a *bzou,* a werewolf or devil. The bzou learns her destination, and upon parting he takes the way of the "pins," while she takes the path of the "needles." But the bzou arrives at the grandmother's house first. He murders the old woman, minces her flesh and decants her blood into a bottle. When the girl arrives, she eats the "meat" and "wine" that he has left in the pantry. Then she removes her clothing piece by piece, from petticoat to stocking, announcing each item before throwing it into the fire, and climbs into bed beside the bzou.

In 1951 the French folklorist Paul Delarue published a study of this bizarre story, which he called "The Grandmother's Tale." Parts of it had appeared in a scholarly journal many years earlier, adapted from a manuscript in the possession of the folklorist Achille Millien, who in turn had been told the tale by Louis and François Briffault, at Montigny-aux-Amognes, Nièvre, in or around 1885. Strange as the story was, it was not unique. During the course of his research, Delarue found dozens of versions of the tale from France and from French-speaking areas, some of which had been passed on by word of mouth for generations. They varied in local color, but the great majority of them shared an abundance of details as well as the same general plot.

What's more, around the time that Delarue was collecting these French tales, scholars and collectors became aware of other, nearly identical tales from elsewhere in Europe and beyond. Italo Calvino included "The False Grandmother," a tale from Abruzzo, in his collection *Italian Folktales*, published in 1956. Its heroine passes through a river and a gate, instead of through the forest, and she encounters an ogress, rather than a bzou, who fries up her grandmother's ears and stews her teeth. Upon climbing into bed, the girl discovers that the ogress is large and hairy and has a tail—much like the French bzou. In Asia, the sociologist and folklorist Wolfram Eberhard documented and analyzed a group of 241 Taiwanese tales that closely resembled the one from Montigny-aux-Amognes except that instead of a bzou, a tiger is tucked under the covers in the grandmother's or grandaunt's bed. He gobbles up the girl's younger sisters and in some versions hands her one of their fingers to chew on. In the Chinese tale "Lon Po Po" a mother goes off through the woods while the wolf, disguised as Grandmother (Po Po), approaches the children in their own home. In these versions there are sometimes two or three girls, not one; yet the tale is undeniably the same.

Bawdy and gruesome, these oral tales share themes of cannibalism, sexuality, defecation, mistaken identity, and an encounter in bed with a dangerous foe. They lack the usual fairy-tale moral that scolds the heroine. And most of them share one more remarkable element: The heroine escapes. In the French story collected by Delarue, she pulls a clever, and typical, ruse. Realizing she has climbed into bed with danger, she pretends she has to relieve herself. In one memorable variation, the bzou tells her to do it in the bed, but she refuses—"Oh no, that will smell bad!" So the bzou ties a cord around her ankle and lets her out on the leash. Once outside, the girl unknots the cord and ties it around a tree. With the bzou in belated pursuit, she makes her escape.

THE DISCOVERY OF THIS GLOBAL sisterhood of oral tales has potentially profound implications for understanding "Little Red Riding Hood" and more broadly the role of women in folklore. Previously, scholars had thought the literary tales of female folly and punishment penned by Charles Perrault and the brothers Grimm to be typical of folk tradition. Many of them believed the Grimms' "Little Red Cap" to be a timeless tale, chock full of details that were either very ancient or archetypal. The heroine's red cloak, in particular, attracted their attention. The myth-ritualist Emile Nourry (who published under the pseudonym P. Saintyves) thought the tale described an ancient rite celebrating the coming of spring. The heroine's red headdress, he said, was a vestigial symbol of the flowers once worn by the May Queens. Folklorist Arthur Lang saw the tale's heroine as a symbol of the sun, the dawn, or the recurring springtime. The advent of psychoanalysis brought alternative, generally sexual theories from two famous sources—Erich Fromm and Bruno Bettelheim. According to Fromm, the tale represented a riddle from the collective unconscious, easily decipherable, in which the red cap symbolized the onset of menstruation, the heroine's bottle of wine symbolized her virginity, and the stones which she later sews in the wolf's belly symbolized sterility.

Bettelheim, whose theories had enormous popular appeal, thought "Little Red Cap" had an antecedent as far back as the Latin story *Fecunda ratis,* written in the year 1023 by Egbert of Lièges, in which a little girl in red is found with a company of wolves. For Bettelheim, the enduring red cloak stood for precocious sexuality:

> Red is the color symbolizing violent emotions, very much including sexual ones. The red velvet cap given by Grandmother to Little Red Cap thus can be viewed as a symbol of a premature transfer of sexual attractiveness, which is further accentuated by the grandmother's being old and sick, too weak even to open a door. The name "Little Red Cap" indicates the key importance of this feature of the heroine in the story. It suggests that not only is the red cap little, but also the girl. She is too little, not for wearing the cap, but for managing what this red cap symbolizes, and what her wearing it invites.

Such interpretations fascinated a generation raised on psychoanalysis and were welcomed in a scholarly climate that embraced theories of universalism. However, with the discovery of "The Grandmother's Tale" and its variants, it became evident that many of the so-called "archetypal" motifs that scholars had latched on to, including the beloved red cloak, were not universal at all but on the contrary relatively recent and unrepresentative inventions. What's more, with the advent of new folkloric methodology, it became increasingly obvious that Charles Perrault—whose 1697 text is the presumed source of the Grimms' "Little Red Cap"—had dramatically revised the original folk tradition.

FOLKLORISTS TRACE TALES just like scientists trace the evolution of species, by collecting, dating and comparing samples and by looking for traits that suggest a common ancestry. For paleontologists, an opposable thumb or a spinal cord can indicate a species' place in the phylogenetic tree. For folklorists, motifs—the tiny, immutable elements of a plot that persist in telling after telling—are the details that suggest a tale's lineage. A motif can be an object, a person, or a particular plot development: a magic key, a wicked stepmother, or the rubbing of a lamp that recurs in tale after tale, from one place to another and from generation to generation. By dating and comparing tales and noting the earliest appearance of particular motifs, folklorists can follow a tale's development.

The so-called "science of folklore"—a seemingly unlikely combination of terms—began with the brothers Grimm, who were among the first to date tales and record their sources (however deceptively). Their results inspired scholarly followers around the world. An annotated bibliography attached to the Grimms' 1850 edition of *Children's and Household Tales* lists hundreds of folktale collections that had appeared since the Grimms' 1812 work. In their introduction to the 1850 edition, the brothers claim that most of these foreign collectors had attributed their inspiration to the Grimms, either by personal letter or in their prefaces. Initially, when these international scholars came across variations of well-known tales, they identified them either by their number in the Grimms' table of contents or simply by a short, descriptive phrase. Soon, however, it became evident that a better and more systematic method was needed—and the Finnish folklorist Antti Aarne emerged as the "Linnaeus of folklore."

In the early twentieth century, Aarne collected vast numbers of tales and classified them according to what he determined to be their most elemental "type." His *Types of the Folktale*, published in 1910 and augmented and updated by his disciple Stith Thompson in 1928 and again in 1961, enabled scholars to distinguish and identify related tales as they appeared around the world. The Aarne-Thompson Tale Type Index, as it is called, has since become standard study for college folklore students and one of the most important folklore reference books. The bizarre, even comical, charm of the index is its complete lack of reverence for the intangible magic of a story. Within its jungle of cross-referenced entries and coded legends, wedged between 333-H, "The Treacherous Cat," and 334, "Household of the Witch," is "Little Red Riding Hood"— tale type 333, a strange cipher of references and cross-references called "The Glutton":

TT 333: *The Glutton (Red Riding Hood)*. The wolf or other monster devours human beings until all of them are rescued alive from his belly. Cf. Types 123, 2027, 2028.

Wolf's Feast. (a) By masking as mother or grandmother the wolf deceives and devours (b) little girl (RRH) whom he meets on his way to her grandmother's.
Rescue. (a) the wolf is cut open and his victims rescued alive; (b) his belly is sewed full of stones and he drowns; (c) he jumps to his death.

[Motifs:] K2011. Wolf poses as grandmother and kills child. Z18.1 What makes your ears so big? F911.3 Animal swallows man (not fatally).

F913. Victims rescued from swallower's belly. Q426. Wolf cut open and filled with stones as punishment.

Just imagine reading *that* at bedtime!

Though its European bias and heavy reliance on the brothers Grimm (whose tales, as we have already seen, were not as representative of oral folk tradition as they claimed) make the Aarne-Thompson index a rough and sometimes unreliable guide, it performs the great service of clearing away local foliage to reveal a tale's trunk and roots, allowing folklorists to see where splits in the family tree begin. Perhaps even more important, since its publication a legion of international folklorists has embarked on the endless task of recording and classifying tale traditions from around the world. These folklorists, followers of the historic-geographic or simply "Finnish" school, after Antti Aarne, have compiled a growing matrix of regional tale-type indices that fill in the gaps between the Aarne-Thompson codes. One such follower was Paul Delarue, who was in the process of creating a French tale-type index when he produced his mid-century study of "The Grandmother's Tale."

Together with fellow folklorist Marie-Louise Tenèze, Delarue classified some 10,000 tales from France and its former territories using the Aarne-Thompson scheme. The particular importance of their work is that it provides a folkloric context and suggests an oral history for what have since become some of the most popular tales in the world. Their collection, *Le Conte populaire français* (The French popular tale), includes parallel versions of "Rapunzel," in which the heroine invites her prince up into the tower to make love (tale type 310); a frightening Bluebeard, who displays his dead wives' corpses on the wall (312); a more cynical set of Cinderellas (510A and 510B); and bawdy variations on "Sleeping Beauty" (410). It includes tales of sex, cannibalism, rape, incest, shitting, pissing, sodomy, cheating the Devil and tricking God. And of course, it includes the thirty-five oral sisters of Little Red Riding Hood—the evidence of her buried past.

Some of Delarue's collected oral cognates of "Red Riding Hood" had been "contaminated" by exposure to Charles Perrault's "Le petit chaperon rouge"; that is, they possessed identifying details like the telltale motif of the red hood, one of Perrault's inventions. But others had not. These tales, which apparently owe nothing to the literary fairy tale, indicate a narrative ancestor that predates Perrault's story. Their discovery has enabled folklorists to say with a fair degree of certainty that "The Grandmother's Tale" is how Little Red Riding Hood's adventure was told many years ago, around the fire or in the fields, long before she found her way to print.

T HE REVELATION about Little Red Riding Hood's oral sisters delivers two lessons: the danger of interpreting a tale without knowing its history; and the importance of examining its broader folkloric patterns. Bettelheim and Fromm made the first mistake. Princeton historian Robert Darnton, who was familiar with "The Grandmother's Tale," made a merciless summation of Fromm's psychoanalytic blunder:

Fromm made a great deal of the (nonexistent) red riding hood as a symbol of menstruation and of the (nonexistent) bottle carried by the girl as a symbol of virginity: hence the mother's (nonexistent) admonition not to stray from the path into wild terrain where she might break it. The wolf is the ravishing male. And the two (nonexistent) stones that are placed in the wolf's belly after the (nonexistent) hunter extricates the girl and her grandmother stand for sterility, the punishment for breaking a sexual taboo.

In contrast to Fromm, who employs the psychoanalyst's universalistic approach, Darnton is an eloquent spokesman for reading the tale as an historical document with clues to the premodern past. In an essay in his book *The Great Cat Massacre,* Darnton applies this historical approach to the French oral tales of the Delarue-Tenèze collection, asking, What if these tales sprang not simply from the imagination, but also from real life? Through the lens of his historical expertise he plucks fascinating insights from previously mysterious fairy-tale motifs.

In the overcrowded, underfed households of France's Old Regime, illiterate peasants sometimes gathered around the fire on cold winter evenings for a *veillée,* to share gossip, work, and stories. Not stories of fantasy, but of observation. Hunger, infanticide, and abandonment—all the cruel "fictions" of popular fairy-tale plots—were very real in these peasant communities at a time when the land was far less fertile than the population and life was a constant Malthusian struggle against starvation. Peasants labored from dawn until dusk on pathetic strips of soil. They survived on porridge made of bread and water. They ate meat only a few times a year. Those who couldn't make it farming became highwaymen and prostitutes. Childbearing was Russian roulette—thus, the stepmother, a trope for family woe in fairy tales, was a fixture of rural France. Step-siblings were extra mouths to feed and, like Cinderella's dreaded sisters, presented direct competition for the patrimony. As for the scatological and sexual elements of oral folktales like "The Grandmother's Tale," households were small, grown children lived at home for a long time, and family members often shared beds—and the chamber pots beneath them. The intimacies and indelicacies of bodily functions were no secret in the Old Regime's peasant households.

Yet while fruitful, Darnton's historical approach fails to explain, just as he fails to notice, the most exceptional element shared by the oral cognates of "Red Riding Hood": the happy ending, with its heroine triumphant. This ending is no mere incidental motif. Its recurrence suggests that it is fundamental.

Scholars know of many tale types, or cycles, that recur around the world. Certain tales are ubiquitous—perhaps even universal. The flood myth of the Bible is echoed in the Epic of Gilgamesh from ancient Babylon, a tale recorded on stone tablets in the seventh century B.C. and composed some 4,000 years ago. There is not one but many quests for the Holy Grail. And the same mythic hero, in many different guises, appears over and over again across the globe. There are several theories as to why this is. Some have suggested that there was once an original tale, a narrative Adam and Eve, or even an entire "mythogenic" zone from which tales first emerged and diffused throughout the world. The *Panchatantra,* a collection of Indian folktales believed to have entered Europe after the eighth century during the Muslim conquest, is thought by some to be the original source of all our tales. Jungians, on the other hand, believe in "polygenesis," rooting the phenomenon in the common human experience: We all possess a human body, a human psyche, and these universal aspects of humanity give rise to collective dreams and symbols, which Jung called "archetypes." But all explanations ultimately lead to the same point: If a tale is important enough, it will be found amongst many peoples and will last a long time.

A narrow focus on history, such as that found in Darnton, can obscure the big picture. The specific details of life under the French Old Regime cannot account for the appearance of "Little Red Riding Hood" cognates in China, Korea, Japan, or Italy. The recurrence of stories remarkably similar to "The Grandmother's Tale" in countries separated by land and sea suggests that only by looking at the tale's global pattern can we get a sense of its broader, older, deeper meaning as an oral folktale—or "wives' tale."

F AIRY TALES TEND TO FOLLOW a familiar pattern, which the anthropologist Arnold van Gennep calls a *rite de passage*. It is the same pattern that characterizes human rituals marking life transitions: birth, death, and especially puberty or initiation rites. This pattern follows a sequence of three stages: a separation, a "liminal" or gestational period, and finally a return to society in a new form or with new status. Indeed, most fairy tales end in marriage, a symbol of social and sexual maturity.

In the popular literary fairy tales, heroines tend to follow a passive version of the rite of passage. Sleeping Beauty, Snow White, and the Grimms' Little Red Cap all wait, asleep or in a deathlike state, for rescue (and resurrection) by a prince (or hunter-woodsman) who frees the heroine from her slumber in a castle, a glass coffin, or the belly of the wolf. But, beyond fairy tales, there is a more heroic version of this pattern that has been widely studied—as it pertains to stories about boys and men.

The myth of the hero, or Hero Cycle, has been written about since the late nineteenth century by such diverse scholars as Carl Jung, the Viennese psychoanalyst Otto Rank, the English folk-lorist Lord Raglan, and most famously, the American mythographer Joseph Campbell. Campbell observed that the same hero appears all over the globe: Theseus, Odysseus, Siddhartha, Buddha, Jacob, Moses, Luke Skywalker, and even (as folklorist Alan Dundes has argued) Jesus Christ. In each incarnation, the hero looks different and has a different name but acts out a remarkably consistent script.

The myth begins when the hero's royal or marvelous birth is concealed from commoners or from those who raise him. Moses is sent downstream in a basket and is found by Pharaoh's daughter. Jesus is born of God but raised by Joseph and Mary. Oedipus, the son of a king, is cast away after birth to avoid the Sphinx's prophesy that he will kill his father. Untested, the young hero may be naïve, perhaps arrogant or even self-doubting, but he is nonetheless full of promise. Clues suggest a great calling—superhuman strength or skill. The youthful David bests Goliath, years before becoming king. Superman the child rescues his mother from a car wreck by single-handedly lifting the vehicle. Still, little beyond this brief foreshadowing is heard of the hero until early adulthood, when he must undertake a journey by which he proves himself. Later he will rise to power and confront his father, as Zeus battled the Titan Cronos (Time) and freed his sibling gods to reign on Mount Olympus. Ultimately he will face death, hung on the cross or in the stars—but not before he has passed his tests and completed his journey. In brief form, this journey parallels the pattern of heroes marching through the fairy-tale woods, a passage that some have called a "wisdom journey."

This journey, the central episode of the hero's voyage, is a test of mettle. The hero's search of self is fraught with danger and promises enlightenment. He faces demons, both literal and figurative. They may be ogres or giants, death in the form of a dark figure, or the underworld itself. The passage is so important that it may become synonymous with the hero's identity: During his thirty-year journey, Odysseus voyages to Hades, where he meets the ghosts of Greek warriors and heroes. Or the hero may encounter the "dark side," the term used by movie director George Lucas, who spent time with Campbell and styled his *Star Wars* epic after the scholar's insights. This dark side is symbolic not only of physical danger but of inner demons, one's doubts and weaknesses.

The fundamental lesson of the hero's journey is self-reliance. Neither Yoda nor Obi Wan Kenobi, Luke Skywalker's warrior mentors, comes to help him when he confronts and defeats his nemesis, the villainous Darth Vadar—his father. The hero must always pass this test alone. His journey leads toward wisdom and maturity, in many forms: acceptance of responsibilities to family, community, kingdom, or God.

Fairy tales, of course, are not myths. Myths are sacred and grand in scope; fairy tales are specific, secular, and local. Campbell observed that the accomplishment of the mythic hero is world-historical, representing macrocosmic human triumphs, whereas the protagonist of the fairy tale achieves a domestic, microcosmic triumph—a personal victory. More frankly, perhaps, myths tend to glorify man's accomplishments, while fairy tales—at least those that are best known today—focus on women. According to Otto Rank, mythic heroes are never female. Campbell limited his early analysis to male heroes, although many of his examples were female—and he later acknowledged childbirth as one form of heroism. Yet, "The Grandmother's Tale" follows a pattern similar to that of the mythic hero's wisdom journey. Might the lesson of her tale—a coming of age, represented by a test of self-reliance—or even heroism—be the same?

In fact this oral ancestor of "Red Riding Hood" contains the classic signs and symbols that might support this interpretation. A girl leaves home heading into the dark area of the forest, beyond the boundaries of society, where danger in all forms—physical, spiritual, and sexual—lurks. She must choose a path of pins or needles—the tools and symbols that appear in female initiation rites around the world, and in particular in France, where sending a young girl to apprentice with the seamstress for a year or so was, according to one scholar, a bit like sending her to finishing school, and carried a sense of sexual maturation. The girl meets a bzou, which some scholars interpret as a nefarious sexual encounter. The bzou might be a male figure; it might also be an ogress, the symbol of maternal oppression, when motherly protection becomes a hindrance to independence. The bzou or ogress attempts to tie the girl to the bed, but she slips the leash and goes off on her own—a classic metaphor for attaining independence.

As for the cannibalistic meal, a motif that Delarue found in a great many of the folk versions of the tale: Perhaps the act of cannibalism is a symbolic reminder that the old will be reborn in the young, in a reversal of the maternal tide. In more literal terms, our bodies carry the genes of our ancestors; we are flesh of their flesh, blood of their blood. Children are born and come of age as grandparents die.

THE HEROIC HEROINE of "The Grandmother's Tale" stands in stark contrast to the passive female protagonists of Perrault and the brothers Grimm. Why? The explanation, perhaps, is that the story and its cognates come from a different set of authors—or rather, tellers. The clues to this lie in the stories themselves. In "The Grandmother's Tale," the girl meets a bzou at the fork in the path between pins and needles. This is no isolated reference. Sewing terms appear in many variants of this oral tale—just as they are practically omnipresent in our surviving literary fairy tales. A princess can't fling a dead cat without hitting a spinning wheel or a loom. Sleeping Beauty pricks her hand on an old spindle. Rumplestiltskin spins straw into gold. None of this is coincidence.

Because today few people sew their own clothes, much less produce the fabric from which garments are made, it is difficult to grasp that for most of history, spinning was *the* consuming labor of women everywhere in the world, and France was no exception. In the seventeenth century, textiles represented France's national industry, a patriotic duty driven by the need to clothe the nation's growing armies. Spinning rooms were attached to orphanages. Jailed or hospitalized women were made to spin, and prostitutes were expected to produce a certain number of bobbins of yarn in their off hours. Prizes were awarded to women who spun the most. And in the countryside, it was the incessant and deforming labor of the peasant woman, who sought distraction and relief in conversation, gossip, and stories. Women told tales to the repetitive rhythm of work, weaving in the signs of their labor, until telling a tale and spinning a yarn became one and the same.

"The Grandmother's Tale" suggests how their tales changed when put on paper. Perrault, the brothers Grimm, and their early Neapolitan predecessor Giambattista Basile all credited female sources for their tales: Mother Goose, Frauen, and the ugliest old crones around, respectively. But the sense of female author- ship—literally, female authority—is absent from their tales. The stories of the fairy tale canon little resemble oral tales like those recorded by Delarue, and the heroine triumphant has all but dis- appeared. The best-known tales have until relatively recently been written and studied almost exclusively by men who lived in a world where women never came of age, where even well into middle age, unmarried women were "girls of the house."

In this vein, it is also particularly interesting to note that in his insightful essay drawing on "The Grandmother's Tale," Darnton hardly considers—and indeed has entirely omitted from his tran- scription—the happy ending recorded by Delarue in which the girl escapes by her wits. This ending's appearance in so many of the oral French variants, as well as in other cultures' versions of the tale, suggests that it is fundamental to the tale's broad mean- ing. But Darnton's interest in the tale is an historical document, and so he misses its broader elements. They are not part of his story—just as, all too frequently, they are left out of history.

IV

Stubbe Peeter, Werewolf: A True Story

The Trial of Stubbe Peeter, Werewolf

A true Discourse

Declaring the damnable life

and death of one Stubbe Peeter, a most

Wicked Sorcerer, who in the liknes of a

Woolfe, committed many murders, continuing this

Divelish practise 25 yeeres, killing and de-

vouring Men, Woomen, and Children,

Shewing the manner and order of his taking, as

Divers persons of credit heere of the Cittie

Doth know and hve seen and

Heard of it.

Who for the same fact was ta-

Ken and executed the 31 of October

Last past in the Towne of Bedbur

Neer the Citti of Collin

In Germany

Truly translated out of the high Dutch, according

Source: This is a redacted version of the account of Stubbe Peeter's crimes, trial, and punishment, from a pamphlet held by London's Lambeth Palace Library, translated from the high Dutch into English in 1590.

To the copie printed in Collin, brought over into
England by George Bores ordinary Poste, the
XI Day of June 1590,
who did both hear and see the same.
At London
Printed for Edward Venge, and are to be
Solde in Fleet-street at the signe of the
Vine.

In the towns of Cperadt and Bedbur near the city of Collin in high
Germany there was nourished one Stubbe Peeter, who from his youth
was greatly inclined to evil, and the practicing of wicked arts, surfeit-
ing in the damnable desire of magic, necromancy, and sorcery,
acquainting himself with many infernal spirits and fiends. The Devil
who hath a ready ear to listen to the lewd motions of cursed men,
promised to give unto him whatsoever his heart desired during his
mortal life, whereupon this vile wretch, having a tyrannous heart and a
most cruel bloody mind, requested that at his pleasure he might work
his malice on men, women and children in the shape of some beast.
The Devil gave unto him a girdle, which being put about him, he was
straight transformed into the likeness of a greedy devouring wolf,
strong and mighty, with eyes great and large, which in the night
sparkled like unto brands of fire, a mouth great and wide, with most
sharp and cruel teeth, a huge body and mighty paws. And no sooner
should he put off the same girdle but presently he should appear in
his former shape, according to the proportion of a man, as if he had
never been changed.

Stubbe Peeter was exceedingly well pleased. He had a fair young
Damsel, his Daughter, after whom he lusted most unnatural, and

such was his inordinate lust and filthy desire toward her that he begat a child by her; but as an insatiate and filthy beast he also lay with his own sister. This lewd sin of lechery did not assuage his cruel and bloody mind, but continuing an insatiable bloodsucker, he accounted no day spent in pleasure wherein he had not shed some blood. He had a son, the first fruit of his body, yet his delight in murder exceeded the joy he took in his son. On a time, he enticed him into the fields and from thence into a forest near by, where, making excuse to stay about the necessaries of nature, while the young man went forward, in the shape and likeness of a wolf he encountered his own son and most cruelly slew him. This done, he presently ate the brains out of his head as a most savory and dainty delicious means to staunch his greedy appetite.

Thus this damnable Stubbe Peeter lived the term of five and twenty years, in which time he had destroyed and spoiled an unknown number of men, women and children, sheep lambs and goats and other cattle, and did act more mischief and cruelty than would be credible, although high Germany hath been forced to taste the truth thereof. Oftentimes the inhabitants of Collin, Bedbur and Cperadt found the arms and legs of dead men and women and children scattered up and down the fields, to their great grief and vexation of heart.

And here is to be noted a most strange thing which setteth forth the great power and merciful providence of God to the comfort of each Christian heart. There was not long ago certain small children playing in a meadow by town, where also animals were feeding and suddenly comes this vile wolf, caught a little girl by the collar with intent to pull out her throat, but luck was and will of God that he could not pierce the collar of the child's coat and being high and very well stiffened and close clasped about her neck, and there with all the rest of the children who escaped so amazed the cattle feeding by, that being fearful to be robbed of their young, they altogether, came running against the wolf and he was compelled to let go his hold and to run away to escape the danger of their horns; by which means the child was preserved from death, and, God be thanked, remains living at this day.

And that this thing is true, Master Tyce Artyne, a Brewer dwelling at Puddlewharfe in London, being a man of that country born, and one of good reputation and account is able to testify, who is near kinsman to this child, and hath from thence twice received letters concerning the same; and for that the first letter did rather drive him to wonder at the act then yielding credit thereunto, he had shortly after at request of his writing another letter sent him whereby he was more fully satisfied; and divers other persons of great credit in London hath in like sort received letters from their friends to the like effect.

Witnesses that this is true.

Tyse Artyne

William Brewar

Adolf Staedt

Geore Bores

With divers others that have seen the same

THE TRIAL OF STUBBE PEETER in Bedpur, Germany, in 1589 was known all over Europe. A pamphlet describing his crimes circulated soon after he was tortured and executed. In it, he confessed to multiple counts of adultery and rape, to committing incest with his daughter and sister, to murdering his son and eating his brain, and to attacking lambs, sheep, goats, cattle and humans and eating their raw flesh. He also admitted that he had made a pact with the Devil and that the Devil had given him a girdle to transform himself into a wolf.

Although Peeter's story strained credibility, or perhaps because it did, the pamphlet included testimony from numerous neighbors and witnesses. Some reported finding the "arms and legs of dead people scattered up and down the fields." Master Tyse Artyne, a German brewer living at Puddlewharf in London, also swore he had received letters confirming a werewolf attack on the daughter of a relative in Stubbe Peeter's vicinity. A print from a woodcut engraving attached to the pamphlet illustrated in eight consecutive panels Stubbe Peeter as a wolf mauling one of his victims; his chase and capture by a group of townsmen; his grisly torture at the hands of his executioners; and finally, his death by decapitation on Halloween day, with severed head hoisted on a high post above a likeness of a wolf and wooden effigies of his sixteen victims, and (for good measure) his headless body burned at the stake along with his daughter and mistress. The image might make anyone think twice before making a pact with the Devil.

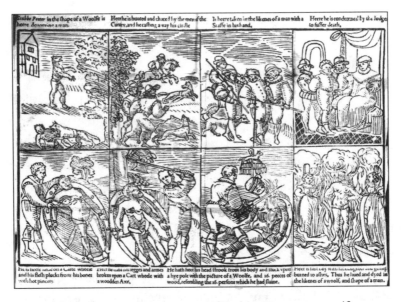

The crimes, trial, and torture of Stubbe Peeter, werewolf, as appearing in a 1590 pamphlet.

Peeter's story stands in stark contrast to the fairy tale today. The story of "Little Red Riding Hood" as we know it has been sanitized by generations of children's book editors. In modern storybook tradition, the heroine is rejuvenated by a helpful hunter-woodsman, who cuts open the wolf with his knife or scissors and lifts her from the belly of the beast as if from a bad dream. The wolf is no more than a temporary setback: a symbolic nightmare, a means of exploring childhood fears or fantasies, as the popular child psychologist Bruno Bettelheim suggested, or an entertaining shock from which the heroine—and the audience—easily recovers. Frequently, the surviving characters end their adventure with a light meal or even a bit of music, as in a 1920 play for children by Caroline Wasson Thomason, in which the heroine, her grandmother and some wood nymphs join in and sing the Marseillaise.

Even the earliest published version of "Little Red Riding Hood," by Charles Perrault, is not particularly disturbing or violent, even though the girl dies. That story dwelt not on gore but instead on the sexual significance of the wolf as the charming, handsome frequenter of the bluestocking salons who seduced and deflowered young girls of the upper crust. Charles Perrault's wolf was a danger, indeed; but a genteel one.

Yet just as Little Red Riding Hood has a premodern antecedent in "The Grandmother's Tale," an oral folktale with radically different meanings and a dramatically different heroine from that of literary tradition, so the wolf also has a premodern antecedent— an historical villain with a meaning and identity far different from that which has been preserved and passed down for generations in the storybook.

I N ITALY *lupus in fabula*, or "wolf in the fairy tale," is the equivalent of the English phrase "speak of the Devil," said when an individual whom people have just been discussing suddenly appears. As the phrase suggests, in fairy tales there is always the potential, even the expectation, of a wolf. The very act of telling a tale seems to call it forth. Red Riding Hood climbs into bed with one. Prokofiev's Peter catches one after it swallows a hapless duck. The three little pigs find refuge from the wolf in the house of brick, but the seven little goats are eaten by one and then rescued from its belly. The wolf also makes an appearance in dozens of popular fables, from Aesop to La Fontaine to Uncle Remus. But why is the wolf the omnipresent villain of our popular fairy tales? Why *lupus in fabula?*

Not all cultures and traditions cast the wolf as evil. Indeed in many traditions the wolf is heroic. In Rudyard Kipling's *Jungle Book,* an Indian boy named Mowgli is raised by wolves. The ancient Roman twins Romulus and Remus were nursed by a she-wolf. Frescoes and mosaics throughout Italy depict this wolf as a nurturing protector, for Romulus later founded Rome. Because the animal was also associated with Mars, the Roman god of war, for early Romans the appearance of a wolf before a battle could be an omen of victory. The Native American wolf was respected and even revered; the most honored warrior among the Cheyenne in the nineteenth century was named Little Wolf. Norse warriors donned wolf skins to sustain courage in battle. Genghis Khan claimed that he descended from a blue-gray "chosen wolf" sired by the sky.

But in places where the wolf was man's great predator, where forests spread over the land and famine brought animals into increasing conflict with humans, the wolf also became in legend and law a beast of ill repute: the projection of evil within and a symbol of evil beyond. In such regions the wolf became a symbol of peasant hardship. To have "the wolf at the door" signified desperate poverty and hunger. The avaricious landlord was a "wolf," as was virtually anything that threatened the peasant's precarious existence. The wolf embodied not only earthly misfortune but also spiritual danger. Witches were depicted in broadsides riding not only on broomsticks but on wolfback. A medieval bestiary records that the Devil "bears the similitude of a wolf, he who is always looking over the human race with his evil eye, and darkly prowling around the sheepfolds of the faithful." In the Bible a wolf appears as the Devil's agent in Jesus' Sermon on the Mount: "Beware of false prophets, which come to you in sheep's clothing, but inwardly they are ravening wolves."

In certain parts of Europe during the sixteenth and seventeenth centuries, particularly in rural territories that now belong to France, wolf attacks were rampant. The Court of Dôle ordered farmers to guard the fields and issued instructions for what to do if a wolf should be spotted: Villagers were to sound the alarm by ringing the church bell, gather at the church, and keep note of anyone suspicious who did not show up. In places like this, all the abstract associations with the wolf converged into a frightening phenomenon. As "The Grandmother's Tale" circulated by word of mouth through the woods of old France, peasants were plagued by a virtual epidemic of werewolves.

THE LURID PAMPHLET and broadside showing Stubbe Peeter's crimes and punishments is now held by London's Lambeth Palace Library. It is one of five "true" histories bound together in a small booklet that once sold on Fleet Street "at the sign of the vine." Because of this pamphlet, and others like it that circulated at the time, Stubbe Peeter's story and fate have become somewhat famous, at least among certain eclectic scholars. But if Stubbe Peeter's trial was sensational, his crime was not unique. Indeed, in certain areas, at this particular moment in history, it seems to have been almost commonplace.

On January 18, 1575, more than fifty witnesses deposed before the Court of Dôle, Lyons, that Gilles Garnier, a *loup-garou,* had devoured children in the nearby vineyards. He confessed without torture to killing a small girl with his hands and teeth, removing her clothes, eating part of her thighs and arms, and then taking home a portion for his wife. The court condemned him to be burned alive. Henri Boguet, judge of the Abbey of St. Claude, documented accusations against an entire werewolf family in 1598. Once in prison, father and son ran on all fours about their cells howling, but they did not transform; perhaps, wrote Boguet, because they did not have the necessary magic salves. That same year, a tailor accused of child murder and necrophilia was burned as a werewolf in Paris. On February 25, 1599, Jacques Verjuz of Baume-le-Nonnes appealed to the Parliament of Dôle after he was accused of sleeping with his mother and banished for practicing witchcraft and changing into a wolf. And fourteen-year-old Jean Grenier, a native of Bordeaux, confessed in 1603 to eating dogs and babies and to biting a small girl to death.

Grenier's story, retold in 1865 by the priest and scholar of the occult Sabine Baring-Gould, included the by then familiar explanation: He claimed that a salve and a wolf pelt transformed him into a wolf. Evidence presented at his trial included the disappearance of local children and the discovery of their partially eaten remains, as well as the usual sighting of a werewolf attacking them—all in keeping with other cases of the time. But Grenier's trial was exceptional, at least in its outcome. On appeal the high court determined him to be mentally deficient, annulled the death sentence and sent him to live in a monastery, a decision that stands out against the hysteria of the times.

However fantastic seeming, the werewolf of trial records gives only the shadowy outline of a far bigger specter: one that existed in the sixteenth-century mind. Today the accounts read like pulp fiction, but 400 years ago they were legal opinions that were representative of broad belief, albeit nuanced by a variety of explanations. Prominent and respected judges throughout the land heard the cases. Henri Boguet was a scholar; his *Discours des Sorciers* was well received and saw many editions between 1590 and 1611, during which time he was a practicing judge. This work recorded both first- and second-hand accounts of werewolves that he deemed reliable. Kings, monks and physicians all debated the nature of *lycanthropy*—the delusion of being transformed into a werewolf. To Boguet it was a form of madness, accompanied by hallucinations in both sufferers and their victims. Heinrich Kramer and Jacob Sprenger, authors of the *Malleus maleficarum*, a fifteenth-century guide for witch hunters, thought it a "glamour caused by witches." The well-known French jurist Jean Bodin believed in the actual physical metamorphosis of man into beast, an opinion that was rare amongst his educated brethren but shared by many European peasants. In Padua in 1541, for example, a farmer who had attacked and killed a number of people confessed that he was a werewolf whose pelt was inside-out. Joham Weyer's widely circulated sixteenth-century critique of the witch hunts, *De praestigiis daemonum* (On Witchcraft), describes the population's response: The villagers "hacked at his arms and legs with a sword and cut them off, to find the truth of the matter. And when they realized that the man was innocent, they handed him over to the surgeons to cure him, but he expired after a few days."

Finally, many believed that the Devil could possess men and

drive them to act as wolves—or that he sometimes possessed wolves themselves. Thus, if men were executed as wolves, so on occasion wolves were executed as men. Barry Holstun Lopez, who has written about wolves, relates that in 1685 the townspeople of Ansback, Germany, identified a wolf as the reincarnation of a local, hated burgomaster. They hunted it down, killed it, cut off its muzzle, dressed it in a suit of flesh-colored cloth, fitted it with wig and beard and a mask fashioned after the burgomaster's face, and hung it in the town square.

Such spectacles and stories provide a clue to the mental landscape of the past shared by those who told stories on dark winter nights around a fire, with perhaps a wolf or two howling in the background. Fairy tales are far from the reality of the modern reader. But to a sixteenth-century peasant, such plots took place just outside the door. "Little Red Riding Hood" was not a frivolous fable but a direct warning from a true story. Her villain was real—maybe even a neighbor.

By the time Charles Perrault first published "Little Red Riding Hood," the belief in werewolves had become less fashionable, at least among the upper classes. Perrault's villain incorporated old peasant beliefs—his wolf walks, talks, and eats humans, just like the bzou of yore. But as he slipped from the courtroom into the realm of fairy tale, the wolf, or werewolf, became no more than a salacious metaphor.

Probably it was the wolf's ravenous appetite that originally led to its association with sexual hunger. Wolves will eat an entire kill at once and sometimes stay at a large carcass for hours on end. Although they may not eat again for days, the impres-

By the time Charles Perrault wrote *Little Red Riding Hood*, the belief in werewolves was waning. Nonetheless his tale resonated with the meaning of the werewolf, even as that figure moved from the court-room to the realm of the fairy tale. His villain talks, walks, and eats girls—like the werewolf in this eighteenth-century print.

sion to the human observer of their feeding is that of rabid appetite (hence, "to wolf down your food"). But if Perrault's villain was the ultimate insider, a silver-tongued dog who insinuated his way into the best skirts of Parisian society, the werewolf of the past was just the opposite—a dangerous outcast, a social misfit, and a warning of the consequences of that status.

Tales of transformation of man into beast stretch back in history. Pliny writes of an ancient race of men with dogs' heads who wore animal skins, lived in caves and barked. Herodotus writes in the fifth century B.C. of a race of Neurians who changed for a few days each year into wolf form. In one of the medieval lais of Marie of France, the werewolf is a nobleman held under a spell. In that story, his treacherous wife hides his clothes (the means of his magical transformation) and he must stay in wolf form. He is freed only when his good manners are recognized by a neighboring king who makes him into a companion.

But according to the Roman poet Ovid who wrote around the time of Jesus, the werewolf was not civil, but rather, a beast of disgrace. Ovid writes that the Greek King Lycaon civilized Arcadia and instituted the worship there of Zeus, King of the Skies and head of the Greek pantheon. But Lycaon was sloppy in his worship and displeased the god. One day, Zeus came to visit him. Lycaon and his many sons welcomed Zeus into their home, but they could not resist the opportunity to test his omniscience. So they devised a grisly plan. They sacrificed one of the brothers, Nyctimus, mixed his guts into a stew along with the meat of sheep and goats, and served him up to the god. Need it be said that Zeus was not fooled? Outraged, he hurled the bowl to the floor and turned Lycaon and his sons—all save Nyctimus, whom he restored to life—into wolves. He then unleashed a flood of biblical proportion to cleanse the earth of sin.

Ovid's story provides the origin of the word *lycanthrope,* as well as an insight into the werewolf's enduring social meaning at the time of the trials of pre-Enlightenment Europe. In the biblical story, Abraham is willing to kill his only son, Isaac, to prove his faith in God. His unquestioning deference exemplifies social order. Jesus, too, is sacrificed to preserve—or rather, restore—order between man and God. But in the Greek myth told by Ovid, the sacrifice is inverted. Lycaon kills his son to test Zeus, demonstrating his *lack* of faith. His trespass symbolizes the height of human arrogance and the depths of human blasphemy—the rebellion of doubt. His sin is so grave that the entire human race must be obliterated. Lycaon was thus a sort of inchoate Antichrist, a figure who rather than dying for mankind's sins, sins and seals mankind's annihilation. The story gives us the werewolf as a figure that marks the boundaries of social and religious order, and separates those within from those whose character or behavior set them dangerously apart.

Stubbe Peeter's trial occurred during the years when Europe was still buckling under the rule of the Inquisition, the ecclesiastical tribunal established in the thirteenth century under Innocent III to suppress heresy. His successors went on to target and root out all forms of social deviance and diversity: Protestants, mystics, men of learning, and under the Spanish, Jews and also those accused of bigamy, seduction and usury. Between 1580 and 1650, a witch hysteria reigned. Confession was the surest proof of wrongdoing and torture the surest means of procuring a confession. Needless to say, the number of confessions was quite high, and so "proof" of the Devil's ascendancy was overwhelming. The death penalty was sometimes exacted in mass *autos-da-fé*.

As for werewolves, many of these trials occurred in secular courts, but the spirit and hyperbole of the Inquisition prevailed. Stubbe Peeter's "ordinary" crimes—rape, incest, murder and cannibalism—would surely have warranted a death sentence on their own. Nonetheless he was accused of relations with the Devil and tortured (civil courts also adopted the Inquisition's methodology) for crimes that, incomprehensible though they were, were not to be questioned. This combination left little to doubt but much to fear. Like Lycaon, the werewolf served up an example, and became a means of controlling Europe's isolated rural population. Those accused were paraded before the population, and their public torture was thought to be educational. Their punishment, often as brutal as the alleged crimes, amplified the accusations and, paradoxically, confirmed guilt; and pamphlets with fantastic descriptions of their bestiality and horrible deaths spread across the Continent instilling fear and distrust, and encouraging social conformity.

In the heyday of these trials, any woman or man who bucked social norms might be accused of being a witch or a werewolf. Women with sexual knowledge or perceived sexual power were frequent targets: Midwives, widows, barren women; any who sought or provided abortions; beautiful women who inspired lust, or those who caused impotence. Indeed, the *Malleus maleficarum* uses "bewitched" as a synonym for impotence. Meanwhile, werewolves manifested aberrant, fruitless sexuality. On rare occasion they were women, but overwhelmingly they were men, and generally men living on the fringes of society: beggars, loners, hermits (like Gilles Garnier), the mentally ill (like Jean Grenier) or other social outcasts. Because these men lived beyond the physical or psychological boundaries of society, they were perceived as closer to the Devil and a key part of his mission to corrupt mankind. Werewolves committed rape, incest, cannibalism or acts of homosexuality. Like Stubbe Peeter, they were adulterers who bore their children's children and then ate them. In some accounts they were the Devil's agents; in others they were the victims of witches who acted as the Devil's agents. And frequently they attacked small girls.

The werewolf account was a morality tale historically related to the story of Little Red Riding Hood, but also very different. It was a warning not to demoiselles but to peasants on the edge. It was not so much about what one might meet as about what one might become. It was a warning—issued in no uncertain terms to the hermit, the outcast, or just the average peasant man—to keep in line.

Today Little Red Riding Hood's villain has lost his occult past, though details occasionally resurface, and when we read them perhaps we feel a shock of the familiar. A curious volume of stories released in the year 1801 under the title *Tales of Terror* offers a surprisingly gory version of "Little Red Riding Hood." Rather than swallowing the girl and her grandmother whole and alive, in a form that can later be rescued, the villain of "The Wolf King" mangles and mutilates them with obvious gusto. First, Grandma:

He dash'd her brains out on the stones
He gnaw'd her sinews, crack'd her bones;
He munch'd her heart, he quaff'd her gore
And up her light and liver tore!!!

An illustration that accompanied the story in an 1808 edition showed the beast disemboweling the grandmother in a bloody tug-of-war.

The wolf disembowels granny in an 1808 edition of *Tales of Terror.*

When Red Riding Hood arrives slightly after, she meets an equally maudlin fate.

His hungry teeth the Wolf-King gnash'd
His sparkling eyes with fury flash'd,
He oped his jaws all sprent with blood,
And fell upon small Red-riding-hood.

He tore out bowels one and two,
—"Little maid, I will eat you!"—

But when he tore out three and four,
The little maid she was no more!

Murder, mutilation, the anthropomorphism of the villain—
"The Wolf King" seems like a lyrical version of Master Tyse
Artyne's testimony about the little girl whom Stubbe Peeter had
mauled and killed.

Odd words also remind us of the wolf's past. Some old English
variants of "Little Red Riding Hood" refer to the villain as a
"gaffer" wolf, or "gossip" wolf, a term also used in the Stubbe
Peeter pamphlet to describe the werewolf's mistress. The ety-
mology of both terms indicate a close family relation. (The
Anglo-Saxon term for a godparent, *godsibb,* being a compound
of *god* and *sib,* "relative," originally denoted a sponsor of a child
at a baptism. From the same roots comes the modern "sibling."
Gaffer is thought to be a contraction of *grandfather* or *godfather.*)
These terms might be used simply to mean an older person, but
in folklore words inevitably take on multiple meanings. In this
case they may be vestigial references to incest—also a common
charge in the werewolf trials. This concept may help to clarify a
puzzling aspect of the story's plot. Why does Red Riding Hood
speak to the beast in the woods? And how, later on, could she
mistake his furry snout for Granny? What if, in the context of
the werewolf's well-known proclivities, the villain of the tale
were understood to be Red Riding Hood's grandfather? This
would account for the girl's total lack of suspicion and fear in virtually all versions of the tale. For who else would she expect to
find in Grandma's bed?

Not for centuries—long after Perrault and the brothers

Grimm were dead—would the werewolf, arch symbol of Evil, of the Devil himself, get a chance at rehabilitation. By the twentieth century, its carnal desires would increasingly become a symbol of manly prowess and even a source of humor. The werewolf would become the hairy-chested Lothario of Lon Chaney, Jr.'s, movies—horror, passion, a swooning date—while Red Riding Hood's dangerous foe would become a harmless, whistling dog.

Red Hot Riding Hood:
A Babe in the Woods

Lil' Red Riding Hood

By Robert Blackwell

Sung by Sam the Sham and the Pharaohs, 1966

OWOOOOOOOOO!
Who's that walking in these woods?
Why, it's Little Red Riding Hood
Hey there Little Red Riding Hood
You sure are looking good
You're everything a big bad wolf could want—Listen to me

Little Red Riding Hood
I don't think that little big girls should
Go walking in these spooky old woods alone
OWOOOOOOOOO!

What big eyes you have
The kind of eyes that drive wolves mad
So just to see that you don't get chased

Source: From the album *Lil' Red Riding Hood* by Sam the Sham and the Pharaohs, recorded by MGM, 1966.

I think I ought to walk with you for a ways

What full lips you have
They're sure to lure someone bad
So until you get to grandma's place
I think I ought to walk with you and be safe

I'm gonna keep my sheep suit on
Until I'm sure that you've been shown
That I can be trusted walking with you alone
OWOOOOOOOOO!

Little Red Riding Hood
I'd like to hold you if I could
But you might think I'm a big bad wolf so I won't
OWOOOOOOOOO!

What a big heart I have
The better to love you with
Little Red Riding Hood
Even bad wolves can be good

I'll try to be satisfied
Just to walk close by your side
Maybe you'll see things my way
Before we get to grandma's place

Hey there Little Red Riding Hood
You sure are looking good

You're everything a big bad wolf could want
OWOOOOOOOOO!
I mean baaaaaaa!
Baaaaaa? Baaaaaaaaaaaa!

WHEN THE GRIMM BROTHERS turned "Little Red Riding Hood" into a children's tale for Victorian audiences of the nineteenth century, the heroine became the embodiment of innocence. She lost all traces of her earlier French sexuality. Not until the twentieth century was the bowdlerized Red Riding Hood defrocked, so to speak, and redressed. Or, in the hands of the legendary animator Tex Avery, simply defrocked. Avery brought the heroine and her wolf from the European forest to the Hollywood nightclub and transformed the fairy tale into a caricature of American courtship. In his *Red Hot Riding Hood,* released in 1943, the sweet heroine of storybook tradition—who in Perrault's seventeenth-century original had served up a warning about the dangers of promiscuity—became her own symbolic opposite: a Hollywood stripper.

Red Hot Riding Hood begins on the corner of Hollywood and Vine, the legendary spot of history's most famous nightclubs, where the wolf, dressed to the nines in top hat and tails, arrives for an evening of carousing. Grandma's house is now a bordello around the corner, a penthouse apartment lit up by a neon sign: "Grandma's Joint—come up and see me." (A neon hand with a wiggling finger, à la Mae West, invites the passerby upstairs.) And on stage at the Sunset Strip, a chic nightclub that advertises "30 gorgeous girls, no cover," Red Hot Riding Hood steps into the spotlight, all dolled up in make-up and cape—which she quickly tosses aside, along with her basket. No kid anymore, this Red's a buxom bombshell in a short (*very* short) red strapless number. She launches into her song and dance—"Hey Daddy, you better get the best for me"—which sends the wolf, seated in the audience, into a frenzy. He hoots and howls, claps and whistles, and employs a clapping and whistling machine to amplify his appreciation. "Hey Daddy! Hi Paw! Say now *Father,*" Red goes on, undulating her hips and shaking her fanny. The wolf's eyes pop out (literally—they fly across the room), his tongue unrolls like a red carpet, and he rises in the air and stiffens into a full body erection.

As soon as Red finishes her routine, the wolf snakes a long arm onto the stage to whip her to his table. "Fly away with me to the Riviera," he says in a smarmy French accent. But after he follows Red to Grandma's Joint, the tables turn. Granny, a hot old dame in a slinky red dress, is besotted. Now *she* whistles and levitates and hoots, as she chases him from door to door with puckered lips. "*That's* a wolf! *Whoo hoo!*"

"Little Red Riding Hood" was apparently Avery's favorite fairy tale. He repeatedly returned to it, or some semblance of it, throughout the 1930s and 1940s, transforming the tale into a full-scale romance, told in multiple episodes. In *Little Red Walking Hood,* the first of Avery's flirtations with the tale in 1937, he gave Red the body of a little girl but the demeanor of a grown woman. She trots along the boulevard, as the wolf—here a pool hall city slicker, all oily charm and questionable intentions—drives slowly behind her in a shiny black car, throwing out pick-up lines as fast as his lips can animate. She eventually interrupts the narrative to commiserate with the women in the audience about lascivious male behavior.

In *The Bear's Tale* (1940), Avery cast Red as a smart-mouthed, freckle-faced kid from Brooklyn. She teams up with Goldilocks to defeat the wolf by leaning over a split-screen line that separates their plots: "Hello, Goldie! This is Red Ridin' Hood. I just found a note from that skunk the Wolf. . . . " (She hands over the note.) In *Little Rural Riding Hood* (1949), the last of Avery's pseudo–fairy-tale burlesques, he drew a gangly, toothy redhead as the country cousin of Red Hot Riding Hood. She opens and closes doors with her long, unsightly toes, and puckers her enormous, almost snout-like lips.

Of all Avery's variations on this theme, however, *Red Hot Riding Hood* gave him his guiding stars. The buxom redhead and the wolf quickly outgrew the plot that inspired them, becoming recurrent characters in numerous animated shorts. Avery placed the couple not only in his "Red Riding Hood" send-ups, but also in other fairy-tale cartoons. The heroine of *Swing Shift Cinderella* (1945) is really Red Hot all over again. She appears in the familiar nightclub set, with the same upswept red hair, gyrating the same va-va-voom figure. She wears the same revealing outfit, only this time it's conjured up by her fairy godmother. (Red: "You do wave a mean wand, don't you old girl?") And of course, as in her first appearance in *Red Hot Riding Hood,* she is paired up with the same eternally aroused wolf, who falls into throes of ecstasy at her song and dance. This time the tune goes, "Oh Wolfie, ain't you the one!"

Avery placed Red Hot and her wolf in cartoon parodies of

Tex Avery's stripper-heroine is *Red Hot*. For MGM, 1943.

other genres as well, including *The Shooting of Dan McGoo* (1945), his mock western, *Wild and Wolfy* (1945), and *Uncle Tom's Cabana* (1947). In his last spoof on the couple, *Little Rural Riding Hood*, inspired by the Jean de La Fontaine fable about a country mouse and a city mouse, Red is again a dancer at the same nightclub, this time performing for two wolves: a hormone-crazed country bumpkin and a supercilious urbane Romeo (who later falls for Red Hot's homely country cousin).

For Avery, the characters of *Red Hot Riding Hood* transcended the fairy tale. The showgirl and her lascivious pursuer were not just a girl and a wolf, but the characters and symbols of the human sexual drama. His heroine is a sex object. His wolf, stiffening and levitating at the sight of her, is the penis personified.

Such gags were not unusual in the cartoons of an earlier era. Avery's Red Riding Hood riffs were only incidentally for children. They were pre-television, shown in theaters before the main attraction for a general audience. Children went to movies, too, but they were an afterthought for Avery. Like other cartoonists working at this time, Avery incorporated details of American life during the war into his animations. In *Blitzwolf,* released in 1942, the three little pigs face their old enemy the wolf, who has now taken on the persona of Adolph Hitler (a break from his trademark role as lascivious nightclub suitor, and a startling contrast to the Nazi interpretation of the wolf as the marauding Jew). Avery's Swing Shift Cinderella is a nod to Rosie the Riveter; she has to flee the nightclub to be on time for her midnight job— the "swing shift" at the Lockheed factory. And his Red Hot Riding Hood is obviously modeled on the pin-up girls who raised the "morale" of World War II soldiers.

Avery subverted the prevailing standards of animation set by Walt Disney, whose *Snow White and the Seven Dwarfs* became the first full-length feature cartoon in 1937. While Disney revered the Grimms' tradition, Avery disrupted his plots with running gags, ridiculed fairy-tale clichés, and blended Old Europe with contemporary America wherever he found a way to make it funny (as in the tavern called "Ye Old Beere Joint"). He mixed and matched tales, provided unorthodox settings, and produced self-aware characters who frequently interrupt the narrative to comment on the plot or make a statement to the audience, completely rupturing any suspension of disbelief. *Red Hot Riding Hood* begins with a traditional Euro-Disney landscape and the conventional storybook plot. ("Good evening, kiddies," the off-screen narrator intones.) But then the characters rebel and demand that it be done a new way. (The narrator agrees and obligingly begins again.) In *Little Red Walking Hood,* the girl and the wolf suspend animation to wait for a pair of late moviegoers to seat themselves; the fictitious offenders' "silhouettes" appear realistically on the screen. Above all, Avery worked in opposition to Disney's saccharine sweetness, epitomized by the bleached heroine of Disney's *Snow White.*

Avery's endless, obvious visual metaphors for sexual excitement earned him the scrutiny of U.S. government censors. He was known to create salacious sequences that he knew would be cut, hoping to distract them from the sex gags that he truly wanted to keep—though not always successfully. In the publicly released version of *Red Hot Riding Hood,* the wolf is driven mad by the attentions of Red Hot's grandma and vows to kill himself if he ever sees another woman. He shoots himself when Red Hot appears on stage again, and his ghost rises to cheer her striptease on. But the original version that Avery animated, struck by the Hays Office for its explicit theme of bestiality, was much racier. In that version, sent to GIs abroad but not shown to civilian audiences, Grandma and the wolf are married in a shotgun wedding (with Red sitting in the seat of an antiaircraft gun pointed at the wolf's back). They appear in the next scene back at the Sunset Strip, for Red's last act, with a litter of howling wolf pups in tow.

Avery's *Red Hot Riding Hood* captured a changing vision of the American woman in the 1930s and 1940s. She was not only more frankly sexual, but also tougher and more self-reliant than the demure woman of the Victorian era. In Avery's animations, the roles of sex object (even stripper) and self-reliant heroine are

Tex Avery's eternally aroused wolf woos
"Miss Riding Hood" at the Sunset Strip.

not mutually exclusive. His Red Riding Hood, no matter which of his cartoons she appears in, can take care of herself: She is easily able to fend off her suitor with a literal cold shoulder (drawn as a snowball in *Little Red Walking Hood*) or to give his ardor a lights-out by hitting him over the head with a nightclub table lamp (in *Red Hot Riding Hood*).

Avery's contemporary, the humorist James Thurber, also captured this new street-smart quality of American womanhood (minus Avery's explicit sexuality) in a cartoon adaptation of "Little Red Riding Hood" that appeared in his *Fables for Our Time and Famous Poems* in 1939. "It is not so easy to fool little girls nowadays as it used to be," reads the moral beneath his drawing of a no-nonsense heroine, arms akimbo, who regards the tongue-wagging wolf who waits for her in bed with evident annoyance. Thurber's cartoon, like Avery's animations, reflects changes in the lives of American women from the 1920s through the 1940s that sparked new ideas and attitudes. Among those changes: Suffragettes won the vote, bras replaced corsets, and women began wearing pants—finally following the advice of nineteenth-century dress reformer Amelia Bloomer. Amelia Earhart flew solo across the Atlantic in 1932; the Gibson Girl gave way to the flapper, who stepped aside for Rosie the Riveter; the "new woman" went to work, wore lipstick, and smoked cigarettes; and in Hollywood, female stars like Joan Crawford and Betty Davis made names for themselves playing tough femmes fatales.

Avery's and Thurber's work capture some of the sexual and political attitudes of this era, with its revolutionized manners. Avery's Red Hot Riding Hood is the new leading lady—she's a sexpot, sure, but no pushover. She's a cross between Rita Hayworth (the market-savvy redheaded sex goddess who dyed her hair and hid her Spanish heritage to become an "Anglo" star) and Mae West, who herself trafficked in fairy tales, but also restaged and rewrote them. West's one-liners captured the public imagination and entered the language as clichés for the same reason that Avery's cartoons became famous: because they put the fairy tale in twentieth-century terms. "I used to be Snow White," West once famously quipped. "But I drifted."

TEX AVERY'S *Red Hot Riding Hood,* with its wartime pin-up girl heroine, captured a slice of American history and gave new meaning to the fairy tale as a courtship story. It also her-

James Thurber's girl is not as easy to fool
as she used to be.

alded the onset of a specific new role for Little Red Riding Hood. In twentieth-century pop culture, she increasingly conveyed adult female ideals and represented a new and growing demographic: the single woman. "*Miss* Ridinghood," as Avery's wolf calls her. Of the best-known fairy-tale heroines, only Red Riding Hood remains unattached at tale's end—there's no wedding, no prince, not even a brother or two. Thus, over the next decades, as fairy tales became increasingly devoted to expressing feminine ideals, she developed a significance very different from that of other fairy-tale heroines, who underwent their own transitions at the time.

Identical Prince Charmings wear matching outfits,
in Hudson Talbott's book adaptation of *Into the Woods*.

It's no secret that today's best-known fairy-tale protagonists
are female: Cinderella, Snow White, Rapunzel, Sleeping Beauty,
and Red Riding Hood, to name just a few. These heroines act
amongst a cast of banal male foils. The men are simply fathers,
beasts, dwarfs or princes, all interchangeable and usually illustrated as one and the same from tale to tale. In Stephen Sondheim's Broadway musical *Into the Woods,* the Prince Charmings
of two interwoven fairy tales swap places without so much as a
ripple in the plot. In an illustration from the book adaptation of
the musical, they wear matching outfits in matching colors, just
as they share a common name and common romantic mission.
("And how do *you* manage a visit?" says one to the other.)

In these fairy tales, the heroines make decisions that illustrate
the expectations of women in real life, while the male figures are
simply metaphors for punishment (misbehave and you'll meet a
wolf) and reward (a prince in the end—if you're good!).

But what a contrast today's feminine fairy tale is to the genre's past. The brothers Grimm, who were prolific collectors, penned twice as many male as female leads. Looking over their table of contents can befuddle the modern reader: Hans my Hedgehog? King Thrushbeard? Where have these tales of male adventure gone? The answer: They have lost out in the game of editorial selection. As folklorist Kay Stone observed, most children's storybooks contain only a handful of the original 212 stories that appear in the Grimms' complete *Children's and Household Tales*—and nearly all of those that survive feature female-driven plots. Tales with female leads are also far more likely to be made into movies. Disney's *Snow White and the Seven Dwarfs,* an overnight success in 1937, along with *Cinderella* in 1950, established the fairy-tale heroine as a collective role model for every girl and woman aspiring to be a wife and mother. Disney's Snow White gives the dwarfs' bachelor pad a spring cleaning, singing "Whistle While You Work" as she washes dishes, sweeps floors, dusts cobwebs and scrubs clothing—with the assistance of birds, deer, rabbits and other forest fauna. In a similar scene in Disney's later *Cinderella,* mice and birds assist the heroine by sewing a gown for the ball while she finishes cleaning house and dressing her stepsisters—chores that anticipate her life as happy housewife to Prince Charming.

These two movies, like the new twentieth-century feminized fairy tale in general, captured the allure of marriage and domesticity that became the dominant ideal for women after the war. In the 1950s, the age of newlyweds dropped, as did the age of first motherhood, and divorce rates plummeted. Men returned to their jobs, and Rosie the Riveter was urged back into the home. With the family as the center of American life, managing the household became the preoccupation of women's lives. Despite new labor-saving appliances, the number of hours devoted to housework increased. Child care took up twice as much time as it had in the 1920s. Joan Crawford posed for pictures mopping floors. Ozzie and Harriet acted out an idealized version of their real-life marriage on TV. And during this time, American culture produced a parallel ideal in fiction: the "fairy-tale wedding"—a romanticized union that in fact has nothing whatsoever to do with the forced matrimonial trades behind Charles Perrault's seventeenth-century fairy tales—which never existed before the twentieth century.

Yet if America idealized the family, behind the trimmed hedges and driveways of suburbia the reality of mid-century life was more complex, as scholars like Stephanie Coontz have thoroughly documented. Despite the cult of domesticity and the prudery of Ozzie and Harriet, the 1950s were a time of new sexual freedoms. Terms like "going steady" and "petting" (or even "heavy petting") came about to describe them. Teenage girls got pregnant, were sent away to have their babies, and came back "rehabilitated." The number of pregnant brides skyrocketed—though with the appearance of better methods of birth control (particularly the pill in 1960), premarital sex became less risky. And alongside the glorified housewife, there was increasingly the woman who did not go straight from father's to husband's arms. Living on her own, she navigated the double standards of the age. This is the demographic that Red Riding Hood, the single heroine, rose to serve.

As Sleeping Beauty, Cinderella and Snow White marched down the aisle, mid-century pop culture depictions of Little to bring the wolves out... ‹

Red Riding Hood seem as if meant to illustrate Helen Gurley Brown's 1962 bestseller *Sex and the Single Girl*. In advertising of the time she is cast as a femme fatale, hawking liquor, make-up and fast cars. Ripe, young "riding hood red" lipstick would "bring the wolves out," Max Factor promised in a poster-sized ad appearing in *Vogue* magazine in 1953 that radically transformed the tale's traditional warning against speaking to strangers. On one side of the spread a red-hooded, red-nailed vixen smiles coyly as she applies a bright shade of red lipstick. On the opposite page, a background shot shows a forest, with a company of Gregory Peck look-alikes peering out from behind the trees, grinning comically lecherous grins. "Wear Riding Hood Red at your own sweet risk. . . . We warn you, you're going to be followed!" says the ad copy: "It's a rich, succulent red that turns the most innocent look into a tantalizing invitation." A 1962 advertisement in *The New Yorker* similarly cast Red as a glamorous femme fatale: this time, on her way to Grandma's in her "little red Hertz." Her car is a racy convertible; her hood now a high-fashion item that might have come from Dior; her coy come-hither smile and sidelong glance is almost identical to that of the Max Factor model. And, "Without red, nothing doing," says a 1983 ad for Johnny Walker red label, which shows a wolf bypassing a girl dressed in white. Who wants to buy a drink for bleached goody-two-shoes?

In pop music, Sam the Sham and the Pharaohs also echoed the new popular version of the tale as a courtship dance, and the heroine's new availability—both social and sexual. In their 1966 smash hit "Lil' Red Riding Hood"—which could easily have been the theme song for Madison Avenue ads or for Avery's *Red Hot*

Riding Hood—the wolf pursues the girl not in search of a meal but in hopes of a date. This time it is *he* who notices what big eyes— not to mention full lips—that the heroine, now a "big girl," has. "Owoo! Little Red Riding Hood—you sure are looking good!"

As Sam the Sham and the ads of Madison Avenue suggest, the new grown-up Red Riding Hood has a suitor; indeed, she may bring out as many wolves as she pleases—but she is defined by her independence from them. Brown's *Sex and the Single Girl*, which described the prototype of the *Cosmo Girl*, offers an insight into the sort of woman who might purchase Max Factor's ripe young "riding hood red" lipstick. Brown's advice, though in opposition to some of the coming ideas of feminism, nevertheless stands in stark contrast to the clichés of 1950s gender stereo- types and epitomizes the sort of power that at the time was avail- able to single women—as "gold-diggers" and flirts. During a woman's best years, Brown counseled, "You don't need a hus- band," just a man, and men "are often cheaper emotionally and a lot more fun by the bunch." She advised flirtation with butchers to get a better side of beef, and counseled single women against having an affair with only one married man—though there was nothing wrong with dating *many*.

F AST-FORWARD to the end of the twentieth century, when a 1998 television spot crafted by Luc Besson for Chanel No. 5 perfume updates the heroine's commercial sex appeal. This time, Red is a Parisian beauty (model Estella Warren, shown in cos- tume in the opening image of the introduction to this book) who calls her own shots. She sashays through a mansion in a red satin bustier-and-petticoats number—reminiscent of the outfit worn by Avery's Red Hot. In her vault, bottles of Chanel No. 5 perfume, stacked ceiling high and wall to wall like bricks of gold, signify her incredible stock of sex appeal, here defined as scent. After dabbing her pulse points, she dons a shiny red satin cloak and heads for the door, where she turns at the last moment and places a finger to her lips to shush a howling wolf—her house pet. Subdued, he sits obediently as she flips her hood over her head and with a smile heads out the door to the Paris skyline for a night on the town with a different set of wolves. "Share the fantasy," exhorts the legendary Chanel tag line.

In just thirty seconds the Chanel ad inverts the tale's traditional message: The admonition to obedience has been redirected—now *he* is tamed—and instead of the womanizing wolf, this time it's the heroine who goes on the prowl. But has the message *really* changed? Although Chanel's "Little Red Riding Hood" has tamed her wolf, her implicit lesson is hardly different from that of Max Factor's femme fatale in 1953: namely, that sexual appeal—or lack thereof—is the source of female power and value, whether in the perfume vault or in the open market of dating and mating.

The sultry single woman has been one of Little Red Riding Hood's great twentieth-century roles, whether *Red Hot* or "ripe, young" or just a fantasy in a perfumed red dress. Chased by a pack of smitten bachelors in the cartoons of Tex Avery, the croonings of Sam the Sham, or the ad copy of Max Factor, by mid-century our heroine emerged as an icon of feminine availability: the image of woman as man desires her, distinguished by her ability to turn his head (or make him levitate, steam, and lose his eyeballs) and always desirous of a romantic romp.

But while the popular understanding of the tale as a parable of puppy love endures into the present day, this version of the story as a romance, crafted by men like Avery, Luc Besson, and the executives of Madison Avenue, contrasts sharply with the way women in the latter half of the twentieth century retold the fairy-tale. Far from romantic fun and games, feminists cast Red Riding Hood's encounter with the wolf in a far more sinister light.

VI

The Waiting Wolf: In the Belly of the Beast

The Waiting Wolf

BY GWEN STRAUSS

First, I saw her feet—
beneath a red pointed cloak
head bent forward
parting the woods,
one foot placed straight
in front of the other.

Then, came her scent.
I was meant to stalk her
smooth, not a twig snaps.
It is the only way I know;
I showed her flowers—
white dead-nettle, nightshade,
devil's bit, wood anemone.

I might not have gone further,
but then nothing ever remains
innocent in the woods.

When she told me about Grandmother,
I sickened. She placed herself on my path,
practically spilling her basket of breads and jams.

Source: From *Trail of Stones,* published by Knopf, 1990.

Waiting in this old lady's ruffled bed,
I am all calculation. I have gone this far—
dressed in Grandmother's lace panties,
flannel nightgown and cap,
puffs of breath beneath the sheet
lift and fall. I can see my heart tick.
Slightly. Slightly.

These are small lies for a wolf,
but strangely heavy in my belly like stones.
I will forget them as soon as I have her,
still, at this moment I do not like myself.

When she crawls into Grandma's bed,
will she pull me close, thinking:
This is my grandmother whom I love?

She will have the youngest skin
I have ever touched, her fingers unfurling
like fiddle heads in spring.

My matted fur will smell to her of forest
moss at night. She'll wonder about my ears,
large, pointed, soft as felt,
my eyes red as her cloak,
my leather nose on her belly.

But perhaps she has known who I am since the first,
since we took the other path
through the woods.

IN 1961 THE POET Anne Sexton, beautiful and suicidal, gave her daughter Linda a blue hard-bound collection of Grimms' fairy tales. Years later, Linda recalled reading at the kitchen table, slurping canned soup to the clatter of her mother's typewriter in the adjacent dining room, and finding solace in the predictable plots. Linda was sixteen when her mother finally became curious about her fascination with the tales and asked her to list her favorites. Sexton wrote them down on a paper napkin. Later Sexton reworked them, with her trademark audacity, into one of her best-selling collections of poems, and one of the most famous revisions of the Grimm fairy tales by a woman. Published in 1971, *Transformations* is not what most people would expect from fairy tales—"very wry, and cruel and sadistic and funny," as Sexton said—and spattered with references to rape, incest, child abuse and pedophilia.

For Sexton, the Grimm fairy tales had a lot to say about real life, if you looked at them with a twisted mind. She found the tales full of dark secrets about men and women, gender and madness (among her favorite themes). In the princesses trapped in towers and dungeons, she saw not romantic fantasy but metaphors for the domestic prison of abused daughters and suburban housewives. The Grimms' heroines were so entirely self-sacrificing that she described them in terms of their edibility: Sleeping Beauty, whose father molests her in the dark years of her coma, is passed along to her husband "like a bowl of fruit." The Maiden Without Hands has a cruel, ogling father who wants to "lap her up like a strawberry preserve." Snow White is like a porcelain doll, mindless—"her glass eyes rolling open and shut, open and shut"—and delectable. When she falls into her poisoned slumber, the dwarfs marinate her like a pot roast: "Though they washed her with wine/and rubbed her with butter/it was to no avail."

Though food is a central metaphor in these poems, Sexton herself rarely cooked. She was intimidated and exasperated by the kitchen, but also more broadly by the role of wife and mother (she had first attempted suicide shortly after Linda's birth). As for the Grimms' happily-ever-after endings, they too rang false with Sexton, whose own marriage—she had eloped, romantically, as a teenager—buckled under the weight of her mental illness, her frequent affairs, and violent fights with her husband, Kayo. Her Cinderella snags a prince in the end, but the fantasy of their perfect union is punctured by ridicule. "Their darling smiles pasted on for eternity/Regular Bobbsey Twins," Sexton dubbed the couple sarcastically. "That story."

Reset amidst the signs and symbols of pop culture, Sexton's sixteen "transformed" Grimm tales contrast the metaphors and promises of fairy tales, especially their idealistic fantasies about men and women, with the disappointments and ambiguities of real life. Her "Little Red Riding Hood" (which is reproduced before Chapter 8) dwells on deception and the peculiarities of gender. The wolf is a transvestite who appears "in his ninth month" after eating the heroine and her grandmother. The woodsman rescues Red with a "carnal knife" and delivers her via caesarian section. It is as if the male characters have taken over the apparatus of womanhood, from clothing to pregnancy, while Red Riding Hood awaits rebirth in the belly of the beast—a space that is vaguely disturbing, and suggestive of a larger darkness. Throughout the poem, there is constant questioning of the trite as well as the fundamental details of the story—of gender, sexuality, villainy and rescue. Yet the heroine and her grandmother remain unaware—they eat wine and cake, "remembering nothing" of being swallowed and trapped in the darkness of the beast's belly, oblivious to their own plight and to how they have been marginalized. Sexton's poem, with its interrogative tone, implies that the reader, too, has been blinded to or deceived by elements of the plot, and perhaps by elements of her own life.

Transformations captures a life of contradictions. These poems, like many others by Sexton, attempt to reconcile her outer image and inner turmoil—the struggle that led her to begin writing poetry in the first place, at the suggestion of her therapist during a stay at a sanitarium. The third daughter of an upper-middle-class New England family, Sexton came from glamorous, rowdy stock. As a girl, she once kidnapped a docile friend and hid her in the bedroom closet overnight until a distraught mother telephoned in search of her lost child. As a young woman, she was a scene-stealing siren with a penchant for small but melodramatic rebellions—the sort of woman who put on gaudy red lipstick and red high heels for a trip to the supermarket, who sunbathed naked atop her mother's mink coat on the backyard snow banks in the dead of winter, and who threw temper tantrums at her own parties. She spoke LOUDLY (and often wrote in capital letters, much to the same effect). In Boston she frequented the Ritz with fellow poets Sylvia Plath and Ted Hughes. "I would always park at a LOADING ZONE sign," she wrote in the fall of 1965 to Charles Newman, editor of *TriQuarterly,* "and tell them 'It's okay, because we are going to get loaded.'"

By the time she was forty, Sexton was a celebrity. She had won virtually every award available to an American poet, published in prestigious magazines like *The New Yorker,* was featured in magazine articles, had won the Pulitzer Prize, and—though she had never graduated from college—had honorary degrees from both Harvard in 1968 and Radcliffe in 1969. On stage at readings she was all cigarettes and dramatic gestures, husky whispers and sultry stares. She arrived late, sometimes smashed, sometimes bringing standing ovations. And she was beautiful: Dark-haired, blue-eyed and svelte, she stood out from the tweedy literary crowd around her, radiating glamour and sex appeal. Her friend Maxine Kumin likened her to a fashion model, which in fact she had once been. A photo from her days with the Hart agency in Boston shows her in a floor-length white gown, cool and poised and iconic.

Yet if in outward appearance she was a real-life version of a fairy-tale "princess"—the pet name by which her husband Kayo called her—in her own mind she was its exact opposite. In *Transformations,* Sexton cast herself as the prototypical fairy-tale villain: "a middle-aged witch, me." Despite her fantastic success, her many admirers, her undeniable glamour, this was her favorite alter ego, conjured up with a wave of a cigarette whenever she read aloud her trademark poem "Her Kind": "I have gone out, a possessed witch,/haunting the black air, braver at night." By the time she published *Transformations*, Sexton was forty-one, a self-described "mad housewife" with dishpan hands and maniacal tendencies, living in the Boston suburbs, and just a few years from death. She was afraid to travel. She checked into and out of sanitariums. Needy and sexually insecure, she carried on numerous extramarital affairs, including one with her psychiatrist during paid therapy sessions. She corresponded with fans in mental hospitals. Much later Linda revealed disturbing stories of her mother sexually abusing her during her adolescence. Kayo took over the household while Sexton wrote, lectured, taught around the nation, and became increasingly focused on death. Her book sales continued to climb throughout her career, even as her mental health teetered. She attempted suicide on nine different occasions before she finally succeeded, gassing herself in the family garage, in 1974.

Sexton's poems were more than a response to her personal struggles, however; they were part and parcel of a broader social dynamic. Sexton documented her life in notoriously intimate terms—"confessional" is the usual adjective attached to her work; yet she also gave voice to contradictions in the lives of American women, and especially to the increasing awareness of such contradictions. Sexton grew into suburban femininity in post–World War II America, when the expansion of the leisure class left more and more women at home, idle and bored. Her poems exposed the rift between a woman's experience and the social ideals of womanhood, a contradiction that Betty Friedan had recently named in her landmark book *The Feminine Mystique* (or the "FEM MYSTIQUE," as Sexton and Maxine Kumin called it). Sexton wrote about her erotic fantasies, and of the exhausting demands of femininity. "I was tired of the spoons and pots, tired of my mouth, my breasts, tired of the cosmetics and the silks," she wrote in 1962; "I was tired of the gender of things." She wrote poems in homage of her affairs and others that challenged her unfaithful lovers. She wrote of abortion, sexual abuse, her sagging midriff. She pondered menopause, masturbation, and menstruation, becoming such a notorious voice of the female body that a reviewer once commented that she "wallowed in gynecology." And her poems in *Transformations,* as the title implies, caught a new female focus on changing the world.

The 1960s marked the beginning of the second wave of feminism—or the Women's Liberation Movement, as it was then called. One of the central insights of this resurgent feminism was that women had been imbued with a false consciousness and thus needed to have their true consciousness raised. Why should men be the ones, they asked, to set the standards of female beauty, behavior and happiness? Protesters burned bras at the 1968 Miss America pageant and occupied the offices of the male editors of the *Ladies' Home Journal* in 1970. The French writer Simone de Beauvoir had already argued persuasively that girls are socialized to become submissive, adored objects. In her landmark book, *The Second Sex,* which reached American audiences in 1953, four years after its French publication, she examined how every book, lesson and signal in a girl's life seemed to conspire to make her into the lesser sex, somewhere between man and eunuch. "A woman is not born, but made," she famously declared. In the 1960s, feminists followed her lead, analyzing art, song, literature, religion, psychology and culture. In particular, they turned their gaze on fairy tales—what they saw as the first training manuals for little girls.

Their analysis: In the time-worn tales of the literary canon, boys go on quests and are rewarded with riches, while girls wait for the ultimate payoff of marriage. While the fairy-tale heroine waits, a series of unfortunate patterns defines her role. First, the beauty pageant: She is always the prettiest girl in all the land. Yet if she is loved for her beauty, her individual features are hardly of note, and her lover may even fail to recognize her altogether. In the Grimms' collection, Cinderella's prince twice mistakes the heroine for her stepsisters, and even in the Walt Disney version he must rely on her shoe size to be sure. Second, her youth: If she has sisters, she is not only the prettiest, but also the youngest. Finally, and above all, the fairy-tale heroine undergoes a ritual preparation for her eventual marriage through a series of humiliating trials so universally recognizable that folklorists refer to an entire genre of tales simply by the descriptive phrase "the innocent persecuted heroine."

Our most popular fairy tales are all, in fact, variations on this genre and its familiar, brutal pattern. Cinderella's stepfamily treats her as a slave, confining her to the kitchen to wear rags and sleep among the hearth ashes; her very name implies as much. Rapunzel's parents give her away at birth to an old witch, who imprisons her for many years in a high tower without door or stairs: The only means of entrance is via Rapunzel's braided locks, which she lets fall like a rope ladder from her window. Snow White's jealous stepmother forces her to flee into the forest, where she becomes scullery maid to a troop of dwarfs. And in "The Handless Maiden" (a somewhat less-known Grimm brothers tale that dramatically exemplifies the genre), a father accidentally trades his daughter to a devilish stranger, then amputates her hands and sends her off, maimed and bandaged, to wander the world as a beggar.

Complete submission to these trials is the heroine's ticket to happily-ever-after—for if the heroine is loved for her beauty, she is *rewarded* for her passivity. The female protagonists of the Grimms' fairy tales are idealized not for their initiative or accomplishments, notes feminist anthropologist Sherry Ortner in her book *Making Gender,* but for the exact opposite: the *renunciation* of agency. "If [the heroine] has been at all active in the early part of the tale, she must invariably pass through severe trials before being worthy of marrying the prince." Other heroines who are proactive—Gretel, who rescues Hansel from a witch, or Red Riding Hood, who is adventurous—never graduate to the state of marriage, the symbolic recognition of maturity. These heroines haven't yet been properly socialized into their adult roles.

But exile and isolation, domestic drudgery, rags and utter submission to humiliating abuses are the least of the fairy-tale heroine's plight. What most aroused feminists' ire is how the fairy tale romanticizes her murder. Indeed, some of our stock sequences might be called "fairy-tale snuff."

The bridegroom of the Grimms' "Fowler's Foul," a variation of Perrault's "Bluebeard," kills and dismembers a series of brides; the heroine of the tale, the current Mrs. Bluebeard, only narrowly escapes his blade. In her feminist revision of that tale, British writer Angela Carter highlights and embellishes on the blood-thirsty bridegroom's perverted fetish fantasies, describing the contents of his medieval torture chamber: the carefully arranged remains of his former wives. The first is naked and perfectly pre-served, embalmed and surrounded by candles, with a smile on her dead lips. Another is locked in the spiked grip of an Iron Maiden; as the heroine opens her cage, a pool of blood forms at her feet. A third floats in the air, a disembodied skull strung up by unseen cords, decorated with a crown of white roses and a veil of lace.

However horrific, Bluebeard's presumed sexual excitement at the sight of these lovely cadavers (or parts thereof) is only typical of the popular fairy-tale's male lead. In Perrault's "Sleeping Beauty," the heroine pricks her finger on a spinning wheel, falls under an evil fairy's spell and slips into a death-like state. She lies motionless for one hundred years, yet magically fresh, her beauty more perfect in seeming death than in life. Prince Charming sees her comatose body and falls to his knees, "trembling in admiration."

The Grimms' Snow White falls under a remarkably similar death spell after being poisoned not once but thrice by her step-mother, the wicked queen. Prince Charming falls in love with her only after she has died and been laid out in a glass coffin—glass, for better viewing, and so that the dwarfs can keep watch for any sign of decay. He even offers to buy the coffin from the dwarfs, so that he can take her home intact and preserved, and share his life with a corpse.

Even Little Red Riding Hood is devoured alive in the course of a titillating bedroom scenario with the anthropomorphized wolf. Sexton's contemporary Sylvia Plath provided the lines that might eulogize these damsels in distress on their epitaph: "The woman is perfected/Her dead/Body wears the smile of accomplishment."

To feminists, these fairy tales filled little girls with dreams of becoming glamorous victims. Simone de Beauvoir wrote: "A whole flock of delicate heroines, bruised, passive, wounded, kneeling, humiliated, demonstrate to their young sister the fascinating prestige of martyred, deserted, resigned beauty." In her 1974 book *Woman Hating,* radical feminist Andrea Dworkin extended de Beauvoir's analysis, deeming the canonical fairy tales the first formative scenarios of patriarchy:

> We have taken the fairy tales of childhood with us into maturity, chewed but still lying in the stomach, as real identity. Between Snow-white and her heroic prince, our two great fictions, we never did have much of a chance. At some point the Great Divide took place: they (the boys) dreamed of mounting the Great Steed and buying Snow-white from the dwarfs; we (the girls) aspired to become that object of every necrophiliac's lust—the innocent, *victimized* Sleeping Beauty, beauteous lump of ultimate, sleeping good.

IN THE CONTEXT of feminist analysis, "Little Red Riding Hood" in particular developed a dramatically new meaning. In her landmark book on rape, *Against Our Will,* published in 1975, Susan Brownmiller examines the cultural glorification of female victimhood. Even before a girl has learned to read,

Brownmiller argues, the stories told to her indoctrinate her into the victim mentality:

> Fairy tales are full of a vague dread, a catastrophe that seems to befall only little girls. Sweet, feminine Little Red Riding Hood is off to visit her dear old grandmother in the woods. The wolf lurks in the shadows, contemplating a tender morsel. Red Riding Hood and her grandmother, we learn, are equally defenseless before the male wolf's strength and cunning. His big eyes, his big hands, his big teeth—"the better to see you, to catch you, to eat you my dear." The wolf swallows both females with no sign of a struggle. But enter the huntsman—he will right this egregious wrong. . . . *Red Riding Hood* is a parable of rape. There are frightening male figures abroad in the woods—we call them wolves, among other names—and females are helpless before them.

Brownmiller's analysis of "Little Red Riding Hood" picks up on symbolic references that extend beyond the fairy tale and suggest how perceptive her point really is. Accounts of prison rape, for example, provide independent confirmation of her assertions about gender, power, rape and the fairy tale. One of the most descriptive of these accounts appears in Haywood Patterson's autobiographical *Scottsboro Boy,* the story of one of the nine young black men accused of raping two white women and sentenced to death in 1930s Alabama. "I learned men were having men," Patterson wrote, shortly after he arrived at Atmore prison. "Old guys, they called them wolves."

Patterson's description of the process that defined and distinguished who was a "wolf" and who was not dramatically reveals our underlying social assumptions of gender:

Soon after I got [to Atmore] I saw how a wolf would trick a young boy. They all worked the same way. First the wolf, he gave the new guy money and bought him what he wanted from the commissary. He told the boy he was a friend. He would protect him from the tough guys. He would fight for him. He didn't tell him right off what he was leading to. After he spent four or five dollars on the boy, he propositioned him.

In the end, however, this courtship inevitably failed to win the young prisoner over, and matters were resolved violently: "The old wolf beat him up unmerciful," initiating the boy into a new identity. "The other prisoners just looked on," writes Patterson. "They knew *a young woman was being born*" (my emphasis).

In Patterson's prison narrative, just as feminists argued more broadly, gender is not a question of biological sex, but of power. Among a population of biological men, there is *still* a separation of inmates into *his* and *hers* categories. A man, or "wolf," is defined not by a penis, but by his ability to physically and sexually dominate others. As in Brownmiller's analysis of "Little Red Riding Hood," the wolf is the rapist. His victim, the "young woman," or "gal-boy" as Patterson writes elsewhere (or "bitch," in the more modern prison lexicon), is the weaker inmate, who is at the mercy of the wolf, and at once in need of his protection. Though anatomically male, the gal-boy does not possess masculine prerogative. *She,* therefore, is defined entirely by her want of power.

IN RECENT DECADES, Brownmiller's reading of "Little Red Riding Hood" as a tale of male dominance and female victimization has become almost common, particularly in women's writing. In her book *Promiscuities* (1997), feminist author Naomi Wolf recalls a childhood episode of sexual assault as a "danger that I experienced in the terms of the fairy tales." Her walk from the bus stop to day camp at the age of ten becomes, in her memory, a version of the famous story of the girl accosted in the woods. "I strode quickly in the straight, safe line my mother had pointed out to me," she writes; but "crouching in the triangular patch of ground where thick foliage grew, a devil waited for me in the underbrush. . . . 'Little girl!' he whispered. 'Little girl!'" Entering the bushes, the naïve ten-year-old Wolf (her own name adds an ironic depth to her memory) is tricked into searching for a contact lens while the "devil" masturbates. And when, in her controversial book on campus sexual politics, *The Morning After,* Katie Roiphe criticizes the anti-rape movement and asserts that "Little Red Riding Hood is just a fairy tale, whatever big bad wolves are out there are out to get all of us, flesh and blood, male or female," she implicitly acknowledges the fairy tale's widespread symbolic value as a parable of date rape.

Modern fiction writers also frequently incorporate themes of sexual assault in their retellings of "Little Red Riding Hood." In her collection *The Rose and the Beast,* Francesca Lia Block retitles the fairy-tale "Wolf" and tells it as a modern American story of sexual abuse in which the heroine is repeatedly raped by her mother's boyfriend. She remembers the villain, "above me in that bed, with his clammy hand on my mouth and his ugly ugly weight." The opening credits for the 1996 movie *Freeway*, based on the "Red Riding Hood" plot (to be discussed in Chapter 10) begin with a lurid sequence of neon-colored cartoons that depict a leering, salivating wolf chasing a series of frightened, fleeing girls. The drawings intentionally stir the hornet's nest about whether a woman ever "asks for it" by contrasting the girls' evident fear with their ridiculously skimpy outfits and by frequently giving the wolf's-eye-view up their skirts—making the audience complicit in the act of sexual assault. More explicitly, in Anne Sharpe's 1985 tale, "Not So Little Red Riding Hood," the heroine, now renamed "Scarlet," brushes off the come-on of a man in a "perfectly cut gray suit," ignoring his wolf whistle and the scent of Brut cologne—thereby "provoking" his rapacious assault: "His body became sheeted steel from which his limbs extended as grappling hooks. He was the last invincible warrior with the ultimate weapon." And Gwen Strauss's 1990 poem, "The Waiting Wolf," reprinted at the beginning of this chapter, contains the legacy of Brownmiller's analysis. Strauss's dark, lurking pedophile of a wolf, with his creepy, self-rationalizing approach to his soon-to-be sexual offense, uses the familiar language of men who accuse women of leading them on: "She placed herself on my path/ Practically spilling her basket of breads and jams." Strauss's poem gives us a woman's perspective on a man's perspective on sexual aggression. All calculation and testosterone, her villain spins the age-old adventure, apparently hoping to justify his actions to the reader while in fact damning himself further.

Yet even as feminism has changed the way many of us read and retell "Little Red Riding Hood," the increasing acceptance of this feminist interpretation of the fairy tale tends to obscure the enormous historical breakthrough that it implies. In his wonderful anthology *The Trials and Tribulations of Little Red Riding Hood,* Jack Zipes, one of the leading experts on the fairy tale, and a scholar of feminist folklore as well, argues that Charles Perrault transformed "an oral tale of the seventeenth century . . . into a literary tale of rape and violence." Certainly Perrault took liberties with oral tradition; but did he *really* pen a tale of rape? In fact, one of the implicit points of feminists' work is that "Little Red Riding Hood" could never have been a story about rape, at least, not as we conceive of that concept today, before the second half of the twentieth century. For as scholars like Brownmiller have documented, throughout most of history rape was considered a crime against men.

In biblical times, wives and daughters were considered the property of the head of the household. According to Brownmiller, in the Hebrew social order virgin maidens were bought and sold at the price of fifty silver shekels. Criminal rape was defined as a property crime: the theft of a daughter's virginity and hence of her fair price on the market. The punishment? The rapist "was ordered to pay the girl's father fifty shekels in compensation for what would have been her bride price, and the pair was simply commanded to wed."

Rape was also a crime against honor—male honor. According to the Bible, Dinah, the virgin daughter of Jacob and Leah, was raped by Shechem, the son of a neighboring chief and a gentile. Later her attacker attempted to make amends in the customary way by offering to marry her. Dinah's family agreed, but with a condition: that Shechem and his men would all be circumcised. Three days after the operation, when the men were in pain, Dinah's brothers Simeon and Levi attacked. They killed all the men, seized their flocks and raped their wives. Dinah's feelings are not recorded—apparently they were not important; only those of the Hebrew men are preserved. Jacob was angry with his sons, the Bible says, but they answered: "Should our sister be treated like a whore?" (Genesis 34).

Although Brownmiller finally locates the first legal recognition of rape as a crime against women in the thirteenth century, when Charles Perrault first published "Little Red Riding Hood," in 1697, the court of Versailles had not much advanced its analysis of the crime. The crime of *rapt,* meaning forceful abduction or seduction (from the same roots we get both "rape" and "rapture"), was not an offense against a woman, but against her *father.* In the seventeenth century, parents controlled marriage arrangements, inheritance and patronage, using their offspring to advance the family status and to enlarge the patrimony. The rapt of an heiress, presumably a virgin, was considered a violation of parental rights and a threat to the family welfare so serious that it was punishable by death. Whether or not the lovers in question wished to marry, or indeed whether the woman had consented to have sexual relations with the man, mattered not at all. French law made no distinction between a woman's willing elopement and her violent rape.

What's more, charges of rapt could be brought against the young woman herself if any of the parents—his or hers—felt entitled to make a better match. French scholar Sarah Hanley has documented a number of such cases. In 1619 Jean Brochard sued his own son, along with the woman whom he had secretly married. His son César got off lightly; he was sent briefly to stay in a monastery. But Susanne Guy, the woman whom he had married, was convicted of rapt and banished from Paris for a decade. By the end of the seventeenth century, when Perrault penned his Mother Goose tales, the dockets were overflowing with cases of rapt. An edict of 1697, the very year Perrault's collection was issued, listed the problems—unions that dishonored the family and ignored inequality of birth; priests and witnesses who could easily be bribed to permit secret, unapproved marriages; and above all, the inability of laws to arrest the force of human passion. Charges of rapt continued to be brought against women well into the eighteenth century, with devastating effect. In 1732, Ferdinande-Henriette-Gabrielle de Brun and Louis-Henri de Saulx de Tavannes attempted to marry secretly, but they were foiled by Ferdinande's father, who obtained a *lettre de cachet* for Ferdinande's cloistration. She spent fourteen years in convents and was released only after her father's death. Even then she was severely disadvantaged because she had been disinherited.

Not until the 1970s did women activists create a new awareness of rape as a crime of aggression against women, finally revising the historical view of rape as a property crime, overturning Freudian notions that women secretly desired to be overcome (hence their rape "fantasies"), and challenging widely held beliefs that women who cried rape had just been "asking for it." Brownmiller was active in the anti-rape movement of the early 1970s, which provided the impetus and context for her book about rape, *Against Our Will*. She belonged to the New York Radical Feminist Organization, which organized a pivotal series of speak-outs on rape between 1971 and 1974. In subsequent years, rape and its corollaries, sexual harassment and date rape, became hot topics of the college campus, of feminist theory and mainstream news reportage. The first rape crisis center opened only in 1971. In the 1980s sociologist and activist Diana Russell's first sophisticated survey on rape gave the startling figures that are now frequently referenced in newspapers: One in four women had been raped, her study asserted; one in three had been sexually abused in childhood. In 1985, *Ms.* magazine published a study on rape by acquaintances, or "date rape." And in 1975, women activists at Cornell University coined the term "sexual harassment," which eventually became, with the 1991 Clarence Thomas–Anita Hill Senate hearings, a household word.

Only now, 300 years *after* Charles Perrault transformed "The Grandmother's Tale" into his "*Le petit chaperon rouge*," has feminism infused the fairy tale with the sense of a patriarchy and given us the vocabulary and statistics to read "Little Red Riding Hood" as a parable of rape.

F ROM CHASTITY WARNING and obedience lesson to budding female hero and sexpot cartoon, now in the second half of the twentieth century Little Red Riding Hood's journey of identity has incorporated a new theme, and a new ominous character—a wolf dramatically different from the love-struck bachelor of the courtship scenarios of Tex Avery and Madison Avenue.

But while some of the stories from or influenced by the women's movement highlight the gap between the way men wrote the fairy tale and the way women read it, others offer a new vision of the fairy tale to bridge that divide. Increasingly, women would reclaim "Little Red Riding Hood" from the belly of the beast and put her in the place, and even in the fur, of the wolf.

VII

The Company of Wolves:
She-Wolf or Bitch?

Little Red Riding Hood and the Wolf

By Roald Dahl

As soon as Wolf began to feel
That he would like a decent meal,
He went and knocked on grandma's door.
When Grandma opened it she saw
The sharp white teeth, the horrid grin,
And Wolfie said, "May I come in?"
Poor Grandmamma was terrified,
"He's going to eat me up!" she cried.
And she was absolutely right.
He ate her up in one big bite.
But Grandmamma was small and tough,
And Wolfie wailed, "that's not enough!
I haven't yet begun to feel
That I have had a decent meal!"
He ran around the kitchen yelping
"I've got to have another helping!"

Source: From *Roald Dahl's Revolting Rhymes,* published by Knopf, 1983.

Then added with a frightful leer,
"I'm therefore going to wait right here
Till Little Miss Red Riding Hood
Comes home from walking in the wood."
He quickly put on Grandma's clothes,
(Of course he hadn't eaten those.)
He dressed himself in coat and hat.
He put on shoes and after that
He even brushed and curled his hair
Then sat himself in Grandma's chair.
In came the little girl in red.
She stopped. She stared. And then she said,

"What great big ears you have, Grandma."
"All the better to hear you with," *the Wolf replied.*
"What great big eyes you have, Grandma,"
said Little Red Riding Hood.
"All the better to see you with," *the Wolf replied.*

He sat there watching her and smiled.
He thought, I'm going to eat this child.
Compared with her old Grandmamma
She's going to taste like caviare.

Then Little Red Riding Hood said, "But Grandma,
What a lovely great big furry coat you have on."
"That's wrong!" cried Wolf. "Have you forgot
To tell me what BIG TEETH I've got?
Ah well, no matter what you say,

I'm going to eat you anyway."
The small girl smiles. One eyelid flickers.
She whips a pistol from her knickers.
She aims it at the creature's head
And bang bang bang, she shoots him dead.
A few weeks later, in the wood,
I came across Miss Riding Hood.
But what a change! No cloak of red,
No silly hood upon her head.
She said, "Hello, and do please note
My lovely furry WOLFSKIN COAT."

F ASHION, IN THE FAIRY-TALE, is a powerful source of identity, and a change of clothing generally heralds deeper
shifts in a character's or a tale's meaning. In a 1972 revision of
"Little Red Riding Hood" by a group of four women called the
Merseyside Women's Liberation Movement, our heroine gets a
new cloak and a new sense of confidence. Shy, skittish and
frightened of everything from thunder to forests to strangers,
she heads off through the woods and encounters the usual
wolf—only this time she has backup. Red Riding Hood's great-
grandmother is a strong old woman who once fought and felled
a wolf in her own youth. Arriving from the kitchen to save the
day (in place of the usual hunter-woodsman), she holds the wolf
at bay with a blazing branch from the stove. As the branch burns
down and the wolf prepares to pounce, Red Riding Hood suddenly remembers the sewing knife in her basket, and she takes it
and plunges it into the wolf's heart. Together, she and her great-
grandmother skin the wolf and stitch its fur into her red cloak,
making a warm new lining—with special powers that the old
woman says will allow any child who wears it to grow brave.

In the second half of the twentieth century, a proliferation of
revisions of "Little Red Riding Hood" turned the tale around to
teach a new lesson. Storytellers from the women's movement and

beyond reclaimed the heroine and her grandmother from male-dominated literary tradition, recasting the women as brave and resourceful, turning Red Riding Hood into the physical or sexual aggressor, and questioning the machismo of the wolf. Their new heroines dominate the plot, sometimes with humor or strength and frequently with a libido more than equal to the wolf's.

In Anne Sharpe's 1985 tale "Not So Little Red Riding Hood," Scarlet neatly dispatches a would-be rapist by using karate. She deals him an eye gouge followed by a quick kick to the groin, and hasn't even got around to striking his solar plexus when he whimpers for mercy. By the time she gets to Grandma's she has forgotten the incident altogether, while her attacker, when he recovers, heads for the local pub to drown *his* memory in beer. In Rosemary Lake's "Delian Little Red Riding Hood," from her feminist collection *Once Upon a Time When the Princess Rescued the Prince,* the old woman has a good laugh with the heroine inside the wolf's belly: "'He told me he was you,' said Grandmother. 'He said you had a bad cold.'" Then the two women use her scissors (in the sewing basket, which the wolf had also swallowed) to snip themselves free—a brief homage to the tools and symbols of women's work that played such a prominent part in old wives' tales of oral tradition.

In James Garner's "politically correct" version of the fairy tale, Grandma is not old, but "in full physical and mental health" and "fully capable of taking care of herself as a mature adult." In "Little Red Riding Hood—the Real Version," by Rachel Yap, Grandma "used to work in the US army." When the heroine screams, Grandma grabs a rifle and kills not one but a whole pack of wolves—and makes wolf soup for dinner. And in Paul Musso's hilarious comic strip, "You Are What You Eat," Grandma is the heroine of a story in which Little Red Riding Hood makes no appearance at all. His plot begins in *medias res*, at a cabin in the woods, in the dark of night. The wolf enters Grandma's house through an open window, "undetected by the hearing aid on the end table." His tail knocks over the Franklin Mint Guardian Angel statue, triggering "the clapper," and the lights go on. Grandma, now awake, is no traditional bedridden biddy. "Our Heroine, a hardy woman who has lived [through] five wars, a depression and 26 different presidents, grabbed a confederate army revolver from its hat box." Fist meets fur and tchotchkes scatter as the old woman and the wolf duke it out. They crash through the door of Grandma's timber cottage, and a screech of pain rings out "as a tooth shatters against a titanium hip replacement." The battle continues through the night and into the dawn, and at daybreak the story ends without revealing the victor. Only a profile in shadow can be seen, of indeterminate species, watching the sunrise amidst a landscape of torn gingham and fur.

Olga Broumas transforms the story's sexual subtext: Her 1977 lesbian retelling of "Little Red Riding Hood" imagines the tale without a wolf at all. Nor has the hunter-woodsman escaped revision. In "Red Riding Hood Redux," by D. W. Prosser, the heroine unloads a 9-mm Beretta into the wolf. As tufts of wolf fur waft down, she sends the hunter off to a self-help group, *White Male Oppressors Anonymous*.

AMIDST THE ABUNDANCE of feminist or pseudo-feminist updates of "Little Red Riding Hood," however, the Merseyside version of the story captured what has turned out to be one of the most fertile and surprisingly recurrent themes: the power of the wolf's pelt to transform the heroine. As in previous centuries, when peasants of Europe thought that by donning a wolf fur a man might turn himself into a werewolf, so in the Merseyside story the heroine assimilates aspects of her nemesis by wearing his fur inside her own eponymous red hood. In recent decades, a number of storytellers, artists and filmmakers have similarly redressed the heroine, exploring (in a seeming clash of feminism and political correctness) the power of a fur coat. By switching her garb and/or trading skins, Red Riding Hood sheds the historical associations of her own red cloak—sin, scandal, blood, sexual availability—and acquires a new set of meanings. These revisions may empower the heroine, enhance her animal instincts, or give her a richer identity. Some challenge the power of the wolf as a symbol of patriarchy. Others merely challenge his status as the tyrant of the fairy tale. Some suggest Red Riding Hood's darker side; others highlight her natural sexuality or her predatory mating tactics. Some of these revisions just give the heroine a change of clothes. Others transform her entirely into a she-wolf—or bitch.

One of the slyest inversions of the traditional "Red Riding Hood" plot is Roald Dahl's "Little Red Riding Hood and the Wolf." Dahl, a master of the absurd rhyme, who wrote for adults as well as children, saw social satire in children's literature. (Among his brilliant and bizarre longer tales: *Willy Wonka and the Chocolate Factory* and *James and the Giant Peach*.) Rather than noting the wolf's big teeth, Dahl's Red Riding Hood notices his thick pelt—and, whipping a pistol from her knickers, she quickly moves to acquire it. When the narrator next bumps into

Red Riding Hood in the woods, she is wearing her slain enemy. An illustration by Quentin Blake that accompanies the farcical verse in *Roald Dahl's Revolting Rhymes* shows her in a thick fur coat that covers her from head to toe.

Like the Merseyside storytellers, Dahl signals a shift in power with a change of clothing. But his heroine seems more excited by her new wardrobe than by the prospect of empowerment—a point made even more clear by Dahl's rhyme about the three little pigs. In that one, the pigs call in Red Riding Hood (whose tough reputation has spread) to assist with *their* wolf problem. Our heroine obliges, killing the second wolf—but in the end she takes home more than just another fur coat.

> A piglet you must never trust
> Young ladies from the upper crust
> For now Miss Riding Hood, one notes
> Not only has *two* wolfskin coats
> But when she goes from place to place
> She has a PIGSKIN TRAVELLING CASE.

Dahl's rhymes subvert the fairy-tale plot and empower the heroine. But they also take a satirical swipe at feminism that confuses female emancipation with the power to consume: Her victory is a fashion statement.

Similarly, if a bit more stylishly, in Stephen Sondheim's Broadway musical *Into the Woods* Red Riding Hood and her grandmother skin the wolf and Red Riding Hood trades her red cloak in for a chichi wolf fur stole and hat. In Hudson Talbott's illustration for the book adaptation of the musical, the heroine looks as if she might be strolling out of a Fifth Avenue boutique.

Red trades her eponymous cloak for wolf fur.
Illustrations by Quentin Blake and Hudson Talbott.

A deeper look at the relationship between fur and female power appears in the stories of Angela Carter and Tanith Lee. In *The Bloody Chamber,* Carter's 1979 collection of dark, feminist fables, the heroines are bestial and ferocious. Her story "The Tiger's Bride," in a reversal of "Beauty and the Beast," features a heroine who licks off her human skin: the sheen of culture, or domesticity, or perhaps just her acquired social sense of femininity. In "The Werewolf" the titular protagonist is a grandmother. And in her 1984 movie *A Company of Wolves,* written with Neil Jordan and based on Carter's short stories, the heroine turns into a she-wolf at tale's end. Told as a series of stories, themselves within the frame of a young girl's dream, the movie is full of details from the folk history of werewolves as well as from the folkloric background of "Red Riding Hood." It recounts the ambiguous sequence of events and feelings concerning a girl's first sexual encounter.

In the frame story, a young British girl sleeps fitfully while within her dream a peasant girl named Rosalee visits with her grandmother. She learns of werewolves, whose eyebrows meet in the middle, and of their carnal desires, and also that not all werewolves are men. She listens to her grandmother tell stories, which Carter has drawn from the legends and historical writings on werewolves by, among others, Henri Boguet, the sixteenth-century French jurist who convicted a number of men, and some women, as werewolves during his tenure. Meanwhile, still within the dream, Rosalee flirts with a local village boy, who takes her for a walk in the woods. They kiss; she runs from him, teasingly, and climbs a tree. The tree rises above the rest of the forest like a great phallic stalk. At its peak, she finds a nest full of symbols: red lip gloss, a mirror, and eggs, which hatch to reveal tiny, sculpted human fetuses.

By the time Carter's dream-heroine sets off for Grandma's house, the traditional fairy tale has become a parable of sexual awakening. Rosalee heads into the woods, carrying her basket and wearing her red cloak. There, she comes across a handsome stranger—his eyebrows meet in the middle—who says he has "something in my pocket which always points north." The seemingly scandalous object turns out to be a compass, which he uses to get to Grandmother's house before Rosalee, who follows the marked path. Mixing old traditions with new ideas, Carter develops the ambiguous ending of "The Grandmother's Tale"—the premodern foremother of "Little Red Riding

Hood"—into a story of mutual lust. The handsome stranger eats Rosalee's grandmother and burns her body in the fire, but a wisp of hair remains to reveal to Rosalee what has happened when she finally arrives. Carter's heroine is far from helpless. She holds the handsome, hirsute stranger at bay with a gun. But instead of fleeing she watches him undress, then throws her own clothing on the fire, garment by garment, and joins him in bed. In Carter's short story, which inspired the movie, she laughs when he threatens to eat her: "She knew she was nobody's meat." By the morning, she, too, has become a wolf. Meanwhile, in the frame-dream of *A Company of Wolves,* the young British girl is awakened by a pack of wolves who burst into her family home, leap over tables, bound up the stairs, and take her crashing through the window.

This revision unravels the tale's underlying sexual currents and imbues the heroine with animal instincts that cause her own transformation. Carter explores female lust—healthy, but also challenging and sometimes disturbing, unbridled and feral lust that delivers up contradictions. Her heroines in other tales inhabit dark sexual panoramas, sometimes pornographic, sometimes masochistic; sometimes they are willing participants in their own exploitation. They are also unabashed: Her Rosalee beds the werewolf with desire and glee and in Carter's story that inspired the movie, even her grandmother admires the beast's genitals ("Ah! Huge!") before her death. But Rosalee's coming of age is not without a cost—her grandmother dies, and she becomes an outcast, transformed into a she-wolf, and must flee her own family. (The movie's ending, which Carter reportedly disliked, differs from the climax of her short story, in which the wolf is tamed, and morning finds the heroine sleeping soundly in his arms.)

In Carter's "Red Riding Hood"–related tales, and in the film, the heroine's wolf is not her oppressor, nor her opponent, nor her ravisher. Rather than besting the beast, the heroine incorporates it. The protagonists—both heroine and villain—move back and forth between the forms of human and beast, and each is by turns tender and aggressive. Their parallel transformations suggest their interrelated identities that encompass darkness and brightness, innocence and evil at once. Her heroine's bestial side is an acknowledgment not only of her natural sex drive but also of her sexual complexity.

If Carter's tales and the movie based on them explore the explosive and complicated properties of sexual attraction and sexual union, Tanith Lee's "Wolfland" explores the sexual divide. In Lee's short tale of matriarchal legacy and dark female power, the young "Lisel" is sent to visit her eccentric, rich grandmother in a château surrounded by wolves. Grandmother, implausibly hearty and imposing, eats raw meat and rules her household with an iron will. She pats a dwarf-servant on the head as if he were a dog. Flashbacks in the story reveal her past: her life with a violent, abusive husband, her pact with a Wolf Goddess that enables her to kill her husband and save her daughter, and the trade-off—in exchange for salvation, Lisel's grandmother becomes a werewolf each night. Unlike Carter's she-wolf, Lee's female werewolf is not sexual; indeed, she transforms to escape the bonds and duties of marriage and afterwards has nothing to do with men at all, save for the dwarf, a disembodied phallic companion, a house pet. Whereas Carter's she-wolf man-

Sexy celebrity Kim Cattrall plays Red Riding Hood *and* the wolf,
flashing a lupine gaze in Pepsi One's 2001 television spot.

ifests sexual power, sparked by her budding attraction for (and
desirability to) men, Lee's Bitch Goddess offers independence
from men. Born into the werewolf line, Lisel will assume her
grandmother's shape. The tale ends with the vague suggestion of
the powerful but lonely future that stretches before her.

A more commercial interpretation of Red Riding Hood's animal instincts appears in a thirty-second television spot for Pepsi
One that aired during the college football "Pigskin Classic" in
the fall of 2001. A wolf howls. Sam the Sham and the Pharaoh's
old 1966 hit plays in the background—*Owooo! Hey there Little
Red Riding Hood!* The actress Kim Cattrall appears in a hot,
spaghetti-strapped paint-the-town red dress and hooded cape.

Striding purposefully through the streets of Prague, she skillfully navigates cobblestone roads in her strappy red heels. She bypasses a group of loitering beefcakes drinking Coke, and another pair drinking Diet Coke, and finally comes upon a handsome male model in black, sipping Pepsi One amidst a forest of lighted candles. He seems to be the wolf—but wait. As she homes in on her object of desire, she narrows her gaze. Suddenly her eyes flash lupine yellow and she gives a mental howl.

Cattrall transforms Little Red Riding Hood into a fantasy contradiction. Designed to appeal to the mostly male audience of college football fans, the ad plays off of Cattrall's well-known role as "Samantha," the forty-something sexaholic on HBO's hit series "Sex and the City" who frequently parodies stereotypical male sexual behavior. As a blend of wolf and Little Red Riding Hood, she plays a paradox: the prospect of female sexual liberation—combined with a warning to diet. The Pepsi One spot also makes for an interesting déjà vu: In 1981 Cattrall played hot gym teacher "Miss Honeywell" in the summer sex-comedy *Porky's*—a character who earned the nickname "Lassie" for her habit of howling during locker room trysts.

Of all the explorations of the heroine's wilder side, one of the most enigmatic is multimedia artist Kiki Smith's sculpture of a young female who is half girl and half beast. Peering from beneath the hood of an ankle-length red cloak, Smith's standing figure, constructed from nepal paper, bubble wrap, methyl cellulose, hair, fabric and glass, possesses a human nose and eyes, entirely surrounded by a face of fur. The sculpture is titled *Daughter*—perhaps the spawn of Red Riding Hood's sexual encounter with the Wolf? *Daughter* falls somewhere on a continuum between identities, and rather than spotlighting the battle of the sexes, the divide between human and beast or the opposition of Good and Evil, the sculpture blurs the lines between the characters and their symbolic associations. In particular, it challenges the gender assumptions that we tend to read into the fairy tale.

Smith says she was inspired by "hirsute women," and indeed the initial confusion and discomfort that *Daughter* evokes is well articulated by Jennifer Miller, the "bearded lady in a well-known American sideshow." In Tami Gold's 1995 documentary film *Juggling Gender,* Miller describes her painful and futile attempts to remove the thick facial hair that began to appear on her chin at the age of seventeen. Depilatories and electrolysis failed to do the job, and ultimately Miller came to see her struggle for hairless conformity, against the natural state of her body, as a denial of her intrinsic worth. Yet as a bearded lady, the battle over her gender did not end. It simply moved from her own personal struggle waged on the battleground of her body to a public struggle located on the street corner, played out in the eyes and minds of passersby. In public, Miller is often mistaken for a man. In the film, she discusses how she came to see this as part of her identity—that she is, ultimately, at least in part what other people think her to be. Her ability to see beyond categories is, at least for the duration of the film, contagious. In one scene Miller appears in the bathtub, splashing water across her beard, hair and breasts, in a visual montage that nudges the viewer to reconsider what is male, what is female, and what is normal.

Like Miller, Smith's *Daughter* also challenges the concept of normalcy; both destroy our comfortable understanding of the world—and ourselves—and more specifically, the sense of binary opposition that the fairy tale cultivates. Which of the characters is good or bad, male or female, human or beast? Are these categories themselves even valid? *Daughter* seems caught in mid-sentence, her glassy eyes looking upward, her mouth slightly open, mute in the face of the questions she herself poses.

THE POWER OF THESE TALES and images that transform heroine into beast is generated not only by our understanding of those categories, but more broadly by our popular understanding of women, men and hair. One enduring cultural myth is that women tame men—or soothe the savage beast—an idea rooted in some of the oldest stories. In the epic from ancient Babylon, the belly of civilization thousands of years ago, the godlike hero Gilgamesh ravaged the city of Uruk with his conquests and philandering. He drove the inhabitants to such desperation that, to drain his energy and balance his deeds, the gods created for him a wild brother of titanic strength, named Enkidu. Covered with coarse hair from head to toe, Enkidu lived among the animals. He ate grass and drank from the watering holes on the steppe; he did not speak. To tame him, Gilgamesh sent a woman—a prostitute—to lay with him. When it was over, Enkido bathed, ate, and dressed, and the wild animals would no longer come near him.

Countless tales feature heroines who turn animal bridegrooms into handsome princes; "Beauty and the Beast" and "The Frog Prince" are among the better known. Some have reinterpreted "Little Red Riding Hood" along these lines as well. As in Angela Carter's short story mentioned earlier, Otto Gmelin's heroine in "Red Cap" tames a wolf to reveal his true character beneath: An illustration accompanying the 1978 tale depicts a girl nuzzling a naked boy atop a wolf pelt. But the idea that women civilize men has also been supplanted by another theme: As Angela Carter put it, "If there's a beast in men, it meets its match in women too."

Carter's words, along with the many versions of "Little Red Riding Hood" in which the heroine wears or becomes her furry nemesis, fall into a modern tradition that might be called "beast feminism." From free love to hairy legs, from "grrrl" bands that defined themselves by a grrrowl to the Wolf Girls of Vassar who brought lesbianism out of the campus closet, from the California sex worker's union C.O.Y.O.T.E. (for Call Off Your Old Tired Ethics), to bestsellers like Clarissa Pinkola Estés's 1992 bestseller, *Women Who Run With the Wolves* (which also inspired a phenomenally popular Wild Wolf Women website), over the past few decades women have increasingly appropriated "masculine" metaphors of bestial power. Helen Reddy's 1972 hit "I Am Woman, Hear Me Roar" provided the ferocious feminist anthem of the 1970s. And in the 1980s the Guerilla Girls, an anonymous group of "art world feminists," donned ape masks to challenge sexism in galleries and museums. They appeared in full gorilla regalia for television interviews, during which they sometimes ate bananas. One of their more famous posters, plastered onto Manhattan walls, kiosks and construction site fences in 1989, depicted the voluptuous, pale body of Jean-August Dominique Ingres's 1814 masterpiece *Odalisque*—one of the most famous nudes ever painted—with a great, hairy gorilla head. "Do women have to be naked to get into the Metropolitan Museum?" the caption (and the gorilla) demanded.

Most plainly, in keeping with beast feminism, the term "bitch" has evolved into a compliment. In the 1970s the term became a radical feminist rallying cry in "The Bitch Manifesto," penned by Joreen Freeman, who correctly identified male fear and resentment of female power as the driving subtext beneath the word's mainstream derogatory connotations. Freeman pointed out: "Bitches were the first women to go to college, the first to break through the invisible Bar of the professions, the first social revolutionaries, the first labor leaders, the first to organize other women." Today "bitch" is a statement of female solidarity, with a variety of nuances. On the front cover of her book *Bitch: In Praise of Difficult Women* (1998), Elizabeth Wurtzel appears topless and flipping the bird to her readers—an image that combines the sensibilities of so-called "pro-sex" or "do-me" feminists with good old-fashioned objectification. Between the covers Wurtzel advocates brashness as a form of female power. "Bitch" also connotes a new kind of feminism. Today's edgy young women's magazine *Bitch* describes itself as a "feminist critique of pop culture" and explains its title as follows: "'Bitch' describes all at once who we are when we speak up, what it is we're too worked up over to be quiet about, and the act of making ourselves heard." ("It's a verb, it's a noun, it's a magazine," their website simplifies.)

"Bitch" is now a street greeting among women, from hip hop to mainstream culture. Whether it's an appropriation of the language of the oppressor or an internalization of patriarchy's terms is moot. Notions of femininity and feminism have changed, and many a young woman today would repond to being called a "bitch" with the unruffled, now-popular retort, "You say that like it's a bad thing."

"Beast feminism" plays against the conventional idea that women "soothe the savage beast," but it also harmonizes with broader and perhaps older narrative traditions. In *Women Who Run With the Wolves,* Estés draws upon the "wild woman" archetype of various cultures, which collectively she calls *la loba:* Wolf Woman. For Estés, the wolf is a more appropriate symbol for woman than for man: "Healthy wolves and healthy women share certain psychic characteristics," she writes:

> keen sensing, playful spirit, and a heightened capacity for devotion. Wolves and women are relational by nature, inquiring, possessed of great endurance and strength. They are deeply intuitive, intensely concerned with their young, their mates and their pack. . . . Yet both have been hounded, harassed, and falsely imputed to be devouring and devious, overly aggressive, of less value than those who are their detractors.

In her book, Estés finds la loba, who stands for a woman "in her natural wild state," in stories all around the world. In her book *From the Beast to the Blonde,* Marina Warner also explores the language of women's hair—from the dumb blondes of popular fairy tales to the hirsute she-beasts of ancient lore. Whereas male heroes tend to become beasts by malignant curses, she points out, female protagonists across the ages often embrace their new skin—be it fur, fleece, scales, or feathers—and wear it willingly as a protective shield.

And if today we are most familiar with delicate fairy tale heroines known for their golden tresses—like Goldilocks or Rapunzel—the she-wolves of this chapter also recall the original

French fairy tales by women of the Parisian salons, who fought against the conventions of the seventeenth-century upper class and who frequently cast their heroines as animals, dressed them as men, and otherwise challenged notions of femininity. In their tales, the skin of a beast often provides an escape from an undesired marriage, or the means to a higher love. In "Bearskin," attributed to Henriette-Julie de Murat, the heroine escapes her marriage to the monster Rhinocerous by shifting shapes, while Marie-Catherine D'Aulnoy's *White Cat* reverses the plot of "Beauty and the Beast," with a woman trapped in an animal skin who is saved by the love of a man. These female beasts remind us that heroines in fur are nothing new, and offer a link between the fair tale's past and Little Red Riding Hood's transformation, centuries later, into she-wolf and bitch.

But this new notion of the heroine leaves us with a question. As Red Riding Hood appropriates some of her nemesis's essence, acquiring his fur and the associations that come along with it, what happens to the wolf? These characters exist in tandem, and as we shall see, if a wolf fur stole transforms the heroine, so fashion can reinvent the wolf.

VIII

Red Riding Hood Redux:
The Cross-Dressing Wolf

Red Riding Hood

By Anne Sexton

Many are the deceivers:

The suburban matron,
proper in the supermarket,
list in hand so she won't suddenly fly,
buying her Duz and Chuck Wagon dog food,
meanwhile ascending from earth,
letting her stomach fill up with helium,
letting her arms go loose as kite tails,
getting ready to meet her lover
a mile down Apple Crest Road
in the Congregational Church parking lot.

Two seemingly respectable women
come up to an old Jenny
and show her an envelope

Source: From *Transformations,* published by Houghton Mifflin, 1971.

full of money
and promise to share the booty
if she'll give them ten thou
as an act of faith.
Her life savings are under the mattress
covered with rust stains
and counting.
They are as wrinkled as prunes
but negotiable.
The two women take the money and disappear.
Where is the moral?
Not all knives are for stabbing the exposed belly.
Rock climbs on rock
and it only makes a seashore.
Old Jenny has lost her belief in mattresses
and now she has no wastebasket in which
to keep her youth.

The standup comic on the "Tonight" show
who imitates the Vice President
and cracks up Johnny Carson
and delays sleep for millions
of bedfellows watching between their feet,
slits his wrist the next morning
in the Algonquin's old-fashioned bathroom,
the razor in his hand like a toothbrush,
wall as anonymous as a urinal,
the shower curtain his slack rubberman audience,
and then the slash

as simple as opening a letter
and the warm blood breaking out like a rose
upon the bathtub with its claw and ball feet.

And I. I too.
Quite collected at cocktail parties,
meanwhile in my head I'm undergoing open-heart surgery.
The heart, poor fellow,
pounding on his little tin drum
with a faint death beat.
The heart, that eyeless beetle,
enormous that Kafka beetle,
running panicked through his maze,
never stopping one foot after the other
one hour after the other
until he gags on an apple
and it's all over.

And I. I too again.
I built a summer house on Cape Ann.
A simple A-frame and this too was a deception—nothing haunts a
    new house.
When I moved in with a bathing suit and tea bags
the ocean rumbled like a train backing up
and at each window secrets came in like gas. My mother, that
    departed soul,
sat in my Eames chair and reproached me
for losing her keys to the old cottage.
Even in the electric kitchen there was

the smell of a journey. The ocean
was seeping through its frontiers
and laying me out on its wet rails.
The bed was stale with my childhood
and I could not move to another city
where the worthy make a new life.

Long ago
there was a strange deception:
a wolf dressed in frills,
a kind of transvestite.
But I get ahead of my story.
In the beginning
there was just little Red Riding Hood,
so called because her grandmother
made her a red cape and she was never without it.
It was her Linus blanket, besides
it was red, as red as the Swiss flag,
yes it was red, as red as chicken blood.
But more than she loved her riding hood
she loved her grandmother who lived
far from the city in the big wood.

This one day her mother gave her
a basket of wine and cake
to take to her grandmother
because she was ill.
Wine and cake?
Where's the aspirin? The penicillin?

Where's the fruit juice?
Peter Rabbit got chamomile tea.
But wine and cake it was.

On her way in the big wood
Red Riding Hood met the wolf.
Good day, Mr. Wolf, she said,
thinking him no more dangerous
than a streetcar or a panhandler.
He asked where she was going
and she obligingly told him.
There among the roots and trunks
with the mushrooms pulsing inside the moss
he planned how to eat them both,
the grandmother an old carrot
and the child a shy budkin
in a red red hood.
He bade her to look at the bloodroot,
the small bunchberry and the dogtooth
and pick some for her grandmother.
And this she did.
Meanwhile he scampered off
to Grandmother's house and ate her up
as quick as a slap.
Then he put on her nightdress and cap and snuggled down into the bed.
A deceptive fellow.

Red Riding Hood
knocked on the door and entered

with her flowers, her cake, her wine.
Grandmother looked strange,
a dark and hairy disease it seemed.
Oh Grandmother, what big ears you have,
ears, eyes, hands and then the teeth.
The better to eat you with, my dear.
So the wolf gobbled Red Riding Hood down
like a gumdrop. Now he was fat.
He appeared to be in his ninth month
and Red Riding Hood and her grandmother
rode like two Jonahs up and down with
his every breath. One pigeon. One partridge.

He was fast asleep,
dreaming in his cap and gown,
wolfless.
Along came a huntsman who heard the loud contented snores
and knew that was no grandmother.
He opened the door and said,
So it's you, old sinner.
He raised his gun to shoot him
when it occurred to him that maybe the wolf had eaten up the old lady.
So he took a knife and began cutting open the sleeping wolf, a kind of
    cesarean section.

It was a carnal knife that let
Red Riding Hood out like a poppy,
quite alive from the kingdom of the belly.
And grandmother too

still waiting for cakes and wine.
The wolf, they decided, was too man
to be simply shot so they filled his belly
with large stones and sewed him up.
He was as heavy as a cemetery
and when he woke up and tried to run off
he fell over dead. Killed by his own weight.
Many a deception ends on such a note.
The huntsman and the grandmother and Red Riding Hood
sat down by his corpse and had a meal of wine and cake.
Those two remembering nothing naked and brutal
from that little death,
that little birth,
from their going down and their lifting up.

A N ADVERTISEMENT in a London magazine displays a
wolf, licking his chops, above the caption: "Any food
tastes supreme with Heinz Salad Cream." It is the "after" image of
a scene whose "before" is more typically rendered in children's
books. The wolf wraps his paws around a bulging belly and
gives a conspiratorial smile, his tongue wrapped around his
snout. This quiet scene of post-dinner relaxation captures a
strange contradiction that often goes unnoticed in the heat of the
fairy tale's denouement. The wolf's dark, straggly fur, wet nose,
sharp bared teeth and lascivious gaze all reveal him as the omni-
vore that he is, an insatiable predator. But something is funny.
The thick fur on the wolf's arms sprouts from frilly sleeves, and
beneath his grin, his bonnet is tied in a neat pink bow. And what
about the pink floral comforter and lace pillows?

The wolf, the ever-present villain of the fairy tale, is one of the
most powerful symbols in Western culture. In the old days, the
wolf represented the Devil, or a demonic emissary in the form of
the werewolf of peasant Europe. In modern times, the wolf is a
symbol of manhood, a womanizer (as the dictionary notes), and
the patron saint of bachelordom. From Lon Chaney to Los Lobos
to Wolfman Jack, all beard, howl and hep-cat jive, he exudes

testosterone, and the wolf whistle, or sometimes a howl, is an almost universally recognized mating call. Yet though the wolf has clear and powerful associations, he is less straightforward than at first he seems. Upon closer reflection, his symbolic meaning in the fairy tale, as in our greater cultural mythology, contains some startling contradictions.

Charles Perrault's wolf deflowered virgins. The French sexual expression "to see the wolf," which Perrault illustrated with his tale, has been incorporated into the art and culture of later centuries, and the image of a wolf, or wolf-like beast, bent over the swooning maiden has since become part of a common visual language. The hairy incubus—perhaps a werewolf?—of John Henry Fuseli's painting *Nightmare* (1795–1780) sits atop the pale arched breast of a sleeping girl, while a horse (a sexual allusion, or so a college art history professor once said), hovers above her. The anonymous eighteenth-century engraving of a werewolf attacking a girl reproduced in Chapter 4 is charged with a sense of sexual carnage. A painting by the French master Paul Gauguin entitled *The Loss of Virginity* (1890–1891), explicitly illustrates the old French slang: A wolf paws a naked, reclining girl. She lies sleeping on her back against a landscape of forest green and sunset amber while the wolf, reduced to a fraction of her size, appears like a welcome metaphor from an erotic dream. And in the twentieth century, the silver screen gave us the metaphor in moving form: Lon Chaney, Jr., as *The Wolf Man* (1941), hunching over the pale, heaving breasts of the actress Evelyn Ankers. Despite the yak's fur, which reportedly took hours to apply, Chaney's Hollywood monster is strikingly anthropomorphized. Our werewolf—who in old literature and trial records ran on all fours and possessed the full aspect of a wolf—now sports a flat-tened nose and distinctly man-like mitts—all the better to paw you with, my Dear!

Lon Chaney, Jr. hunches over his "date" in
The Wolf Man, 1941.

Chaney's monster perfectly captures the slang meaning of Per-rault's wolf, the seducer. The underlying premise of his perform-ance, evident to anyone who has seen a poster or publicity shot for the movie, is that beneath the horror and the camp, what is actually taking place is a date. Later titles from the werewolf movie genre, like *Werewolf in a Girl's Dormitory* (1962), make this theme comically explicit, and more recent films offer varia-tions on it. In the horror-comedy hybrid film *American Werewolf in London* (1981), a young man's testosterone levels surge after he is mauled by a wolf, and in *Wolf* (1994), Jack Nicholson's gradual physical transformation into a beast parallels his metaphysical transformation from mouse to man. He plays Will Randall, a timid, aging publisher whose wife and job are snatched away by a younger coworker. But after being bitten by a wolf, Randall becomes increasingly virile, gets up the nerve to win his job back, and chases his boss's lovely daughter (Michelle Pfeiffer). His charisma grows as his manners decline. In one memorable scene, he stands at the urinal beside his unscrupulous coworker, and "marks his territory" on the young man's shoes.

The wolf (or Wolf Man, or werewolf) in these scenes and movies is an admirably masculine figure, who stands in contrast to the domesticated and emasculated dog. (The hilariously coiffed, pedigreed poodles and terriers of the spoof documentary *Best in Show* [2000], for example, invariably call to mind henpecked husbands as they are put through their paces by their nagging owners.) Taken to an extreme, however, the manly wolf also carries associations of feral machismo and misogyny. In 1990, when a roving gang of young men raped and battered a young jogger and left her for dead in New York's Central Park, the newspapers quickly dubbed them a marauding "wolf pack" and created a new term for their criminal activities: "wilding." The film *Magnolia* (1999) contains a scene that fleshes out the predatory mythology underpinning this vocabulary. Speaking in the language of testosterone, Tom Cruise plays macho television guru Frank T. J. Mackey, buffed and tough with a sock in his jock, leading a men's group in chants of manly affirmation: "Respect the cock! Tame the cunt!" The call-in number 1-800-TAME-HER appears on the screen as, in the background, a huge banner comes in and out of focus on which an enormous, muscular, slathering wolf (dressed like Mackey, in a black leather vest) chases a frightened cat. The pussy's obvious terror has as much significance in this scenario as the wolf's invigorated rapacious glee. The banner reads: "Seduce and Destroy."

Mackey's performance presents the wolf as male warrior in a battle of the sexes in which sexual intercourse is a symbolic act of male conquest—and hatred. The aftermath of Mackey's belligerent vision of sexual conquest is revealed by the old, bad joke about a woman who is "coyote ugly": If a man wakes up after a drunken night to find this woman sleeping on his arm, the joke goes, he says he'd rather gnaw off his limb than wake her up. It takes a moment to register that it is not the woman, as one might at first presume, who is cast as the animal in this scenario. Rather, in the rubric of modern mating, last night's macho wolf becomes this morning's coyote.

Curiously enough, the macho playboy wolf of the human imagination has little place in the animal kingdom. The real *Canis lupus,* it turns out, is not a rakish womanizer at all (or a manizer, for that matter). Indeed, some have called it a hopeless romantic. Wolves fall into the tiny fraction of the animal kingdom that is more or less monogamous, and legends of their fidelity abound. The naturalist Ernest Thompson Seton (founder of the Boy Scouts of America) tells of tracking the infamous Old Lobo of Currumpaw, a huge he-wolf who carried a $1000 bounty on his pelt. His paw prints measured five and a half inches in length—a full inch over the norm—and he terrorized ranchers of New Mexico for years in the late nineteenth century. Despite the ranchers' concerted and long-standing efforts to rid themselves of the beast, who killed their livestock, Old Lobo easily eluded capture time and again. He even defe-

Red Riding Hood visits her grandma in Queens
in a 2000 ad for eLuxury.com.

cated on the more elaborate traps in what the ranchers took as a
show of derision for their ploys. But Old Lobo turned out not to
be the macho wolf of legend after all. When Seton et al. captured
and killed Blanca, his mate, Old Lobo followed the trail of her
corpse straight into the hunters' yard and seemingly gave himself up to their traps. "Poor old hero," writes Seton, obviously
moved by the unexpected love story. "He had never ceased to
search for his darling."

IN POPULAR CULTURE the fairy tale frequently reiterates our dominant if unfounded associations with the wolf, especially in modern advertising that pairs Little Red Riding Hood with a dangerous playboy. A 1997 fashion spread in the *New York Times* redressed Red Riding Hood's wolf in high alpha-male style. In it, a lupine model runs through the woods under the caption "The Skirt Chaser." "He's a bounder, a cad, a wolf in lamb's(wool) clothing," the text reads. On the next page the "bounder" moves in on a blonde Red Riding Hood in a slit-up-to-there skirt, who leans against a tree, looking ravishing. Or rather, looking like she's about to be ravished: "She's an earnest but clueless ingénue dressed in the sexiest skirts of the season."

Another recent advertisement, this time for eLuxury.com, shows the wolf as a goateed ogler in black leather. He sits astride a motorcycle and fingers the hem of a bright red dress worn by a pert, blonde, cherry-lipped model. Her mouth is open in a Betty Boop "ooh." The caption reads: "Is this a) Little Red Riding Hood visiting her grandma in Queens, b) the latest from Salvatore Ferregamo, c) a man with a late-night hankering for squash"—all three options managing to capture, in somewhat different terms, the image's sexual innuendo.

Yet while the fairy tale expresses our dominant cultural myth of the wolf, it has also been used to subvert it. As the Heinz Salad Cream ad picked up on, the fairy tale offers us the wolf as a contradiction, a predator in frills and lace, in a plot that can play out in more than one way. In recent years, as Little Red Riding Hood has grown more bestial and red-blooded, the wolf has developed a softer side. Indeed, our hairy-chested swain has even become a bit of a nance. "Long ago there was a strange deception," Anne

Sexton writes in her 1971 revision of the Grimms' fairy tale: "a wolf dressed in frills,/a kind of transvestite."

Modern takes on "Little Red Riding Hood" now feature *his* wardrobe as prominently as the tale once spotlighted hers. The story has become fodder for drag theater and gender-bending literature. A recent performance from Sydney's Gay and Lesbian Mardi Gras featured Reg Livermore as "the precocious latex-skirted" Red Riding Hood *and* the "frightfully-frocked" grandma/wolf. A poem in an independent magazine called *Flatter* suggests that our villain's taste in food is only slightly kinkier than his taste in clothing: "The wolf lifted the latch, the door sprang/Open, and without saying a word he went straight to the grandmother's bed/And devoured her,/Stopping only to don grandmother's/Best garter belt and heels."

And a 1989 Gary Larson cartoon casts the wolf, wearing a floral nightgown, on a psychiatrist's couch. "It was supposed to be just a story about a little kid and a wolf," our villain says. "But off and on I've been dressing up as a grandmother ever since."

Larson's cartoon is funny in part because cross-dressing is kinky, and in part because the psychiatrist's couch is, in fact, where childhood fantasies are called up: Here, an archetype has come to life to analyze the titillating meaning of his tale that Freudians like Bruno Bettelheim postulated. Like Sexton's poem, or the lines from *Flatter,* the cartoon gets a giggle because it captures an element of the tale that was there all along, but which for most people until now escaped notice. But even more, the cross-dressing wolf has the power to shock and amuse because it plays so forcefully against the fairy-tale villain's more established associations.

Cross-dressing is by definition subversive. Dress is in large part how we distinguish men from women, and when a man or a woman cross-dresses, he or she challenges our understanding of gender. But the cross-dressed wolf is not merely a man in a dress; he is *the* man in a dress—that is, our Western symbol of manhood itself, in frills. The transvestite wolf takes gender-bending to its symbolic extreme. He is the ultimate challenge to our understanding of male and female, a contradiction in terms, what Marjorie Garber, in her encyclopedic study of transvestitism *Vested Interests*, calls a "categorical crisis."

Or perhaps the transvestite wolf is not the *ultimate* representation of a categorical crisis. While some have made fun of his feminine dress, others have noticed the far more shocking matter of his pregnancy. After swallowing Red Riding Hood whole, Anne Sexton writes, "He appeared to be in his ninth month." A drawing by Barbara Swan that accompanied the poem in Sexton's collection depicted the "expecting" wolf lying in bed, with the hunter pressing an ear to his belly, listening for a fetal heartbeat. In a similar vein, a 1991 children's book by the Italian illustrator Beni Montressor gives a full-color sonogram of the wolf's pregnant uterus. Rendered in shades of red and gold, Red Riding Hood floats, alive and well, in an amniotic trance. The fairy tale's brutal end has been entirely reconceived: The sleeping wolf smiles in maternal bliss, with the girl safe and sound in his belly, protected and enveloped, and perhaps kicking, inside him. The wolf's associations with evil and with manliness have been erased; he is, as Sexton writes, "wolfless." And what's a pregnancy without a delivery? In Sexton's poem, the huntsman cuts the wolf's belly open with a knife, performing "a kind of caesarian section." Red

Riding Hood comes "out like a poppy/quite alive from the kingdom of the belly./And grandmother too."

Thus the wolf, our arch symbol of masculinity and even misogyny, is also a transvestite, a mother-to-be, and even sometimes a grandmother: On the cover of *The Nation*'s 1997 Fall Books issue, the wolf, dressed in bonnet and robe, cuddles Red Riding Hood in his arms and reads her a tale. Once a macho rake, our ferocious villain has now become what he once only pretended to be: the maternal, protective matriarch.

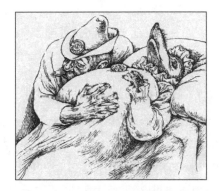

Barbara Swann's "expecting" wolf, 1971.

Beni Montresor's sonogram of the wolf's belly, 1989.

SEXTON'S POEM and the various revisions of "Little Red Riding Hood" that rehabilitate, feminize, or impregnate the wolf reflect the temperature of the times. Perhaps more than ever our assumptions about what women do (and are) and what men do (and are) are under siege. If, as feminists have argued, women can do what men do, then the reverse must also be true. Accordingly, in increasing numbers twentieth-century men have sought out their "feminine" side—indeed, our culture has made it fashionable for them to do so. Today the modern man is supposed to be able to cry. He eats quiche. Perhaps he, like Jerry Seinfeld, carries a "man purse." And the SNAG—a modern acronym for the "sensitive new age guy"—changes his baby's diaper in the men's room, where there are now fold-down changing tables, just like in women's rooms. In his men's movement book *Iron John* inspired by the Grimms' fairy tale, Robert Bly seeks to toughen up his followers with prototypes of manliness from the tales of an earlier age, even as he laments that the "soft male" is everywhere.

Challenges to male dress codes reflect (or even force) changing norms—calling into question not just the duties and roles of men but our understanding of masculinity itself. Boy George, RuPaul and Divine have set the standards for glamorous drag, projecting an image that is at once hyper-female and at the same time abundantly male, thereby magically transcending categories. A decade ago the Ken doll (Barbie's boyfriend) appeared in stores in San Francisco's Castro district repackaged as Cross-Dressing Ken, wearing a pink toile skirt and carrying a baby blue plastic purse. On his box, the caption read, "He's a handsome prince!" In 1993, Barbie and GI Joe underwent transgender operations of a sort: A group called "the Barbie Liberation Organization" switched their voice boxes and then returned the dolls to store shelves, so that Barbie would growl, in baritone, "Dead men tell no lies," while GI Joe, in falsetto, squealed, "Want to go shopping?" Even Lon Chaney's werewolf has taken a drag form, in a low-budget spoof called *The Curse of the Queerwolf* (1988). This bizarre, utterly politically incorrect, low-budget parody of *The Wolf Man* subverts the machismo of Chaney's legendary alter-ego. Instead of virile tufts of fur, the protagonist afflicted with the titular curse develops "big hair" and crimson lips at the onset of the full moon. Instead of the famous special-effects transformation scene showing a man's hand sprouting enormous knuckles and claws, we see a man's hand rapidly growing long, perfectly manicured, siren red fingernails.

Even the fantasy of male motherhood has become part of mainstream culture: witness such movies as *Mr. Mom* (1983), *Mrs. Doubtfire* (1993), *Three Men and a Baby* (1987), and *Junior* (1994), in which Arnold Schwarzenegger plays a pregnant man. Or, more bizarrely, consider the "Empathy Belly." Developed in 1989 by Linda Ware and produced by Birthway Inc., the 35-pound Empathy Belly consists of a canvas waistcoat filled with water and lead weights and a pendulum that swings when jostled to simulate a baby kicking. According to promotional literature, it allows a husband to experience some of the physical symptoms of pregnancy, including weight gain, difficulty in movement, shortness of breath, and (yes) even incontinence: A separate bag of water rides directly above the bladder, causing the need to urinate frequently. Lest one imagine that this device is popular only among dutiful husbands, take note that in 1997 members of Oklahoma State's Alpha Tau Omega fraternity traded off wearing the faux bellies for a month to raise money for the March of Dimes. With such devices on the market, it seems it was only a matter of time before Little Red Riding Hood's wolf got pregnant.

New times generate new tales . . . but is the cross-dressed, pregnant wolf just a sign of the times? If the feminized fairy-tale wolf seems rooted in modern ideas, it is not rooted in new practices. There is nothing particularly novel about transvestitism, for example. From Shakespeare to Tootsie to Tony Curtis and Jack Lemmon in *Some Like It Hot* (1959); from Joan of Arc to George Sand to Madonna, crossing has been a regular part of mainstream culture all along. A December 1895 issue of the *Ladies Standard Magazine* featured patterns for a "Little Red Riding Hood" ensemble suitable not only for "the wee New Woman" but also for the "Little Brother" who has "not yet had his curls cut nor displayed a taste for trousers." And in the seventeenth century of Charles Perrault, men as well as women wore frills.

In high heels, popularized by Louis XIV, who was only five foot four, male aristocrats of Versailles painted their faces and powdered their wigs, wore beauty patches, and dressed as elaborately as their wives. The King's bisexual brother, known as Monsieur, presented himself as a man or a woman, depending on the occasion. What's more, Charles Perrault was himself the suspected coauthor of a sensational novella about cross-dressing. The incredible *History of the Marquis-Marquise of Bannerville,* published anonymously in the popular *Mercure Galant* in 1695 and 1696 (in extended form), tells the story of Marianne, a young boy who is raised as a girl so he can be kept from the battlefield, and the fate that took his father. Shaped by iron stays, he develops hips and breasts and is happily unaware of his biological sex throughout adolescence. At the age of twelve, he arrives in Paris with his mother where he is presented at Court as a young beauty. There, the Marquis-Marquise is courted by a young man, a *bonhomme* who paints his face, wears patches and is as pretty as he is handsome—and who turns out to be a girl, crossdressed as a man!

Marianne and the young man fall in love, a passion that seems destined for disappointment and generates a great deal of narrative tension as they head toward marriage, each unaware of the other's true sex. But all works out astonishingly well: On their wedding night they remove their bodices and waistcoats, corsets and stays, and delight in the fate that brought them together. They decide to continue to live their drag genders in public, while in private enjoying the benefits of their biological sex. They even conceive a child (much to the dismay of Marianne's uncle, who had hoped the barren union would result in Marianne's inheritance transferring to his own family, and is baffled by her seemingly miraculous conception).

Incredible as it seems, the *History of the Marquis-Marquise of Bannerville* was no mere fiction. Charles Perrault is believed to have penned this fantastic tale with his colleague in the French Academy, the abbé de Choisy, who was himself among the most prominent transvestites of the day. A courtier, diarist and historian, the abbé's memoirs establish him as one of the more bizarre characters of the Court of Louis XIV, and the real-life inspiration for the *History of the Marquis-Marquise*—and perhaps for "Little Red Riding Hood" as well.

From a young age François Timoléon, the future abbé de Choisy, was dressed by his mother as a girl. She had his ears pierced and applied a depilatory lotion to his face. He enjoyed playing with the King's brother, Monsieur, and dressed as a girl on these occasions. As an adult, Choisy continued to dress as a young noblewoman and was, at least in some locales, accepted as such. He appeared as an actress in the provinces. In Paris he had a love affair with a young woman, whom he made dress as a man. They carried on a lengthy cross-dressing affair and even married in a mock ceremony.

Though he was a famous transvestite, the abbé de Choisy was also an enthusiastic heterosexual seducer who often exploited his cross-dressing expertise when pursuing an amorous conquest. In seventeenth-century aristocratic society, it was customary for women to receive guests while lying in bed, and perfectly acceptable for a young female visitor to share an elder hostess's bed. In his memoirs, the abbé relates his delight in bedding young girls while dressed as a woman, and even in making love under the noses of mixed company without being discovered.

While Charles Perrault's wolf does not actually dress in women's clothes (that detail was added to the story in later versions), the abbé's ruses suggest the same boudoir trickery that Perrault's wolf employs, while the abbé himself represented exactly the sort of man that Perrault's tale warned against.

PERHAPS THE ABBÉ'S proclivities were not "gender bending" in the way we understand that term today. Scholars of French history like Joan DeJean suggest that in the seventeenth century gender was an *état*, an impermanent state, rather than a permanent identity. Gender was something that could be acquired, as opposed to something inalterable and established from birth. When the abbé cross-dressed, or the marquis for that matter, s/he didn't *bend* gender inasmuch as gender already included the possibility of ambiguous dress.

Yet the enduring phenomenon of cross-dressing, the age-old need to cross boundaries and create "categorical crises," suggests that when Little Red Riding Hood's wolf dresses in frills, or when for that matter Red Riding Hood dresses in wolf fur, they are not acting out the cultural concerns of the times so much as expressing enduring cultural laws. To add to the point, let us consider another long-established aspect of the wolf's character as it has dramatically shifted in recent years.

Long hated, the wolf was hunted for ages. Barry Holsten Lopez, who has researched wolves, writes that to clear the English forest of wolves in the tenth century, King Edgar the Peaceful let men pay their taxes in wolf heads and their legal fines in wolves' tongues. Nearly a millennium later across the ocean that plot reached its denouement. In the nineteenth and twentieth centuries the U.S. government placed a bounty on the beast's pelt and put wolf hunters on the federal payroll. Ranchers also hunted it down, with the same fury their ancestors had once unleashed against the werewolves. By the twentieth century in the continental United States, they had hunted the wolf to virtual extinction.

But whereas Old Father Wolf was once a symbol of absolute Evil, even this *ne plus ultra* villain over time became a victim. With the Endangered Species Act of 1973, the wolf gained an almost revered status, and a legion of protectors have come to its defense. Today dozens of wolf advocacy groups—virtually all founded in the past twenty or so years—urge sponsors to "adopt-a-wolf." They promote wolf repopulation efforts like that in Yellowstone National Park and even sell cuddly stuffed "teddy-wolves" for children. Environmentalists like those at the International Wolf Center in Minnesota now blame Little Red Riding Hood for perpetuating the fear of wolves that has led to their persecution and near extinction in the United States. Accordingly, today retellings of the fairy tale sometimes cast *her* as the villain. "Little Red Riding Hood lied: Restore the wolf!" reads a popular bumper sticker today. "Last chance, sister! Get your hands off that endangered species!" the woodchopper screams, before he decapitates Red Riding Hood in a version of the tale circulating on the Internet.

Today, on its website for kids, the U.S. Department of Justice even features a "conflict resolution" version of "Little Red Riding Hood" that suggests how the story might end differently if only we could "change our stereotype or opinion of wolves" and just hear each other out. (Red to wolf: "You think that I have started unfair rumors about you, and you are miserable and lonely and don't understand why Granny didn't tell your side of the story.") As for the wolf's place in children's literature, in a recent children's storybook, wolves watch humans, warily, from a distant hilltop. "Aren't they supposed to be dangerous?" asks a cub.

The wolf in drag, and the heroine in fur, or the villain who suddenly becomes a victim while his prey becomes predator, are not exceptions to the norm but expressions of the norm itself.

The underlying truth of all our cultural myths is that they ebb, flow and invert. As Joseph Campbell has written,

> The hero, whether god or goddess, man or woman, the figure in a myth or the dreamer of a dream, discovers and assimilates his opposite (his own unsuspected self) either by swallowing it or by being swallowed. One by one, the resistances are broken. He must put aside his pride, his virtue, beauty, and life, and bow or submit to the absolutely intolerable. Then he finds that he and his opposite are not of differing species, but one flesh.

IN THE FAIRY TALE, opposites attract, and over time, they tend to swap skins. Red Riding Hood and the wolf trade fur and frills, and their associations of masculinity and femininity. The effeminate wolf of the revised fairy tale, dressed in his flowered maternity wear, is the inevitable complement to the hairy-chested womanizing alpha male. He is his alternate état. The costumes we wear, or rather those worn by our alter-egos in the fairy tale, are part of an extensive wardrobe, an evolving equation of fashion, gender and identity. Or as the six-foot-seven, mulatto-skinned, blonde-haired bombshell drag queen RuPaul once put it, "Honey, you're born naked. Everything else is drag."

The Punishment of Red Riding Hood: Fairy-Tale Fetish

A Popular Joke

"Aha! Little Red Riding Hood!" says the Big Bad Wolf, upon finding the girl in the woods. "Now I'm going to take off your little red cape, lift up your little red skirt, pull down your little red panties and fuck your brains out!"

"Oh no you're not, Mr. Wolf," Red Riding Hood retorts, pulling a pistol out of her basket and drawing a bead on the wolf. "You're going to eat me just like the book says!"

T̲HE VIDEO BOX COVER shows a dungeon scenario, with a woman suspended by her wrists from leather bindings. She wears stockings, garters, stiletto heels and a red merry widow, with half moons cut out to reveal her breasts. On either side, two blondes in G-strings and dog collars hold her by the thighs, and behind them a third wields a black paddle-whip. *The Punishment of Red Riding Hood* (1996) stars porn veteran Red Riding Hood in "probably her final video performance." According to its distributor's plot summary, this lesbian bondage epic culminates with one of the characters being "whipped and clipped on the dreaded over-head donut."

Never mind that "dreaded" and "donut" are two words you don't normally find so close together. How has Little Red Riding Hood traveled such a long road from the heroine of a chastity and obedience tale to the namesake of a lesbian S & M porn star? As it turns out, she has not made her voyage alone. Other films mining the rich folkloric tradition include *Cinderella in Chains, Alice in Bondageland* and *Goldilocks and the 3 Bares.* Adult Internet sites routinely traffic in fairy tales, and erotic literature plunders the plots, departing from one kind of fantasy into another. Bestselling author Anne Rice, under the pen name A. N. Roquelaure, transforms "Sleeping Beauty" into a cornucopia of S & M. The opening lines of part three of her trilogy suggest just how quickly that leap can be made: "After her century-long slumber, the Sleeping Beauty opened her eyes at the kiss of the Prince to find her garments stripped away and her heart as well as her body under the rule of her deliverer. At once, Beauty was claimed as the Prince's naked pleasure slave to be taken to his Kingdom."

Pornography—by which I mean simply the realm of material that can be found arousing—has a bad name. The debate about whether or not it should be allowed to exist—whatever "it" is—has forged all sorts of unlikely alliances, pitting free-speechers and perverts (on the pro side) against feminists and conservatives (on the con side). But, as Laura Kipnis argues eloquently in her short, provocative book *Bound and Gagged,* the debate over its merits is moot—since porn is here and here to stay. The more interesting question is, what does porn tell us about our culture, what does it say about us? More specifically, in the limited world of this book, what can it tell us about fairy tales?

The fact that pornography has discovered the fairy tale is unremarkable, since porn exploits virtually *any* scenario: from the boardroom, to the classroom, to the tennis court. Kipnis introduces us to gay geriatric porn, fat porn, and of course transvestite porn—the range of possibilities is almost beyond comprehension. In the realm of fantasies, fairy tales are the tip of the iceberg: The options are as astounding as they are amusing. "Mistress Vena" (who once appeared on the photo-montage cover of *Spy* magazine as the leather-clad body of Hillary Clinton) lists on her website her expertise in such scenarios as "NURSE/patient, INTERROGATOR/spy, TEACHER/student, MOTHER SUPE-

RIOR/schoolboy, POLICE OFFICER/bad boy and EQUESTRI-ENNE/horse." She has also given lectures and demonstrations on, among other things, sensory deprivation and mummification. The fairy tale may indeed be pornography's least surprising fantasy. But if finding a children's fairy tale on the shelf of the adult video store doesn't tell us anything new about porn, what it chooses to develop and explore in fairy tales can be enlightening.

Fairy-tale porn is not concerned with fidelity to tradition. Of the four videos mentioned above, none follows, even remotely, a storybook fairy-tale plot. Rather these films pick up on a few motifs, the most compelling elements or memorable twists of plot. A color, a shoe size, a stand-out quality of a character, or a stern lesson—that is not perhaps *exactly* the lesson we think it to be in the traditional fairy tale. In so doing, they isolate for us what makes the fairy tale itself so memorable, durable and fascinating. Peripheral as it may seem at first glance, the booming subgenre of fairy-tale porn distills the fairy tale's most pivotal preoccupations and offers surprising glimpses of its underbelly.

Most obviously, porn uncovers the fairy tale's erotic pulse. Even seemingly little things become magnified erotic elements. Cinderella's shoe size (an unlikely standard of beauty in the West, but some have suggested the motif comes from the tale's Asian ancestry) is eroticized: *Cinderella in Chains* is listed by one video distributor under the category of "foot fetish." Goldilocks experiences a gang bang with the "bares." (A recent television ad for Pepsi One makes the same joke, only soft core, with Kim Cattrall playing Goldilocks, enjoying the jacuzzi in the locker room of the Chicago Bears.) And in *The Punishment of Red Riding Hood,* the heroine's red cloak has been transformed from outer garment to undergarment; a scandalously small item of fetish lingerie that exaggerates the usual costume's sexual charge.

The titillation factor of these videos is in part through transgression—fairy tales are meant, we believe, for children; and meant, we believe, to express morality. But the excitement these scenarios have power to provoke is also at a deeper level. Fairy tales are at their core about sexuality—about the codes and manners and qualities and behaviors that society deems desirable, and thus which make us desirable to each other. They are about establishing and defining our ideas about gender—what makes a man, what makes a woman—at the most basic level. In their early forms, fairy tales were frequently explicit in their sexuality. Boccaccio, an early source for Perrault and other tale-tellers, had a flair for the pornographic. Giambattista Basile's seventeenth-century collection of fifty stories (or really forty-nine, with a frame story), *The Tale of Tales,* offers numerous sexy stories, some of which might be classified as sex comedies. In one, a stoic princess is finally made to laugh when a passing crone trips and her skirts fly up—revealing the "woodsy landscape" beneath. Basile's Sleeping Beauty tells a darker sex tale. In his seventeenth-century version of the story, Beauty is raped and impregnated in her sleep by a passing king, who then abandons her in the woods. She awakens only after one of the twins to whom she gives birth suckles the poison splinter (the cause of her slumber) from her finger. And Charles Perrault's first published "Red Riding Hood," with its hot illustrated boudoir scene and cleverly suggestive verse moral, provides only a small taste of the French fairy tale's erotic literary history. Porn merely uncovers the fairy tale's continuing central preoccupation, which still lurks under the veneer of children's literature.

Fairy tale porn also tells us something about how sexuality is defined, and the terms in which it is understood. It is no coincidence that so much of fairy-tale porn and erotica feature bondage and domination and sadomasochism—or B & D and S & M, in the fetish alphabet. Cinderella is a natural submissive; Snow White's wicked queen is the fairy-tale version of a dominatrix. And Red Riding Hood's story seems obsessed with her punishment, whatever form it may take. In *The Punishment of Red Riding Hood*, the fairy-tale plot has been entirely thrown out to focus exclusively on this theme. The video begins not with a walk in the woods but a straight cut to the bedroom scene followed by a bit of dungeon drama. There is no wolf, no grandmother, no woodsman. The only preserved motifs are the color red—on the star's boobless bustier—and her disobedience. The video begins, then, where the fairy tale ends: with the heroine's punishment, drawn out into a twenty-minute treatment involving tickling, wax, suspension, handcuffs, riding crops and, of course, the "overhead donut," an ideal prop for spanking. Upon reflection it seems obvious that fairy tales should fuel the fetish film. These films make explicit the fairy tale's obsession—and our fascination—with rules, obedience and punishment.

ONE THING FAIRY TALE pornography *doesn't* reveal is absolutes—either about sexuality or about power—much as some people like to argue it does. Feminists like Andrea Dworkin have drawn the link between fairy tales and pornography, both of which in her view signal the menace of male power; fairy tales and porn depict the oppressed, passive heroine as a sexual delicacy for men and supply narratives of the cultural omnipresence of rape and violence toward women:

> Literary pornography is the cultural scenario of male/female. It is the collective scenario of master/slave. It contains cultural truth: men and women, grown now out of the fairy-tale landscape into the castles of erotic desire; woman, her carnality adult and explicit, her role as victim adult and explicit, her guilt adult and explicit, her punishment lived out on her flesh, her end annihilation —death or complete submission.

Dworkin focuses on how fairy tales are the blueprints for gender and sexual relations that we practice later in life (as we have seen in Chapter 6). She moves her analysis smoothly along from fairy tales to pornography, finding the same sort of scenarios in both, only made more explicitly sexual in the latter. Her analysis, eloquent and provocative, provides powerful observations about gender. She sees these plots as institutionalized female victimization: The same patriarchal patterns of oppression in "Sleeping Beauty" are at work in "The Story of O"—both glamorize the passive, beautiful object, making perfect death the ultimate goal of femininity.

But what she misses is a sense of the fluidity of both genres. Read Dworkin, and you'd think every porn film was a snuff film; every fairy tale set in stone. In effect she makes the same blunder that Fromm and Bettelheim made in their psychoanalytic treatments of "Little Red Riding Hood." Both fairy tales and pornography—and the combination—have a social history, and they *change.* Dworkin overlooks the fact that these genres are a form of theater—albeit, as Kipnis notes, in a low idiom—where cultural and social values and desires play out. Both fairy tales and pornography provide a stage and the characters to explore our norms, our fantasies, what it means to be a man or a woman, and the outer limits of the acceptable. They are created and understood within the spectrum of broader social dynamics. They may be socializing forces, but they are also reflective surfaces that tell us things about ourselves and that change as we do.

Angela Carter, in contrast to Dworkin, sees both fairy tales and pornography—and the greater myths to which both belong—as part of a malleable dynamic, the power of which can be deflated, debunked, redirected, appropriated—*if* we can overcome our reverence for them. Carter observes the dominant image of woman in porn, fairy tale, or myth as passive and mute.

> Pornography involves an abstraction of human intercourse in which the self is reduced to its formal elements. In its most basic form, these elements are represented by the probe and the fringed hole, the twin signs of male and female in graffiti. . . . In the stylization of graffiti, the prick . . . always . . . points upwards, it asserts. The hole is open, an inert space. . . . The male is positive. . . . Woman is negative. Between her legs lies nothing but zero, the sign for nothing, that only becomes something when the male principle fills it with meaning. . . . Graffiti directs me back to my mythic generation as a woman and, as a woman, my symbolic value is primarily that of a myth of patience and receptivity, a dumb mouth from which the teeth have been pulled.

Like Dworkin, who sees the "Story of O" as a sort of porno–fairy tale hybrid that defines woman by the hole between her legs—a "zero"—Carter deplores the dominant pornographic myth of woman as negative, or nothing. What angers her isn't the myth itself, however; it's the implication that she, as woman, is incapable of staging her own scenarios—good or bad—and choosing her own narrative. Carter's retellings of "Little Red Riding Hood" feature a grandmother who lusts after a villain and notices his genitals ("huge!"), a villain whose womanizing can be interrupted by fear, and a heroine who knows she's "nobody's meat."

Even the briefest perusal of fairy-tale porn reveals that the genre is as malleable and complicated as any of Carter's stories. Fairy tale pornos feature Dworkin's submissive females, for example; but just as often, they favor the female dominatrix. Consider the following invitation to join an Internet porn site, which features both. The Prince stumbles upon Sleeping Beauty:

> Leaning over her in their beautiful moment of newly found intimacy, he awkwardly notices that her blouse is open . . . her nipple standing to attention. . . . He reaches to clasp her exposed flesh, when suddenly . . . the door flies open and the Witch bursts in. She is a towering figure with her long black luminescent hair drooped over a leather dominatrix outfit, shimmering in the limelight. . . . She sees the Prince's hand over Sleeping Beauty's breast and excitedly rushes towards him.

Or consider how the submissive female so colorfully illustrated on the cover of *The Punishment of Red Riding Hood* has her natural counterpart in a surprising number of variations of *Little Red Riding Crop*—featuring a heroine dominatrix. One humorously illustrated adult postcard shows the wolf tied up for a session of bondage and S & M, enjoying his submissive side. Suspended by his paws from ceiling handcuffs, he wears pink lacy knickers, matching powder-puff slippers, and a stiff, conical bra à la Jean Paul Gaultier. He also wears a dog collar—normally a fetish item, though of course in this case he *is* a dog.

Unlike the cross-dresser of Larson's cartoon, this wolf seems comfortable with his alternative sex life—as does the heroine he is paired with: "Red Riding Crop" appears in dominatrix duds, wearing thigh-high red boots with fishnet stockings and holding a riding crop and whip. Her basket of "goodies"—a variety of dildos—sits nearby.

The drama of Little Red Riding Crop is popular all over. In 2000, the Bad Attitude Boutique in Oregon put on a play by the same title in which the wolf and Grandma have a moment of sexual intimacy—doggy style, of course—when Red catches them in the act. "Bad dog," she cries, whipping him furiously. And in a play by the Raleigh Ensemble Players, *It Could Have Happened Once Upon a Time* (2000), Little Red Riding Crop is more taken with the woodsman, whom she affectionately calls "Woodie." His ax, propped between his legs, illustrates the eponymy.

The dominatrix, of course, may as likely be a figment of the patriarchal imagination as a figure of female empowerment. The point, however, is that the fairy tale has the ability to portray both—and more. The joke that appears at the head of this chapter shows the impact of social change upon the fairy tale. Its heroine takes control of her own sexual enjoyment. The fact that she can

With a crack of her whip, "Little Red Riding Crop"
obviates the age-old need for either seducer or
savior, in a post card by Carlos Aponte.

deliver a bawdy line about oral sex is telling, given that Little
Red Riding Hood began her literary life as a warning against the
female libido.

Gender, power and fairy tales—all are malleable—and the
multiplicity of messages in the images of fairy-tale porn are complicated and reflective of society. They make clear that while on

the one hand fairy tales are about social conformity, on the other they are about transgression. They present a vision of morality, but at the same time they present just the opposite: a roadmap for perversion. And in our theaters of fantasy—both porn and fairy tale—no one scenario of man and woman, weak and strong, can last forever.

X

Freeway:
A Ride in the Hood

Freeway

A MOVIE WRITTEN AND DIRECTED BY

MATTHEW BRIGHT

Fifteen-year-old Vanessa Lutz (Reese Witherspoon), an illiterate southern-California white-trash teenager, comes home from remedial reading class one day to find her mother hustling tricks on the corner and her hirsute, lupine stepfather smoking crack. Inside their ramshackle flat, Vanessa's stepfather sexually molests her, while in the background a television newscaster reports the latest on the "I-5 killer," a serial sex-murderer who has abducted yet another girl victim. Outside, Vanessa's mother unwittingly solicits an undercover policeman; the cops arrive, and both adults are seized and arrested. A social worker whom Vanessa already knows all too well shows up to place Vanessa in yet another foster home. Instead, Vanessa handcuffs her to the bedpost and decides to head north to Stockton in search of her long-lost grandmother.

Vanessa hits the road in a stolen car, stopping only to beg her boyfriend Chopper Wood (Bokeem Woodbine), a black inner-city gang youth from her remedial reading class, to come with her. Since

---

Source: Freeway Productions, 1996. Starring Reese Witherspoon, Bokeem Woodbine, Kiefer Sutherland and Brooke Shields.

he has to be in court for a parole hearing the next morning, Chopper instead gives her his gun for protection. She sets off, heading north. In the next scene, Chopper, defenseless without his gun, is shot down by members of a rival gang. Meanwhile Vanessa's hot rod breaks down. She gets a lift from smooth-talking, clean-cut child psychologist Bob "Wolverton" (Kiefer Sutherland).

As they share the ride, Wolverton encourages Vanessa to open up and share her family problems. He treats her to a roadside dinner and wins her confidence; she shows him a photograph of her grandmother. But soon his probing questions become increasingly lurid and twisted, and when he pulls out a straightedge razor and cuts off her ponytail, Vanessa realizes that she's in the car with the I–5 killer. "You that guy that's been killing all them girls on the freeway, Bob? Why you killing all them girls, Bob?!" Things seem bad until she remembers Chopper's gun and hits Wolverton on the head with it. "See where bad manners get you?" she says. At gunpoint, Wolverton pulls off the freeway at a deserted exit, where Vanessa asks him if he accepts Jesus as his personal savior, then blows his brains out. Only slightly flustered, she heads to a nearby truck stop for breakfast. "I must look a fright," the blood-spattered runaway apologizes to a speechless waitress.

Soon however, Vanessa is waylaid again. Wolverton, it turns out, has not been killed but only severely mutilated. His face is disfigured and his vocal cords injured. He now speaks through a mechanical contraption hanging around his neck that renders his words in a low growl. He has become on the outside the monster that he always was on the inside. Yet the police and the media still don't see his true nature. On television he is portrayed as a victim, whose "courage is a real inspiration." His annoyingly picture-perfect wife (Brooke Shields) cries with outrage at his fate; and in no time flat Vanessa is found, arrested and incarcerated.

Vanessa stages a violent escape with a group of fellow inmates and continues on her way to Grandma's house. Meanwhile a skeptical police officer returns to the scene of the crime, where he finds Vanessa's severed ponytail on the ground, and he begins to believe her story. He and his partner search Wolverton's house and find the skeletons in his closet—literally: Wolverton stores the decaying girls' corpses in a shed—and they set off after him. Wolverton is already on his way to the address written on the back of the photo Vanessa had shown him. All cast members converge on Grandma's trailer park.

Amidst a postmodern landscape of inflatable giraffes and plastic lawn ornaments, Vanessa arrives to find her "grandmother" in bed, in a shower cap and floral nightgown. It's the old fairy-tale trick, and Vanessa is not fooled for a second. Her face drops in disappointment. "Some big ugly fucking teeth you got, Bob."

Grandmother, the camera soon reveals, has already been dispatched in a fetish-style sex crime; but Vanessa is used to taking care of herself. A neighbor wanders in for a moment, and the distraction gives our heroine a split second to smack Wolverton's gun from his hands. She wrestles him to the ground, climbs on top of him, and knocks him out, perhaps for good. Enter the police officers—as always, one beat too late.

As they approach, cautiously and fearfully, Vanessa is already waiting outside her grandmother's front door, mascara running in sweaty streaks down her cheeks. They survey the scene in awe, and she lets out a relieved laugh, dazed but not half as amazed at her victory as they are. "You got a cigarette?"

—SYNOPSIS BY CATHERINE ORENSTEIN

I N THE 1990s, Little Red Riding Hood became a Gen-X girl. Make that *grrrl*. *Freeway,* Matthew Bright's startling 1996 screen adaptation of "Little Red Riding Hood," transplants the story to the underprivileged neighborhoods and byways of southern California, contrasting fairy-tale ideals with a less-than-ideal society. Our heroine, Vanessa, now sports a red leather jacket. Her mother is a crack whore working out of a squalid apartment; her lecherous stepfather is a drug addict on the dole. The forest has been paved over. And when her would-be guardians are arrested and hauled off to the pokey, Vanessa ditches town and heads north in search of Grandma. When her stolen car breaks down, she catches a ride with Bob Wolverton, a clean-cut, nice-looking child psychologist. Unfortunately, Bob is also the I–5 serial sex-killer, predator of young female hitch-hikers.

Filmed in the bright colors of a comic strip, *Freeway* is a fairy tale for the fast, furious and merciless. On the surface, it parodies the lives of the down and out, with each fairy-tale character transformed into a different stereotype, acting out a plot straight from the tabloids. Dressed in the baggy pants and combat boots of hip-hop, the attire of the social underclass, Vanessa is the embodiment of marginalized youth as she heads off on her voyage. Her southern twang (Texan?) sets her even farther apart from the social mainstream, well outside the trendy hip-hop culture of Los Angeles. Her boyfriend Chopper Wood (Bokeem Woodbine) is a black inner-city gang youth from her remedial reading class, with a shaved cranium and hulking presence. As a going-away present, he gives her a gun. Then, defenseless, he is killed by rival gang members in a drive-by shooting.

And the paved-over forest is full of real-life dangers: gangs, guns, and wolves everywhere. The camera zooms in eerily on Vanessa's hairy, doped-up stepfather, who sexually molests her; a leering police officer; and a middle-aged lecher looking for a blow job, who tries to cheat the teen runaway out of a few bucks. Above all, *Freeway* explores the theme of sexual abuse and the conditions and assumptions that make adolescent girls, especially those from the wrong side of the tracks, its repeated targets. Vanessa is so used to being molested that she brushes off her stepfather's groping paws with more annoyance than outrage. Later, she refers to Wolverton's psychopathic habits—he threatens to kill her and have sex with her corpse—as "bad manners."

As it loosely follows the familiar fairy-tale plot, *Freeway* spins a black comedy of social injustice. When Vanessa manages to turn the tables, pulling out Chopper's gun and shooting Wolverton in self-defense, no one will believe her story over his. After all, she's a runaway with a record, while Wolverton is a "respectable" member of society. In jail, Vanessa's plight is magnified by a motley crew of fellow inmates, kindred souls from society's least powerful demographic: poor, uneducated, young and female. Social misfits, minorities, outcasts. Girls who have learned to fend for themselves, sometimes in disturbing and violent ways. Girls with whom no one wants to deal, all trapped in a system that traffics in tranquilizers and "rehabilitation" rather than addressing the causes of their social malaise. By contrast, news reports cast Wolverton as the courageous victim. He may be a psychopath, but he's a well-socialized one. He has the right pedigree, the right skin tone, the right manner of speech. Even after he is horribly disfigured by the shooting, so that he looks as monstrous on the outside as he is within, no one can see through the veneer of his social status. Supported by the law, the media and his wife (dressed in outfits and bows vaguely reminiscent of Disney's Snow White), he can literally get away with murder.

Freeway's underlying theme is social inversion, challenging the line that separates tragedy from happily-ever-after. Its perspective and message come from below. We see the plot through Vanessa's eyes, right from the film's opening shot, as the camera pans, backwards, across a blackboard in her remedial reading class, catching the phrase "klim sknird tac eht" from the illiterate heroine's perspective. Even Vanessa's capacity for violence, and to a lesser extent, that of her fellow juvenile prison inmates, becomes understandable if not justifiable in the context of her daily oppression. And while Vanessa's life is no fairy tale, our heroine is no shrinking violet, and this time The End comes with a twist. In the final bedroom brawl Vanessa bests her age-old nemesis, leaving him in a lump on Grannie's floor—and turning the fairy tale, along with its moral lesson, on end.

Freeway transforms the fairy tale into a critique of modern society—exaggerating and then debunking stereotypes of race, class and gender and mocking the fairy tale even as it carries on the tradition. The film not only gives the characters of "Little Red Riding Hood" a new set and wardrobe; it also restores the original lesson in self-reliance contained in "The Grandmother's Tale," the wives' tale from Old Regime France, with its heroine triumphant. The resurrection of its early themes suggests how far the fairy tale has come, and at the same time, how it has come full circle. What goes around comes around, it seems—though not quite! Unlike the oral tradition of long ago, *Freeway* is viewed (or read) not only in contemporary context but also against the fairy tale's long history. It plays off of the literary canon and its legacy of messages, cleverly manipulating audience expectations and generating a virtual meta-plot. In its irreverent treatment of fairy-tale conventions, *Freeway* provides a chance to recap the tale's stock characters and themes and to reexamine the laws by which they survive and adapt.

IN THE EARLY twentieth century, the Russian folklorist Vladimir Propp pioneered the study of the fairy tale's structural building blocks. In his *Morphology of the Folktale,* translated into English in 1958, thirty years after its Russian publication, Propp compared and deconstructed 100 "wonder-tales" by nineteenth-century Russian writer A. N. Afanas'ev—the Eastern European equivalents of Western fairy tales, grouped together in the Aarne-Thompson index. As he compared them, breaking them down into their fundamental plot elements, he noticed that most seemed to share the same basic form. He found that he could reduce the significant actors in all the tales to a very small number of distinct characters—a hero, a villain, a magical helper, for example—and that these characters moved the plot along through a series of developments that, when viewed in terms of their significance or "function" in the plot, were always the same. He came to the startling conclusion that all fairy tales, in their tremendous diversity of detail, can be reduced to a small number of tale types, and even to a *single* plot.

Propp's fairy-tale "ur-plot" begins as follows: A family member leaves home. S/he is given an "interdiction" or warning, but the interdiction is violated. Then, the villain attempts to contact the hero and obtains information about the him/her, which he uses to trick him/her. The victim is fooled and unwittingly helps his/her enemy, who causes harm or injury to a member of the family. By now the reader has probably already noticed that Propp's scheme is exactly like "Little Red Riding Hood." Following the plots of the Grimms' "Little Red Cap," and of *Freeway,* Propp's terminology might be applied as follows:

1. Absentation: Red/Vanessa leaves home for Grandma's house/trailer park.
2. Interdiction: Red is warned not to stray from the path (or not to speak to strangers); Vanessa is warned about "the I–5 killer."
3. Violation: Red strays to pick flowers and speaks to a wolf; Vanessa steals a car and heads out on the freeway.
4. Reconnaissance: The wolf/Bob "Wolverton" makes contact with the heroine.
5. Delivery: Red gives the wolf directions to Grandma's; Vanessa shows Wolverton a family photo with her grandmother's address written on the back.
6. Trickery: The wolf poses as Red Riding Hood to enter

Grandma's house; Wolverton poses as an innocent victim to have Vanessa arrested.

7. Complicity: Grandma is fooled and lets the wolf in; the police are fooled and arrest Vanessa.
8. Villainy: The wolf eats Red's grandmother; Wolverton kills Vanessa's grandmother.

Here, "Little Red Riding Hood" and *Freeway* part ways. Propp notices a distinction between tales that concern "victim heroes," who are rescued by "seekers" (as heroines are rescued by princes in the most popular literary fairy tales), and those in which victims save themselves (as the protagonists of male-driven stories usually do, and also as the heroine of "The Grandmother's Tale" does). In Propp's scheme, the Grimms' Little Red Cap represents a victim hero who must be rescued, while *Freeway*'s Vanessa will come to her own rescue.

Of the thirty-one "functions" that Propp identifies, not all occur in every tale; but those that do always appear in the same order. The remaining functions of Propp's ur-plot do not apply to "Little Red Riding Hood," but they contain all the plot elements of the fairy tale as a genre, and give us a remarkable sense of our storytelling code.

8a. Lack: One member of a family lacks something or desires something.
9. Mediation: Misfortune or lack is made known; hero is approached with a request or command; he is allowed to go or he is dispatched.
10. Counteraction: the seeker agrees/decides upon counteraction.

11. Departure: S/he leaves home.

12. Donor tests the Hero: the hero is tested, and receives a magical helper.

13. Hero reacts by either passing or failing test.

14. Provision of Magical Aid.

15. Transference to another Kingdom.

16. Struggle: hero and villain join in direct combat.

17. Branding: hero is marked.

18. Victory: hero defeats villain.

19. Initial Misfortune Remedied.

20. Return of hero.

21. Pursuit of hero.

22. Rescue of hero.

23. Unrecognized return of hero (either to home or to another kingdom).

24. Unfounded claims are presented by a false hero.

25. Difficult task is proposed to the hero.

26. Solution: task is resolved.

27. Recognition of hero.

28. Exposure of false hero/villain.

29. Transfiguration: the hero is given a new appearance.

30. Punishment of villain.

31. Wedding: hero marries and ascends the throne.

ONE OF THE BOONS of Propp's analysis is that it offers a new layer to our understanding of the fairy tale's enduring power, and in particular of its so-called "survival forms"—that is, the modern appropriations and adaptations of "Little Red

Riding Hood." In the early twentieth century, Antti Aarne's *Types of the Folktale* had already established that any given tale might have infinite variations, fleshed out by an endless supply of motifs. Like a change of wardrobe, motifs come and go without altering a body of tales. Little Red Riding Hood may wear an aristocratic velvet hat like that of Perrault's character, a small cap like that pictured on the frontispiece of the Grimms' 1847 edition of tales (reproduced in Chapter 2), a red riding habit from the English countryside, or a red leather jacket. Or even no cloak or hood at all. She may encounter a wolf, a bzou, a werewolf, the Devil, a handsome suitor in a gray flannel suit, or a deranged highwayman. The forest may transform into a Hollywood nightclub, the cobblestone streets of Prague, or a stretch of interstate in southern California, yet it is still the symbolic place where danger lurks and strangers meet, and the essential story remains the same.

What Propp pointed out, however, is that not only individual tales but *also* entirely different tale types share the same basic structure and fundamental characters: the villain; the donor (provider of magical agents); the helper; the princess (or sought-for person) and her father; the dispatcher; the hero; the false hero.

The precise application of Propp's terms is less important than his underlying point: that the basic characters recur, not only in the variations of any given tale, but also throughout the corpus of tales that we come across. We know these recurrent characters as our familiars; they are part of a collective mental universe, and even as they change names and swap plots, we recognize and come to expect things from them, sometimes without even realizing it. In short, Propp's schema suggests the structure not only of the fairy tale, but of our greater cultural mentality, or what Jungians might call our collective unconscious. The fairy tale is, in essence, a human code that we ingest in the form of a story.

If we look closely through Propp's lens, the recurrence of, variations on, and even mutations in this cultural code become clear. Consider function number four of Propp's ur-plot, the "reconnaissance," as it has been rendered over the centuries in three different media, against the background of three very different social contexts. In Walter Crane's six-penny Victorian storybook intended for children, an early color print (reproduced in Chapter 2) shows a timid, fearful-looking heroine adorned in peasant clothes, mostly covered by her long hooded cloak. She faces an enormous, standing wolf, dressed in a peasant hat and sheepskin, who blocks her way on the path through the woods. To Victorian audiences, this was a spiritual confrontation between a foolish girl and a symbol of the Devil that dramatized her vulnerability and the need for her absolute obedience to father or perhaps husband. In the background, just over the heroine's left shoulder, two woodsmen watch on, suggesting this child-woman's need for protection and foreshadowing her eventual rescue from disaster.

More than a century later, in an age of new sexual politics, Tex Avery's animated version of the same encounter transforms horror into humor. His cartoon sequence (a still from which appears in Chapter 5) occurs at the Sunset Strip nightclub, where saucy stripper Red Hot Riding Hood shares a table with her wolf in between her song-and-dance routines. Our villain is no longer a spiritual threat, or indeed a threat at all; rather, he is a besotted suitor in tie and tails, beside himself with lust. The changed nature of his designs upon the heroine are readily apparent: He leans forward eagerly to kiss Red Hot's hand. Accordingly, he now has both a snout *and* lips. To mid-century audiences, this wartime cartoon offered humorous relief from real life. The stern morality of Crane's print is replaced by light-hearted escapism, and Avery's comically harmless villain is paired with a sex-object heroine who is anything but naïve. The fairy tale maintains its recognizable, underlying structure, but the scene has become a parody of new American courtship rituals.

In contrast, *Freeway* resituates "function four" in Wolverton's car as he and Vanessa speed down the interstate. The scene is again charged with fear—this time, his. Our heroine has traded her basket for a gun, which she holds to Wolverton's head. Her glare and grip are unwavering. The scene could hardly differ more from the one Walter Crane imagined. Now predator and prey have swapped places, the fairy tale has jumped down the rabbit hole, and the audience is urged to make an uncomfortable moral choice. Within the context of the film, the moviegoer is driven to root for Vanessa over Wolverton—in essence, to cheer for one would-be murderer over another.

Each of these scenes depicts the same moment in the fairy-tale plot. Each presents the same characters in a new guise. At first sight, the three images evoke a small shock of the familiar, since we know this scene not only from "Little Red Riding Hood" but also as a quintessential encounter occurring throughout the fairy-tale genre—and even beyond. But at the same time, these images deliver the shock of the new because in them the old tales have been so radically reconfigured. Set against different social

Our heroine (Reese Witherspoon) holds her attacker,
Bob Wolverton (Kiefer Sutherland), at gunpoint
in a dramatic reversal of the fariy tale order.

backdrops, they are endowed with new motifs and dramatically
new meanings. And each subsequent interpretation is further
nuanced when it resonates against the story's past.

Though *Freeway*'s writer-director Matthew Bright claims to
have had no knowledge of folklore scholarship when he wrote
his script, *Freeway* exposes and explores the fairy tale's underpin-
nings in sophisticated ways, and in particular plays with the conventions that shape the fairy tale's stock cast. Since, from a
structural perspective, the fairy tale's functions are defined inde-
pendently of the characters who are "supposed" to fulfill them, the
characters can swap places, playing against readers' (or viewers')
expectations of both the fairy tale and of real life. In this sense, they

resonate not only with our internalized sense of who they are but also against our constant awareness of who they are *not*.

Vanessa's boyfriend Chopper Wood, for example, is the inversion of the Grimms' goodly woodchopper not only in name, but in every other sense. As a black, inner-city gang tough, Chopper's mainstream association is not that of the heroic savior, but the anti-hero. He represents poor, rebellious, distrusted youth—the sort of character most likely to be cast as a villain in the tabloids. Meanwhile, his function within the fairy tale has also changed. Instead of a rescuer, he is the helper or donor, a character who provides a hero with the means of success. The helper, a well-known figure both within and beyond the fairy-tale genre, can be of either sex: A fairy Godmother in "Cinderella," for example, provides her with a gown and coach to attend a royal ball—and glass slippers that snag her a prince. In *Star Wars*, an epic that shares many of Propp's elements, Obi Wan Kenobi bequeaths Luke Skywalker his weapon—a Jedi light saber. The magical donor exists to provide the hero with the means of salvation, and once his or her function is fulfilled, may even take the sacrifice one step further. In *Freeway* Chopper gives Vanessa his gun, providing her with a means of saving herself from Wolverton, but sealing his own death.

Like Chopper, who has a new role to play in the story that challenges mainstream cultural understandings of his character, Wolverton plays against type and expectation. He is an educated, white, middle-class psychologist, a symbol of influence and affluence. If the film followed mainstream presumptions, he would be its hero. Wolverton lives the proverbial American dream, in a suburban house with a perfect wife. In short, he seems to represent the modern-day Prince Charming. Only here he is the I–5 serial killer. The popular psychologist Bruno Bettelheim once presented fairy tales as a safe landscape for children to explore their inner fears and forbidden desires; psychologists themselves are supposed to be trusted confidants. *Freeway* turns modern psychology on its head and casts a psychologist as the villain. What more appropriate update of Crane's wolf in sheep's clothing than a psychopath posing as a shrink? Wolverton's role in *Freeway* simultaneously subverts a multitude of cultural assumptions and fairy-tale conventions. As a killer with a hankering for young dead girls, Wolverton makes an ironic rejoinder to the Prince Charmings of yore, themselves necrophilic pedophiles: Think Snow White, Sleeping Beauty.

Above all, *Freeway*'s heroine challenges the dominant cultural fairy tale. Rather than a passive victim in need of rescue, like the heroine of the brothers Grimm, Vanessa is her own savior. She plays the role of Propp's "seeker"—the self-reliant protagonist. Her capacity for violence, her disregard for the law, her refusal to be cowed by the upper class (or the educated class) make her antisocial. But that, in the end, is what empowers her to work out her own salvation. As *Freeway* constantly contrasts ideals with harsh reality, it also inverts any sense of conventional moral vision. Though she is illiterate, poor and at the bottom of the social bucket, it turns out that Vanessa sets the moral standards for the movie. *Freeway* ends by directing our outrage not at the heroine, who in the past was blamed for being foolish, unchaste or disobedient; nor even at the fiendish Wolverton: On the contrary, *Freeway* points its finger back at society, and at the false fairy tales it peddles. The movie's moral outrage is directed at a social system—Vanessa's, and implicitly ours—that marginalizes girls and women, distrusts the poor, and preaches happily-ever-after while creating and condoning the social injustices that lead to real-life tragedy.

Propp's vision helps explain the central paradox of the fairy tale: why it is both timeless and universal, and yet always true to the time and day in which it is told. The fairy tale's plot functions remain fixed in perpetuity, but motifs are subject to endless variation, and all are read against a kaleidoscope of social and cultural patterns. Thus a story like "Little Red Riding Hood" both retains and challenges its "traditional" meanings over the centuries with each retelling, and the fairy tale code is passed down, like cultural DNA, from one generation to the next.

Epilogue: Under the Cloak

WHEN I WAS LITTLE, I played with a doll that incorporated the entire cast of "Little Red Riding Hood." In one position, the doll was a plump girl in a gingham skirt and red cape, with freckles and ponytails. But turn her upside down and flip over her skirt, and suddenly the doll became the Big Bad Wolf, dressed up for the finale in Granny's nighty, with her bonnet pulled over his furry head, having already dispatched with the rightful owner of those garments. Granny, it turns out, was not in his stomach but, as logistics demanded, on his back. Flip over the bonnet to cover the lupine snout, turn the doll about face, and there was Grandma's smile, framed by spectacles and a gray bun.

Even when I was little, this doll must have suggested to me what I now think of as the central lesson of the fairy tale. Somehow the little girl, wolf and grandmother were all three one and the same. There was no way to play with them at the same time; no way to make the wolf eat Grandma, and no way to put Red Riding Hood and the wolf in bed together, at least not side by side, as the plot demands. In short, there was no way of dealing with the characters as physically separate entities. Like Superman and Clark Kent, or Jekyll and Hyde, they were multiple aliases for the same body.

The greatest power of the fairy tale may be that it shows us the spectrum of human possibility. It presents us with archetypes that seem, at first glance, extreme. Each is defined in relation to its opposite: The wolf is all the more evil because Red Riding Hood is innocence incarnate. She is female, and the wolf is male—at least so we assume when considering the tale from the perspective of gender. She is human and so represents the civilized world, while the beast is wild. She is young; her grandmother, old. There is the forest, representing the unknown, and there is home, representing the safety of society and family. All is neatly spelled out, or seemingly so.

The French anthropologist Claude Lévi-Strauss talks about how humans see the world, and themselves, in binary opposition. The plots of human narratives, he says, are reducible to bipolar extremes; their meaning ultimately resides in this structure. But the human sense of identity is full of tricks. Absolute categories are elusive. Ideas about who and what we are shift over time and indeed, as the fairy tale suggests, inversions are also part of human nature. Characters and ideas may be defined in opposition to each other, yet none is truly exclusive of the other.

Take the seemingly simple matter of distinguishing men from women—a question of perception that has been explored, through the lens of the fairy tale, throughout this book. It was Freud who first said that when you meet a human being, the first distinction you make is "male or female" and you are accustomed to making that distinction with unhesitating certainty. But the matter is not so simple. The dilemma is not merely in postmodern notions of gender performance—that is, that masculinity and femininity are socially defined categories, hence there can be gender chameleons like Boy George, Divine and RuPaul. The dilemma is more fundamental. Consider, for example, anatomy—something that most people think of as more or less objective and fixed.

Anatomically speaking, what is a man, and what is a woman? Scholars and journalists have described the very curious difficulty that the International Olympic Committee had over the years in answering just this question—seemingly the simplest in the world. When the Olympics began, sex testing was not much of an issue: Only men competed, and they competed naked. In the early twentieth century the committee allowed women and men to sort themselves. But it seemed that some men were cheating. In 1936, a German athlete named Hermann Ratjen bound up his genitals and, calling himself "Dora," competed in the high jump. He placed fourth. Then the Olympic Committee started to use genital exams; athletes called it the "peek-and-poke." But more than a few cases seemed confusing: Some people—"more than is generally assumed," according to Alice Domurat Dreger, author of *Hermaphrodites and the Medical Invention of Sex* (1998)—are born with anatomy different from "standard" male or female bodies. Thus in 1968, when it became feasible, Olympic officials moved to buccal smears and checked the "sex chromosomes" of female athletes, XX indicating a woman and XY being a man. Surely, it seemed, this procedure would resolve the dilemma once and for all. But it didn't. Some people who are "androgen insensitive" may have the XY (male) genotype, but they cannot respond to testosterone. Thus, though genetically male, these people have the look and experience of being female. They have no ovaries or uterus, but they are often considered beautiful by Western standards—tall, slender and with scant body hair.

Hermaphrodites defy our absolute categories and expose how the physical world is subject to the vacillations of the human mind. They are the exceptions that prove the inadequacy of our rules, the permeability of our borders, and the revocability of our convictions. Something as seemingly unquestionable as whether one is man or woman—the first distinction we make about another person and perhaps the single most guiding assumption we harbor about ourselves—is at its core a matter of perspective. Man and woman are not discrete, absolute concepts, but entwined and related and always shifting. Like the fairy tale, our physical bodies are cultural texts that are continually revised. No one story will last for long, inasmuch as we are constantly reinventing ourselves.

The Janus-faced doll that I played with as a child suggests the power of "Little Red Riding Hood" in the fairy-tale kingdom, and in our greater lives. Like a prism that refracts light and delivers the spectrum of the rainbow, "Little Red Riding Hood" splits and reveals the various elements of human identity. The truth is that in the real world, as in the fairy tale, we are all a bit of everything: a spectrum of possibilities, interwoven and interrelated. Over the years, by intention or by intuition, the tale of "Little Red Riding Hood" has explored the shifting fault lines of morality, sexuality and gender. The girl may trade her red cloth hood for one of wolfskin. The wolf will insist on frills and pregnancy. The old woman leaps from bed to grab her service revolver or wrestle her attacker to the floor. The rescuer is upon occasion rendered helpless, and even Mother Goose can at times become wolfish, as when the storyteller is depicted mimicking the wolf for an audience of children, her eyes glaring, teeth bared. The fairy tale runs through us like a current. Each of us carries within an intuitive understanding of what it means to be wolf, Grandma, woodsman, and Little Red Riding Hood.

Notes

Introduction

page

3 Walt Disney's first cartoon: *People* magazine detailed the recent discovery of Disney's long-lost first animated film *Granny Steps Out*—the title given by a British distributor to "Little Red Riding Hood." The seven-minute short, purchased by London film editor and researcher David Wyatt at a liquidation sale in 1978, and rediscovered in 1996 by Disney archivists, was drawn by Walt Disney in 1922 at the age of twenty-one. See *People,* September 21, 1998, p. 86.

3 Charles Dickens's first love: Charles Dickens, "A Christmas Tree," in *Christmas Stories* (London: Chapman and Hall, 1898), p. 8.

5 "Prisons and policemen": John B. Gruelle, *All About Little Red Riding Hood* (New York: Cupples and Leon, 1916).

7 Condoning the use of alcohol: An editorial on the matter ran in the *New York Times*, May 9, 1990, p. A30.

9 Aarne-Thompson Tale Type Index: See A. Aarne, *The Types of the Folktale: A Classification and Bibliography*, 2nd rev. ed., translated and enlarged by S. Thompson (Helsinki: Academia Scientiarum Fennica, 1981; rev. ed., 1961); originally published as *Verzeichnis der märchentypen*, FF Communications, no. 3 (1910; reprint, Helsinki: Academia Scientiarum Fennica, 1959).

10 Popularity of the Grimm tales: According to Jack D. Zipes, *Fairy Tales and the Art of Subversion: The Classical Genre for Children and the Process of Civilization* (New York: Routledge, 1991), p. 5.

11 Fertility narrative: "The sperm saga" is a fascinating subgenre not only of science fiction but, more broadly, of human myth. It follows the same

narrative pattern that hero myths from cultures all around the world follow—the Hero Cycle, discussed in more detail in Chapter 3. However,
more recently scientists have found that in real life, the "conquering"
sperm is far weaker than has long been presumed, while the egg is far
more active, capturing and tethering sperm *before* the sperm penetrates.
See, among other discussions, "The Egg and the Sperm: How Science
Has Constructed a Romance Based on Stereotypical Male-Female Roles,"
by Emily Martin, *Signs* 16, no. 3 (1991): 485–501. See also Gerald Schatten and Helen Schatten, "The Energetic Egg," *Medical World News* 23
(Jan. 23, 1984): 52–53.

12 The psychoanalyst Bruno Bettelheim: Much later, in the weeks after
Bettelheim's suicide in 1990, it was learned that he had fabricated a
dossier of credentials, including a degree (summa cum laude no less) in
psychology from Vienna—and that in fact, prior to arriving in America
in the 1940s, he had not been a psychologist at all but an upper-middle-
class lumber merchant. See Richard Pollak, *The Creation of Dr. B: A Biography of Bruno Bettelheim* (New York: Simon and Schuster, 1997).

CHAPTER 1

24 Court of the Sun King: G. Zeigler, *The Court of Versailles in the Reign of
Louis XIV* (London: George Allen and Unwin, 1966).

24 Royal lechery: The incident is described by Voltaire in his *Le Siècle de
Louis XIV* (The age of Louis XIV), translated by Martyn P. Pollack (New
York: Dutton, 1978), p. 103.

24 Monsieur Le Duc d'Orleans: N. Mitford, *The Sun King* (New York:
Harper & Row, 1966), p. 55.

24 The Princess de Soubise: Ibid., p. 75.

25 "I was delighted": F. Mossiker, *Madame de Sévigné: A Life and Letters*
(New York: Columbia University Press, 1985), p. 95. This collection presents about fifty years of Sévigné's correspondences.

26 *Elle avoit vû le loup:* The phrase "to see the wolf" was common enough
to make it into contemporary dictionaries, and its sexual meaning is
made particularly clear in the preface to Perrault's four-volume master-
work, *Parallèle des Anciens et des Modernes en ce qui regarde les arts et les
sciences*, 4 vols. (Paris: Jean-Baptiste Coignard, 1688–1997). Paraphras-
ing a tale by the Greek poet Theocritus, he writes that a young woman

blushes because *"elle avoit vû le loup"*—a double entendre, because her lover is also named Loup.

28 "The stories they amuse the ladies with": Sévigné in a letter to her daughter dated August 6, 1677. For more on Sévigné and the early development of the French literary fairy tale, see Mary Elizabeth Storer, *Une épisode littéraire de la fin du 17eme siècle: La mode des contes de fées, 1685–1700* (Geneva: Slatkine Reprints, 1972).

32 Prominent bluestockings: The salon women's fairy tales, when eventually published, became expressions of their progressive political goals. D'Aulnoy's *Island of Happiness* questioned the cruelties of arranged marriage. Married at fifteen to a husband thirty years her elder, D'Aulnoy was said to have arranged an attempt on his life. The Countess Henriette-Julie de Murat, banished from Louis XIV's Court for publishing a political satire about him, wrote about true love but did not always end her tales happily. Marie-Jean Lhéritier de Villandon, the niece of Charles Perrault and a well-known figure of the salons, dressed her heroines as boys, had them outfox wicked princes, and condemned the royal historian Nicolas Boileau to be bitten by Cerberus—the dog who guards the entrance to Hell—as many times as he had insulted women. In Catherine Bernard's version of "Ricky with the Tuft" (penned in 1695, before the publication of Perrault's version), a prince magically smartens up his beautiful girlfriend, then offers her the choice of marriage or losing her intelligence; she takes the former, but keeps a lover on the side. And the heroine of Lafayette's *The Princess of Clèves* (1678), a fairy tale-esque roman à clef whose heroine was thought by some to be the real-life Madame de Sévigné, is wrongfully accused of adultery. But when finally freed by her husband's death, she chooses not to marry the man she has for so long chastely loved. Sévigné, widowed at twenty-five and left in control of her own fortune, considered widowhood to be a great boon for a woman. Perhaps she also felt, like Lafayette's Princess of Clèves, that marriage destroys love.

32 "A carousel horse": Phyllis Stock, *Better Than Rubies: A History of Women's Education*. (New York: G. P. Putnam & Sons, 1978), p. 16.

33 Abbé Fénélon: He wrote *De l'education des filles* (The education of daughters) in 1687 with the King's official mistress, thought by many to have become his second wife in a secret marriage. Madame de Maintenon oversaw a conservative girls' school at Saint Cyr. Fénélon was

one of the school's confessors, as well as Maintenon's spiritual counselor.

35 "Your large, beautiful château": Mossiker, *Madame de Sévigné: A Life and Letters,* p. 468.

36 A form of *rapt:* Sarah Hanley gives a detailed discussion of fifteen seventeenth-century marriage laws, including rapt, in "Engendering the State: Family Formation and State Building in Early Modern France," in *French History Studies* (1989): 4–27; and "Family and State in Early Modern France: The Marriage Pact," in *Connecting Spheres: Women in the Western World, 1500 to the Present,* edited by M. J. Boxer and J. H. Quataert (New York: Oxford University Press, 1987).

36 Discussed his marriage plans: In his memoirs Perrault describes a discussion with Colbert about his marriage plans. Colbert thought her dowry of 70,000 livres was not enough: "'I will find you a girl, from a family or business who will bring you a more advantageous dowry. But,' [Colbert] pursued, 'is this not a marriage of affection you speak of?' 'I have only seen the girl,' I replied, 'one time since she was out of the convent, where she was put at the age of four.'" Perrault, *Memoires de ma vie* (Paris: Patte, 1769), p. 106.

37 The *chaperon,* or hood: The experienced married woman shelters the youthful *débutante* as a hood shelters the face, both the Oxford English and French Littré dictionaries now explain.

37–38 A literal translation of Perrault: My translation.

38 "Unsuitable suitor": Folklorist Caroline Oates uses this term in a forthcoming article "Rippers, Trippers and Strippers," *Folklore* (forthcoming).

CHAPTER 2

48 Storyteller of the German countryside: Since only first names were recorded in the margins of the Grimms' first edition, much later some confusion ensued about Marie's true identity. In a retrospective essay about his father published in 1895, Herman Grimm insisted that "Marie" was not Marie Hassenpflug, but "old Marie," a servant woman in the house where Wilhelm's wife (Herman's mother), Dorothea Wild, grew up. Scholars until recently accepted this claim, but the German scholar John Ellis has sharply refuted it. See John Ellis, *One Fairy Story Too Many* (Chicago: University of Chicago Press, 1983), pp. 29–31.

48 Altered their collection: Ibid. Ellis writes that the Grimms deliberately, persistently and completely misrepresented the status of their tales and that their son Herman and numerous scholars have preserved the Grimms' myth and ignored evidence of bourgeois input despite obvious evidence of their deception.

49 Prolonged period of childhood: The publication of Philippe Ariès's *L'Enfant et la Vie Familiale Sous l'Ancien Regime* initiated a broad public debate into the history of childhood as a distinct life stage that was largely an invention of the nineteenth-century middle class. See Philippe Ariès, *Centuries of Childhood: A Social History of Family Life* (New York: Vintage, 1962). In the seventeenth century, children died in great numbers, thus bearing many children was key. A wealthy woman might raise six or seven; a poor woman was lucky even to have one live through the perils of a sixteenth-century childhood. See N. Z. Davis, *Society and Culture in Early Modern France: Eight Essays* (Stanford, Calif.: Stanford University Press, 1975).

50 Books were a luxury: In terms of relative income prices of books have dramatically dropped over the ages. In the seventeenth century, only the truly wealthy could afford them. According to Lucien Febvre and Henri-Jean Martin, in the seventeenth century publishing was subject to authority and relied on the "tried and true." Old chivalric romances made up a significant part of book sales, along with the items mentioned here—but in much smaller quantities than today. See L. Febvre and H. J. Martin, *The Coming of the Book* (London: Verso, 1976).

53 The Grimm brothers: For details on the Grimms' life, see, among other studies, Murray Peppar's biography titled *Paths Through the Forest: A Biography of the Brothers Grimm* (New York: Holt, Rinehart and Winston, 1971).

53 "This new edition": Maria Tatar translates the prefaces to the Grimms' first and second editions in *The Hard Facts of the Grimms' Fairy Tales* (Princeton: Princeton University Press, 1987), p. 220.

54 "A manual of manners": Ibid., p. 217.

55 Exaggerated violence: Ibid.

58 The red riding habit: For details of the English history of the red riding hood, as well as the myths regarding halted French invasions, see A. Oakes and M. H. Hill, *Rural Costume: Its Origins and Development in Western Europe and the British Isles* (London: B. T. Batsford, 1970).

59 Education was minimal: A description of such a woman's life appears in Penny Kane, *Victorian Families in Fact and Fiction* (New York: St. Martin's, 1995).

59 Description of boarding school: Jane Austin, *Emma* (New York: Random House, 2001), first published 1816.

60 "The girls at home": For details of the Victorian woman's social isolation, education and drive to marry, see, among others, Kane, *Victorian Families in Fact and Fiction*.

CHAPTER 3

68 A scholarly journal: Excerpts of "The Grandmother's Tale" first appeared in a folklore journal, *Mélusine* 3 (1886–1887): 428–429.

69 Versions of "The Grandmother's Tale": Delarue discussed the tale and its variants in a multipart essay, "Les contes merveilleux de Perrault et la tradition populaire: I. Le petit chaperon rouge," *Bulletin folkorique d'Ile-de-France* (1951), pp. 221–228, 251–260, 283–291, and (1953), pp. 511–517. Delarue also summarized his findings in a brief note on the tale in *The Borzoi Book of French Folktales* (Canada: Knopf, 1956). Besides "The Grandmother's Tale," he found twenty versions from the oral tradition, two versions that were offshoots of Perrault's literary tale, and a dozen that incorporated elements of Perrault as well as motifs from the otherwise independent oral tradition. The text of "The Grandmother's Tale" and its French variants appeared in P. Delarue and M.-L. Tenèze, *Le conte populaire français* (The French popular tale) (Paris: Erasme, 1957). The Italian variants mentioned appear in I. Calvino, *Italian Folktales* (New York: Pantheon, 1956). Wolfram Eberhard's study on "The Story of Grandaunt Tiger" originally appeared in *Studies in Taiwanese Folktales,* Asian Folklore and Social Life Monographs, vol. 1 (Taipei: The Orient Cultural Service, 1970), pp. 14–17, 27–76, 91–95. I have cited the essay as it appears in *Little Red Riding Hood: A Casebook,* edited by Berkeley folklorist Alan Dundes (Madison: University of Wisconsin Press, 1989). A version of *Lon Po Po,* translated and illustrated by Ed Young, is available as a children's book (New York: Scholastic, 1989).

70 Memorable variation: Jack Zipes, *The Trials and Tribulations of Little Red Riding Hood,* vol. 2 (New York: Routledge, 1993), p. 5. Zipes draws from the collection of French folklorist Charles Joisten.

71 Celebrating the coming of spring: See P. Saintyves, "Little Red Riding Hood or The Little May Queen," in Dundes's *Little Red Riding Hood: A Casebook,* pp. 71–88.

71 "Red is the color": B. Bettelheim, *The Uses of Enchantment: The Meaning and Importance of Fairy Tales* (New York: Random House, 1977), p. 173.

74 Aarne-Thompson index: See A. Aarne, *The Types of the Folktale: A Classification and Bibliography,* 2nd rev. ed., translated and enlarged by S. Thompson (Helsinki: Academia Scientiarum Fennica, 1981; rev. ed., 1961); originally published as *Verzeichnis der märchentypen,* FF Communications, no. 3 (1910; reprint, Helsinki: Academia Scientiarum Fennica, 1959). The index is limited by inevitable incompleteness, a geographic bias toward Europe, and sometimes confusing organization (the division of animal and human tales, for example, obscures the link between identical stories told in one instance with a human protagonist and in another with a beast). Omissions include local legends and literary tales not found in oral tradition. Regarding geographic bias, Thompson writes in the foreword to his 1961 updated edition that *Types of the Folktale* would be better titled *Folktales of Europe, West Asia and the Lands Settled by These People.*" The index also relies heavily on the brothers Grimm, as the entries related to "Little Red Riding Hood" suggest. Thompson references Delarue's work in his 1961 update, but the happy ending of "The Grandmother's Tale" did not make it into the index.

76 "Fromm made a great deal": R. Darnton, *The Great Cat Massacre* (New York: Vintage, 1985), p. 11.

78 A *rite de passage*: Van Gennep's rite de passage is not exclusive to fairy tales; but others have focused more tightly on the patterns of fairy-tale plots. Russian folklorist Vladimir Propp showed that wondertales—the Russian equivalent of fairy tales—could be broken down into a limited number of elements, always occurring in the same sequence. By breaking their plots into elementary "functions" he discovered that all fairy tales could be reduced to a very small number—or even a single!—plot. The female half of the plot differs from the typical male version, however—at least in the fairy tales that most of us know. I will return to this in Chapter 10.

79 The Hero Cycle: See O. Rank, "The Myth of the Birth of the Hero"; L. Raglan, "The Hero: A Study in Tradition, Myth and Drama"; and A. Dundes, "The Hero Pattern and the Life of Jesus," all published together

in Otto Rank et al., *In Quest of the Hero* (Princeton: Princeton University Press, 1990). Also see J. Campbell's *The Hero with a Thousand Faces,* Bollingen Series, vol. 17 (Princeton: Princeton University Press, 1949), and C. J. Jung's "The Psychology of the Child Archetype" in his book *The Archetypes and the Collective Unconscious,* 2nd ed. (Princeton: Princeton University Press, 1969). Also for more on Jung's hero, see Marie-Louise von Franz, *An Introduction to the Psychology of Fairy Tales* (New York: Spring, 1970), pp. 41–46.

81 Microcosmic triumph: Campbell, *The Hero with a Thousand Faces,* pp. 37–38.

81 Focus on women: One of the old canards of folklore is that sacred myths (i.e., about men) over time devolved into fairy tales (about women). In her essay "Is Female to Male as Nature Is to Culture?" in her book *Making Gender: The Politics and Erotics of Culture* (Boston: Beacon Press, 1996), feminist anthropologist Sherry Ortner discusses how the masculine realm is presented as grand and sophisticated, while the feminine is cast as simple, lower in the cultural order: e.g., men are "chefs," women are "cooks."

81 A sense of sexual maturation: See Yvonne Verdier's "Little Red Riding Hood in Oral Tradition," *Marvels and Tales: Journal of Fairy Tale Studies* 11, nos. 1–2 (1997), pp. 101–123.

83 The rhythm of work: For details on spinning in France see S. I. Spencer, *French Women and the Age of Enlightenment* (Bloomington: Indiana University Press, 1984); for a general history of spinning see E. W. Barber, *Women's Work: The First 20,000 Years: Women, Cloth, and Society in Early Times* (New York: W. W. Norton, 1994).

83 Female sources: There is an interesting contradiction between the term "wives' tale"—meaning a lie—and these male authors' need to authenticate their stories through a female voice—they are only "real" if from a woman. Sandra M. Gilbert and Susan Gubar discuss the parallel between authorship and authority in men's and women's writing in their book *The Mad Woman in the Attic: The Woman Writer and the Nineteenth-Century Literary Imagination,* 2nd ed. (New Haven, Conn.: Yale University Press, 2000).

CHAPTER 4

87–88 "A true Discourse": The spellings and format of the original have been retained for the introduction to the Stubbe Peeter account; in the remainder, spellings have been modernized.

94 Native American wolf: In *Of Wolves and Men* (New York: Simon and Schuster, 1978), B. H. Lopez lists a number of Native American stories and names that reveal the wolf as revered, pp. 114–121.

95 Pamphlet and broadside: The Stubbe Peeter account is one of five "true histories" bound together in a small pamphlet now held at London's Lambeth Palace Library. Among the other stories included in the pamphlet are: (1) "Newes out of *Germanie* A most wonderfull and true discourse of a cruell murderer, who had kylled in his life tyme, nine hundred, threescore and odde persons among which six of them were his owne children," 1584; (2) "A breife discourse of the late murther of master George Saunders, a sworshipfull Citizen of London," murdered by his wife in what seems to be 1573; and (3) "A true report of the late horrible murther committed by William Sherwood, upon Richard Hobson, Gentleman, both prisoners in the Wueenes Benche, for the profession of Poperie," of June 18, 1581. The broadside folded in thirds and inserted at the end of the pamphlet gives the following captions: (1) "Stubbe Peeter in the shape of a Woolfe is heere devouring a man"; (2) "Heer he is hunted and chaced by the men of the Cuntry, and he casting away his girdle"; (3) "Is heere taken in the likenes of a man with a Staffe in his hand"; (4) "Heere he is condemned by the Judges to suffer death"; (5) "He is heere laaide on a Carte wheele and his flesh pluckt from his bones with hot pincers"; (6) "Heer he hath his legges and armes broken upon a Car wheele with a wooden Axe"; (7) "He hath heer his head strook from his body and stuck upon a hye pole with the picture of a Woolfe, and 16 peeces of wood, resembling the 16 persons which he had slaine"; (8) "Heer is his body with his daughter and gossip burned to ashes. Thus he hued and dyed in the likenes of a woolf, and shape of a man."

95 Werewolf accounts: Folklorist Caroline Oates, who writes on werewolves, notes a similar broadside circulated in Augsburg, Germany, in 1589, which depicted a variation of the story: A man cuts off Stubbe Peeter's paw, which then reverts into a human hand, proving the crimi-

nal's demonic identity. See Caroline Oates, "The Trial of a Teenage Were-wolf, Bordeaux, 1603," *Criminal Justice History* 9 (1988): 1–29.

96 Grenier's story: For a creative synopsis of the trial of Jean Grenier, see the classic nineteenth-century study by Sabine Baring-Gould, *The Book of Werewolves* (London: Senate/Studio Editions, 1995). For a scholarly summary and description of Grenier's trial and others in the region of Franche-Compté, see Oates's "The Trial of a Teenage Were-wolf"; also her essay "Metamorphosis and Lycanthropy in Franche-Compté, 1521–1643," in *Fragments for a History of the Human Body,* edited by M. Feher (Cambridge, Mass.: MIT Press, 1989). For authors writing on the subject of witchcraft during its peak years, among others see Henri Boguet's well-circulated *Discours des Sorciers,* first published in 1590–1611 but translated by E. Allen Ashwin as *An Examen of Witches* (London: John Rodker, 1929); Jean Bodin's *De la demonamanie de sorciers,* Renaissance and Reformation Texts in Translation, vol. 7 (Toronto: Centre for Reformation and Renaissance Studies, 1995); and Johann Weyer's authoritative *De praestigiis daemonum,* found in abridged form in *On Witchcraft,* edited by B. G. Kohl and H.C.E. Midelfort, translated by J. Shea (Asheville, N.C.: Pegasus, 1998). *A Lycanthropy Reader: Werewolves in Western Culture,* a collection of historical and contemporary writings edited by Charlotte F. Otten (Syracuse: Syracuse University Press, 1986), provides context as well as summaries and analysis of some of the more famous trials; it also contains an excerpt from Boguet. William Monter's essay, included therein, is particularly useful for its overview of trials in different regions. The story about the burgomaster-wolf appears in Lopez, *Of Wolves and Men,* p. 150.

97 *Malleus maleficarum:* Written by Heinrich Kramer and Jacob Sprenger, the *Malleus maleficarum* (Witch's hammer) was first published in 1486–1487 and, thanks to numerous editions issued over the course of the next several centuries from the leading German, French and Italian presses, continued to serve as a guide for witch hunters into the seventeenth century. It describes the different forms of witchcraft—including a memorable section entitled "What is to be Thought of Wolves which sometimes Seize and Eat Men and Children out of their Cradles. Whether this also is a Glamour caused by Witches"—and explains the harsh legal procedures to be used in prosecuting witches. It also pro-

vides a theological basis for the judgments of those, like Bodin and Boguet, who tried werewolves.

102 Spirit of the Inquisition: Oates writes that the Inquisition's role in Franch-Compté seems to have been limited, perhaps due to the efforts of the Dôle Parliament to control all criminal proceedings in the territory. See Oates, "Metamorphosis and Lycanthropy."

103 The heyday of witch trials: The historical witch set the foundation for her modern equivalent, the bitch. As witch was to werewolf, so today the bitch is to the wolf—opposing gender archetypes transmuted over time, given different nomenclature. It is interesting to compare the witch in the *Maleficarum* with today's bitch to see how the archetype has continued into modern times—and how it has changed.

105 "The Wolf King": Translated by Jack Zipes in *The Trials and Tribulations of Little Red Riding Hood* (New York: Routledge, 1993), pp. 129–132.

CHAPTER 5

119 "Not so easy to fool little girls": James Thurber's "The Girl and the Wolf" appeared in *Fables for Our Time and Famous Poems* (New York: Harper, 1939).

122 Female-driven plots: Very few modern translations of the Grimms' *Nursery and Household Tales* offer more than twenty-five tales. Female-driven stories are only 20 percent of the original collection, but often make up 75 percent or more in today's children's books. "In this sense the fairy tale, a male-oriented genre in Europe, becomes a female-oriented genre in North American children's literature," according to K. Stone, "Things Walt Disney Never Told Us," in *Women and Folklore,* edited by C. R. Farrer (Austin: University of Texas Press, 1975), pp. 43–44.

123 Domesticity in the 1950s: See Stephanie Coontz, *The Way We Never Were* (New York: Basic Books, 1992), pp. 23–28.

123 Navigating the double standards: Ibid.

CHAPTER 6

135 Linda Sexton's fascination with fairy tales: The story about Linda's collection of tales appears in Linda Gray Sexton, *Searching for Mercy Street* (Boston: Little, Brown, 1994), pp. 147–148. Linda Sexton also tells the

same story in an essay, "Bones and Black Pudding: Revisiting 'The Juniper Tree,'" in *Mirror, Mirror on the Wall*, edited by Kate Bernheimer (New York: Doubleday, 1998)—but in this version she, rather than her mother, writes on the napkin.

135 "Very wry, and cruel": Quoted in Diane Wood Middlebrook, *Anne Sexton: A Biography* (Boston: Houghton Mifflin, 1991), pp. 336–337.

138 "LOADING ZONE": Quoted in Linda Gray Sexton and Lois Ames, eds., *Anne Sexton: A Self-Portrait in Letters* (Boston: Houghton Mifflin, 1977).

139 Background on Anne Sexton: For details on Sexton's life, see Diane Wood Middlebrook's *Anne Sexton: A Biography*. For Sexton's correspondences, see *Anne Sexton: A Self-Portrait in Letters*, edited by her daughter Linda Gray Sexton with Lois Ames. See also Linda Sexton's *Searching for Mercy Street* and Anne Sexton's *Complete Poems* (Boston: Houghton Mifflin, 1981), which brings together Sexton's life's work and includes an insightful foreword by Maxine Kumin.

140 "Tired of the spoons": From "Consorting with Angels" in Sexton, *The Complete Poems*.

140 "Wallowed in gynecology": Raymond Sokolov, "Shushing the Dead and the Dying," in the *Wall Street Journal*, Aug. 21, 1991.

141 "The innocent persecuted heroine": The tales of this genre share both motifs and general plot episodes as well as a common plot outline. In "The Innocent Persecuted Heroine Genre: An Analysis of Its Structure and Themes," in *Western Folklore* 52 (1993): 13–41, Steven Swann Jones gives an analysis of this genre first proposed in 1927 by Aleksandr Isaakovich Nikiforov. Nikiforov divided female fairy tales into two predominant schemes—those about the heroine winning (usually a groom); and those about her suffering and being persecuted. As Sherry Ortner later observes, however, it's possible to see these two schemes as part and parcel of the same plot—and that the former (marriage) is merely the reward for the latter (suffering and acceptance of subjugation).

142 Not properly socialized: S. B. Ortner, *Making Gender: The Politics and Erotics of Culture* (Boston: Beacon Press, 1996), p. 9.

144 "The woman is perfected": Sylvia Plath, "Edge" (1963), in *The Collected Poems* (New York: HarperCollins, 1981).

144 "Flock of delicate heroines": Simone de Beauvoir, *The Second Sex* (New York: Knopf, 1953), p. 319.

144 "Fairy tales of childhood": A. Dworkin, *Woman Hating* (New York: Dut-

ton, 1974), pp. 32–33. Dworkin focuses on how fairy tales are the blueprints for gender and sexual relations that we practice later in life. She moves her analysis smoothly along from fairy tales to pornography, where she finds the same sort of scenarios, only now made explicitly sexual. I'll bring this up again in Chapter 9.

145 "Full of a vague dread": S. Brownmiller, *Against Our Will: Men, Women and Rape* (New York: Ballantine, 1975), p. 309.

146 Patterson at Atmore prison: H. Patterson and E. Conrad, *Scottsboro Boy* (Garden City, N.Y.: Doubleday, 1950), p 82.

147 Walk from the bus stop: N. Wolf, *Promiscuities: The Secret Struggle for Womanhood* (New York: Fawcett Columbine, 1997), pp. 31–32.

147 "Out to get all of us": K. Roiphe, *The Morning After: Sex, Fear and Feminism on Campus* (Boston: Little, Brown, 1993), p. 48.

148 Remembering the villain: Francesca Lia Block, *The Rose and the Beast: Fairy Tales Retold* (New York: HarperCollins, 2000).

148 Sharpe's tale: Anne Sharpe, "Not So Little Red Riding Hood," in J. Zipes, *The Trials and Tribulations of Little Red Riding Hood* (New York: Routledge, 1993), p 324.

149 "Literary tale of rape": Zipes, *Trials and Tribulations*, p. 1.

149 "was simply commanded to wed.": S. Brownmiller, *Against Our Will: Men, Women and Rape* (New York: Ballantine, 1975), p. 9.

151 Unapproved marriages: For a discussion of paternal dominance over offspring and specifically for details on rapt, see Sarah Hanley, "Engendering the State: Family Formation and State-Building in Early Modern France," in *French Historical Studies* (1989): 4–27.

152 Russell's survey: Diana Russell, *Sexual Exploitation: Rape, Child Sexual Abuse, and Sexual Harassment* (Beverly Hills, Calif.: Sage, 1984).

152 The term "sexual harassment": Brownmiller describes the origin of the term "sexual harassment" in *In Our Time: Memoir of a Revolution* (New York: Delta, 1999), pp. 279–281.

CHAPTER 7

160 Tale by the Merseyside Fairy Story Collective: This story was written collectively by Audrey Ackroyd, Marge Ben-Tovim, Catherine Meredith and Anne Neville, and illustrated by Trevor Skempton. One of Skempton's illustrations precedes the chapter.

161 "Not So Little Red Riding Hood": In Jack Zipes's anthology, *The Trials and Tribulations of Little Red Riding Hood* (New York: Routledge, 1993), pp. 324–327.

161 "Delian Little Red Riding Hood": Rosemary Lake's *Once Upon a Time When the Princess Rescued the Prince* (Guerneville, Calif.: Dragon Tree Press, 2001).

161 "Politically correct" version: "Little Red Riding Hood" in James Finn Garner's *Politically Correct Bedtime Stories: Modern Tales for Our Life and Times* (New York: Macmillan, 1994), pp. 1–4.

161 "The Real Version": The story appears on the Internet, attributed to Rachel Yap, a middle-school student at the Canadian Academy in Kobe, Japan.

162 "You Are What You Eat": Paul Musso's story appears in *Flatter* 3 (1996): 46–47. Edited by Jaina A. Davis, *Flatter* is a small, independent alternative 'zine that describes itself as "the Journal of Oblate Puffery."

162 Broumas's tale: In Zipes, *Trials and Tribulations*, pp. 272–273.

162 "Little Red Riding Hood Redux": This tale, circulating on the Internet, is dated 1993 and attributed to D. W. Prosser.

164 "A piglet you must never trust": Roald Dahl, *Roald Dahl's Revolting Rhymes* (New York: Knopf, 1983), p. 39.

167 "The Tiger's Bride": Angela Carter's version appears in Zipes, *Trials and Tribulations*, p. 290.

173 "Red Cap": Otto Gmelin, in Zipes, *Trials and Tribulations*, pp. 274–277.

173 "If there's a beast in men": Quoted from the movie *A Company of Wolves* (1984).

173 Wolf Girls at Vassar: Their experiences are compiled in a book of the same title: *Wolf Girls at Vassar*, edited by Anne Mae Kay (New York: St. Martin's, 1992).

174 "Bitches were the first": J. Freeman, "The Bitch Manifesto" appears in Barbara Crow's reader, *Radical Feminism: A Documentary Reader*, (New York: New York University Press, 2000), pp. 226–232.

175 "Healthy wolves and healthy women": Clarissa Pinkola Estés, *Women Who Run With the Wolves*, 2nd ed. (New York: Ballantine, 1995), p. 2.

CHAPTER 8

191 "He had never ceased" : Ernest Thompson Seton's *Wild Animals I Have Known* (New York: Scribner, 1898/1991).

193 "The wolf lifted the latch": *Flatter,* vol. 8 (1996), p. 12.

194 "Categorical crisis": Marjorie Garber, *Vested Interests: Cross-Dressing and Cultural Anxiety* (New York: Routledge, 1997). Garber's exuberant study of cross-dressing ends with a conclusion entitled, "*A Tergo:* Red Riding Hood and the Wolf in Bed."

201 Gender was an *état:* Joan Dejean, *Ancients Against Moderns: Culture Wars and the Making of a Fin de Siècle* (Chicago: University of Chicago Press, 1997), pp. 120–121.

202 "Last chance, sister!": Circulating anonymously on the Internet as "Politically Correct Red Riding Hood."

202 "Conflict resolution" version: U.S. Department of Justice Kid's Page, http://www.usdoj.gov/kidspage/getinvolved/2_2_01.htm.

203 "The hero, whether god or goddess": Joseph Campbell, *The Hero With a Thousand Faces,* Bollingen Series, vol. 17 (Princeton: Princeton University Press, 1949), p. 108. Campbell also leads us to James Joyce, who says it this way: "Equals of opposites, evolved by a one-same power of nature or of spirit, as the sole condition and means of its himundher manifestation and polarised for reunion by the symphysis of their antipathies (*Finnegans Wake,* 1939).

CHAPTER 9

209 "After her century-long slumber": A. N. Roquelaure, *Beauty's Release: The Continued Erotic Adventures of Sleeping Beauty* (New York: E. P. Dutton, 1985), p. ix. It is the sequel to *The Claiming of Sleeping Beauty* and *Beauty's Punishment.*

209 Porn is here and here to stay: See Laura Kipnis, *Bound and Gagged: Pornography and the Politics of Fantasy in America* (Durham: Duke University Press, 1999), pp. vii–xiii, which makes this argument convincingly. The book is a wild ride through pornography's "dimly lit corridors."

213 "Literary pornography": Andrea Dworkin, *Woman Hating* (New York: Dutton, 1974), p. 53.

214 "Pornography involves an abstraction": Angela Carter, *The Sadeian Woman: An Exercise in Cultural History* (London: Virago Press, 2000), pp. 4–5.

215 "I can hint at dreams": Ibid.

CHAPTER 10

228 A single plot: See Vladimir Propp, *The Morphology of the Folktale,* 2nd
   ed., revised and edited by Louis A. Wagner, American Folklore Society
   Bibliographical and Special Series 9 (Austin, Tex.: University of Texas
   Press, 1968). In his essay "The Structural and Historical Study of the
   Wondertale," in *Theory and History of Folklore,* translated by Ariadna Y.
   Martin and Richard P. Martin, edited by Anatoly Liberman (Minneapolis: Minn.: University of Minnesota Press, 1984), Propp explains how he
   came to his insights on the fairy tale's structure: In a series of wonder-
   tales about the persecuted stepdaughter I noted an interesting fact: in
   "Morozko" . . . the stepmother sends her stepdaughter into the woods
   to Morozko. He tries to freeze her to death, but she speaks to him so
   sweetly and so humbly that he spares her, gives her a reward, and lets
   her go. The old woman's daughter, however, fails the test and perishes.
   In another tale the stepdaughter encounters not Morozko but a *lesij* [a
   wood goblin], in still another, a bear. But surely it is the same tale!
   Morozko, the *lesij,* and the bear test the stepdaughter and reward her
   each in his own way, but the plot does not change. . . . It is obvious that
   Morozko, the *lesij,* and the bear performed the same action. To
   Afanas'ev these were different tales because of different characters in
   them. To me they were identical because the actions of the characters
   were the same. The idea seemed interesting, and I began to examine
   other wondertales from the point of view of the actions performed by
   the characters. As a result of studying the material (and not through
   abstract reasoning), I devised a very simple method of analyzing wondertales in accordance with the characters' actions—regardless of their
   concrete form. To designate these actions I adopted the term "function."
229 Propp's ur-plot can be applied: "Little Red Riding Hood" is not technically a "wondertale." It may more accurately be called a folktale; but
   Propp's schema still applies.

BIBLIOGRAPHY

Aarne, A. *The Types of the Folktale: A Classification and Bibliography*, 2nd rev. ed. Translated and enlarged by S. Thompson. Helsinki: Academia Scientiarum Fennica, 1981; rev. ed., 1961. Originally published as *Verzeichnis der märchentypen*, FF Communications, no. 3, 1910. Reprint, Helsinki: Academia Scientiarum Fennica, 1959.

Ariès, P. *Centuries of Childhood: A Social History of Family Life*. New York: Vintage Books, 1962.

Backer, D.A.L. *Precious Women: A Feminist Phenomenon in the Age of Louis XIV*. New York: Basic Books, 1974.

Barber, E. W. *Women's Work: The First 20,000 Years: Women, Cloth, and Society in Early Times*. New York: W. W. Norton, 1994.

Barchilon, J., and P. Flinders. *Charles Perrault*. Boston: Twayne/G. K. Hall, 1981.

Baring-Gould, S. *The Book of Werewolves*. London: Senate/Studio Editions, 1995.

Basile, G. *Il Pentamerone*. 1847. Published as *The "Pentamerone" of Giambattista Basile,* edited and translated by Norman Penzer, 2 vols. London: John Lane and The Bodley Head, 1932.

Beauvoir, de, S. *The Second Sex*. New York: Alfred A. Knopf, 1953.

Bernheimer, K., ed. *Mirror, Mirror on the Wall*. New York: Doubleday, 1998.

Bettelheim, B. *The Uses of Enchantment: The Meaning and Importance of Fairy Tales*. New York: Random House/Vintage Books, 1977.

Bly, R. *Iron John: A Book About Men*. Reading, Mass.: Addison-Wesley, 1990.

Bodin, J. *De la demonomanie des sorciers*. Renaissance and Reformation Texts in Translation, vol. 7. Toronto: Centre for Reformation and Renaissance Studies, 1995.

Boguet, H. *An Examen of Witches*. London: John Rodker, 1929.

Bottigheimer, R. B. *Grimm's Bad Girls and Bold Boys*. New Haven, Conn.: Yale University Press, 1987.

Brownmiller, S. *Against Our Will: Men, Women and Rape*. New York: Ballantine Books, 1975.

_____. *In Our Time: Memoir of a Revolution*. New York: Delta, 1999.

Burguiere, A. "Family and Sexuality in French History: Introduction." In *Family and Sexuality in French History*, edited by R. Wheaton and T. Hareven. Philadelphia: University of Pennsylvania Press, 1980.

Calvino, I., ed. *Italian Folktales*. New York: Pantheon Books, 1956.

Campbell, J. *The Hero With a Thousand Faces*. Bollingen Series, vol. 17. Princeton: Princeton University Press, 1949.

Campbell, J., and B. Moyers. *The Power of Myth*. New York: Doubleday, 1988.

Carter, A. *The Bloody Chamber*. New York: Penguin Books, 1979.

_____. *The Sadeian Woman: An Exercise in Cultural History*. London: Virago Press, 2000.

Chafe, W. H. *The Paradox of Change: American Women in the 20th Century*. New York: Oxford University Press, 1991.

Choisy, de, A. *The Transvestite Memoirs*. London: Peter Owen Publishers, 1973.

Coontz, S. *The Way We Never Were*. New York: Basic Books, 1992.

Covington, C. "In Search of the Heroine." *Journal of Analytical Psychology* 34 (1989): 243–254.

Darnton, R. *The Great Cat Massacre*. New York: Vintage Books, 1985.

Davis, N. Z. *Society and Culture in Early Modern France: Eight Essays*. Stanford, Calif.: Stanford University Press, 1975.

DeJean, J. *Ancients Against Moderns: Culture Wars and the Making of a Fin de Siècle*. Chicago: University of Chicago Press, 1997.

Delarue, P. *The Borzoi Book of French Folk Tales*. Canada: Alfred A. Knopf, 1956.

Delarue, P., and M.-L. Tenèze. *Le Conte populaire français: catalogue raisonné des versions de France et des pays de langue française d'outre-mer: Canada, Louisiane, îlots français des Etats-Unis, Antilles francaises, Haïti, Ile Maurice, La Réunion*. Vol. 2. Paris: Erasme, 1957.

Dewald, J. *Aristocratic Experience and the Origins of Modern Culture: France, 1570–1715*. Berkeley: University of California Press, 1993.

Dreger, A. D. *Hermaphrodites and the Medical Invention of Sex*. Cambridge: Harvard University Press, 1998.

Dundes, A. *Analytic Essays in Folklore*. The Hague: Mouton, 1975.

———. "The Hero Pattern and the Life of Jesus." In *In Quest of the Hero*, by Otto Rank et al. Princeton: Princeton University Press, 1990.

———, ed. *Little Red Riding Hood: A Casebook*. Madison: University of Wisconsin Press, 1989.

Durant, A., and W. Durant. *The Age of Louis XIV*. The Story of Civilization, vol. 8. New York: Simon and Schuster, 1963.

Dworkin, A. *Woman Hating*. New York: Dutton, 1974.

Ellis, J. M. *One Fairy Story Too Many*. Chicago: University of Chicago Press, 1983.

Estés, C. P. *Women Who Run With the Wolves*, 2nd ed. New York: Ballantine Books, 1995.

Faguiet, P .M. E., ed. *Madame de Maintenon-Institutrice: Extraits de ses lettres, avis, entretiens, conversations et proverbes sur l'éducation*. Nouvelle édition ed. Librairie Classique. Paris: H. Odin, 1885.

Faludi, S. *Backlash: The Undeclared War Against American Women*. New York: Doubleday, 1991.

Febvre, L., and H.-J. Martin. *The Coming of the Book*. London: Verso, 1976.

Fenelon, A. *The Education of a Daughter*. Baltimore: John Murphy & Co., 1847.

Freeman, J. "The Bitch Manifesto." In *Radical Feminism: A Documentary Reader*, edited by Barbara A. Crow. New York: New York University Press, 2000.

Friedan, B. *The Feminine Mystique*. New York: W. W. Norton, 1963.

Fromm, E. *The Forgotten Language: An Introduction to the Understanding of Dreams*. New York: Grove Press, 1951.

Garber, M. *Vested Interests: Cross-Dressing and Cultural Identity*. New York: Routledge, 1997.

Gennep, van, A. *The Rites of Passage*. Chicago: University of Chicago Press, 1960.

Gilbert, S. M., and S. Gubar. *The Mad Woman in the Attic: The Woman Writer and the Nineteenth-Century Literary Imagination*, 2nd ed. New Haven, Conn.: Yale University Press, 2000.

Gilligan, C. *In a Different Voice*. Cambridge: Harvard University Press, 1982.

Gilligan, C., and L. M. Brown. *Meeting at the Crossroads: Women's Psychology and Girl's Development*. New York: Ballantine Books, 1992.

Gottlieb, B. "The Meaning of Clandestine Marriage." In *Family and Sexuality in French History,* edited by R. Wheaton and Tamara Hareven. Philadelphia: University of Pennsylvania Press, 1980.

Hanley, S. "Family and State in Early Modern France: The Marriage Pact." In *Connecting Spheres: Women in the Western World, 1500 to the Present,* edited by M. J. Boxer and J. H. Quataert. New York: Oxford University Press, 1987.

————. "Engendering the State: Family Formation and State Building in Early Modern France." *French Historical Studies* 16, no. 1 (1989): 4–27.

Herman, J. L., M.D. *Trauma and Recovery: The Aftermath of Violence—from Domestic Abuse to Political Terror.* New York: Basic Books, 1992.

Herodotus. *Herodotus: The Histories.* New York: Penguin, 1954.

Jones, S. S. "The Innocent Persecuted Heroine Genre: An Analysis of Its Structure and Themes." *Western Folklore* 52 (1993): 13–41.

Kane, P. *Victorian Families in Fact and Fiction.* New York: St. Martin's Press, 1995.

Kipnis, L. *Bound and Gagged: Pornography and the Politics of Fantasy in America.* Durham: Duke University Press, 1999.

Kirk, G. S. *Myth: Its Meaning and Functions in Ancient and Other Cultures.* Sather Lecture Series, vol. 40. Berkeley: University of California Press, 1970.

Kramer, H., and J. Sprenger. *Malleus maleficarum.* New York: Dover Publications, 1971.

Lang, A. *Popular Tales.* New York: Arno Press, 1977.

Leeming, D. A. *Mythology: The Voyage of the Hero.* Philadelphia: J. B. Lippincott, 1973.

Lopez, B. H. *Of Wolves and Men.* New York: Simon and Schuster, 1978.

Lougee, C. C. *Le Paradis des Femmes: Women, Salons and Social Stratification in Seventeenth Century France.* Princeton: Princeton University Press, 1976.

Martin, E. "The Egg and the Sperm: How Science Has Constructed a Romance Based on Stereotypical Male-Female Roles." *Signs* 16, no. 3 (1991): 485–501.

McGlathery, J. M. *Grimm's Fairy Tales: A History of Criticism on a Popular Classic.* Columbia, S.C.: Camden House, 1993.

Middlebrook, D. W. *Anne Sexton: A Biography.* Boston: Houghton Mifflin, 1991.

Mieder, W. "Survival Forms of 'Little Red Riding Hood' in Modern Society." *International Folklore Review* 2 (1982): 23–24.

Mitford, N. *The Sun King.* New York: Harper and Row, 1966.

Monter, E. W. *European Witchcraft.* New York: Wiley, 1969.

————. *Witchcraft in France and Switzerland: The Borderlands During the Reformation.* Ithaca, N.Y.: Cornell University Press, 1976.

Mossiker, F. *The Affair of the Poisons: Louis XIV, Madame de Montespan, and One of History's Great Unsolved Mysteries.* New York: Alfred A. Knopf, 1969.

————. *Madame de Sévigné: A Life and Letters.* New York: Columbia University Press, 1985.

Myers, R., and M. Harris, eds. *A Genius for Letters: Booksellers and Bookselling from the 16th to the 20th Century.* Newcastle, Del.: Oak Knoll Press, 1995.

Oakes, A., and M. H. Hill. *Rural Costume: Its Origins and Development in Western Europe and the British Isles.* London: B. T. Batsford, 1970.

Oates, C. "The Trial of a Teenage Werewolf, Bordeaux, 1603." *Criminal Justice History* 9 (1988): 1–29.

————. "Metamorphosis and Lycanthropy in Franche-Compte, 1521–1643." In *Fragments for a History of the Human Body,* edited by M. Feher. Cambridge, Mass.: MIT Press, 1989.

Ortner, S. B. *Making Gender: The Politics and Erotics of Culture.* Boston: Beacon Press, 1996.

Otten, C. F., ed. *A Lycanthropy Reader: Werewolves in Western Culture.* Syracuse: Syracuse University Press, 1986.

Patterson, H., and E. Conrad. *Scottsboro Boy.* Garden City, N.Y.: Doubleday, 1950.

Peppard, M. B. *Paths Through the Forest: A Biography of the Brothers Grimm.* New York: Holt, Rinehart and Winston, 1971.

Perrault, C. *Memoires de ma Vie.* Paris: Patte, 1769; Renouard, 1909.

Pollak, R. *The Creation of Dr. B: A Biography of Bruno Bettelheim.* New York: Simon and Schuster, 1997.

Propp, V. *The Morphology of the Folktale,* 2nd ed. Revised and edited by Louis A. Wagner. American Folklore Society, Bibliographical and Special Series 9. Austin: University of Texas Press, 1968.

————, ed. *Theory and History of Folklore.* Translated by Ariadna Y. Martin and Richard P. Martin. Edited by Anatoly Liberman. Minneapolis, Minn.: University of Minnesota Press, 1984.

Raglan, L. "The Hero: A Study in Tradition, Myth and Drama." In *In Quest of the Hero,* by Otto Rank et al. Princeton: Princeton University Press, 1990.

Rank, O. "The Myth of the Birth of the Hero." In *In Quest of the Hero,* by Otto Rank et al. Princeton: Princeton University Press, 1990.

Roheim, G. "Fairy Tale and Dream: 'Little Red Riding Hood.'" *The Psychoanalytic Study of the Child* 8 (1953): 394–403.

Roiphe, K. *The Morning After: Sex, Fear and Feminism on Campus.* Boston: Little, Brown, 1993.

Russell, D. E. H. *Sexual Exploitation: Rape, Child Sexual Abuse, and Sexual Harassment.* Beverly Hills, Calif.: Sage, 1984.

Schatten, Gerald, and Helen Schatten. "The Energetic Egg." *Medical World News* 23 (Jan. 23, 1984).

Seton, Ernest Thompson. *Wild Animals I Have Known.* New York: Charles Scribner's Sons, 1898. Reprinted 1991.

Sexton, A. *Transformations.* Boston: Mariner Books/Houghton Mifflin, 1971.

———. *The Complete Poems.* Boston: Houghton Mifflin, 1981.

Sexton, L. G. *Searching for Mercy Street.* Boston: Little, Brown, 1994.

Sexton, L. G., and L. Ames, eds. *Anne Sexton: A Self-Portrait in Letters.* Boston: Houghton Mifflin, 1977.

Shavit, Z. "The Concept of Childhood and Children's Folktales: Text Case—'Little Red Riding Hood.'" In *Little Red Riding Hood: A Casebook,* edited by A. Dundes. Madison: University of Wisconsin Press, 1989.

Soriano, M. *Les Contes de Perrault: Culture savante et traditions populaires.* Paris: Gallimard, 1968.

Spencer, S. I., ed. *French Women and the Age of Enlightenment.* Bloomington: Indiana University Press, 1984.

Stone, K. "Things Walt Disney Never Told Us." In *Women and Folklore,* edited by C. R. Farrer. Austin: University of Texas Press, 1975.

Storer, Mary Elizabeth. *Une épisode littéraire de la fin du 17eme siècle: La mode des contes de fées, 1685–1700.* Geneva: Slatkine Reprints, 1972.

Tatar, M. *The Hard Facts of the Grimms' Fairy Tales.* Princeton: Princeton University Press, 1987.

———. *Off With Their Heads!: Fairy Tales and the Culture of Childhood.* Princeton: Princeton University Press, 1992.

Turner, V. *The Ritual Process: Structure and Anti-Structure*. Symbol, Myth and Ritual Series. Ithaca, N.Y.: Cornell University Press, 1969.

Verdier, Yvonne. "Little Red Riding Hood in Oral Tradition," *Marvels and Tales: Journal of Fairy Tale Studies* 11, nos. 1–2 (1997), pp. 101–123.

Voltaire. *Le Siècle de Louis XIV* (The Age of Louis XIV). Translated by Martyn P. Pollack. New York: Dutton, 1978.

Warner, M. *From the Beast to the Blonde*. New York: Farrar Straus and Giroux, 1994.

_____, ed. *Wonder Tales*. New York: Farrar, Straus and Giroux, 1996.

Weyer, J. *On Witchcraft: An Abridged Translation of Johann Weyer's De Praestigiis Daemonum*. Edited by B. G. Kohl and H. C. E. Midelfort. Translated by J. Shea. Asheville, N.C.: Pegasus Press, 1998.

Wiesner, M. E. *Women and Gender in Early Modern Europe*, 2nd ed. New Approaches to European History. Cambridge: Cambridge University Press, 2000.

Wolf, N. *The Beauty Myth*. New York: Doubleday, 1991.

_____. *Promiscuities: The Secret Struggle for Womanhood*. New York: Fawcett Columbine/Ballantine, 1997.

Wurtzel, E. *Bitch: In Praise of Difficult Women*. New York: Doubleday, 1998.

Zarucchi, J. M. *Perrault's Morals for Moderns*. American University Studies, Series II, Romance Languages and Literature, vol. 28. New York: Peter Lang, 1985.

Ziegler, G. *The Court of Versailles in the Reign of Louis XIV*. London: George Allen and Unwin, 1966.

Zipes, J. *Breaking the Magic Spell: Radical Theories of Folk and Fairy Tales*. Austin: University of Texas Press, 1979.

_____. "A Second Gaze at Little Red Riding Hood's Trials and Tribulations." *The Lion and the Unicorn* 7–8 (1983–1984): 78–109.

_____. *Don't Bet on the Prince: Contemporary Feminist Fairy Tales in North America and England*. New York: Methuen, 1986.

_____. *Fairy Tales and the Art of Subversion: The Classical Genre for Children and the Process of Civilization*. New York: Routledge, 1991.

_____. *The Trials and Tribulations of Little Red Riding Hood*. Vol. 2. New York: Routledge, 1993.

Sources

I AM GRATEFUL to those who granted permission to use the following copyrighted works:

Max Factor "riding hood red" lipstick advertisement reprinted with the permission of Procter & Gamble Cosmetics/ Noxell Corporation.

Still image from Chanel No. 5 television commercial reproduced with permission by Chanel Inc., director Luc Besson and actress Estella Warren.

Engraving of Little Red Riding Hood in bed with wolf from Charles Perrault, "Le petit chaperon rouge," in *Histoires our contes du temps passé*. Paris, 1697, p. 47. Courtesy of the Rare Books Division, The New York Public Library, Astor, Lenox and Tilden Foundations.

Image of Mother Goose from the manuscript of Charles Perrault, *Les Contes de Perrault,* 1695. Courtesy of The Pierpont Morgan Library, New York. MA 1505, Frontispiece

Walter Crane's woodcut of hunter rescuing Red Riding Hood, from *The Blue Beard Picture Book,* illus. Walter Crane (London: G. Routledge, 1875) . Courtesy of the de Grummond Children's Literature Collection, The University of Southern Mississippi.

Victorian "Toy book" covers and inside pages from Lydia L. Very, *Red Riding Hood* (Boston, MA: L. Prang, 1863). Courtesy of the de Grummond Children's Literature Collection, The University of Southern Mississippi.

Image of grandmother putting cap on girl from Grimm, J. L. K. *Kinder und Hausmärchen, gesammelt durch die Brueder Grimm*. Berlin, 1847, frontispiece. Courtesy of the Rare Books Division, The New York Public Library, Astor, Lenox and Tilden Foundations.

Francis Wheatley, "A Woodman Returning Home, Evening," 1795. Courtesy of Christie's Images, New York.

Folded woodcut depicting the crimes and trial of Stubbe Peeter. Courtesy of Lambeth Palace Library, London.

"Lil' Red Riding Hood" written by Ronald Blackwell. Copyright 1966, Renewed 1994 Acuff-Rose Music, Inc. International Rights Secured. All Rights Reserved. Used by permission.

Two cartoon images from Tex Avery's "Red Hot Riding Hood," 1943. Red Hot Riding Hood © Turner Entertainment Co. An AOL/Time Warner Company. All Rights Reserved.

Drawing from James Thurber's "The Little Girl and the Wolf" in *Fables for Our Time* © 1940 James Thurber. Copyright © renewed 1968 by Helen Thurber and Rosemary A. Thurber. Reprinted by arrangement with Rosemary A. Thurber and The Barbara Hogenson Agency. All rights reserved.

Image of two princes, from *Into the Woods* by Stephen Sondheim and James Lapine, adapted and illustrated by Hudson Talbott, copyright © 1988 by Hudson Talbott. Used by permission of Crown Publishers, a division of Random House, Inc.

Image of Red Riding Hood stabbing the wolf, grandmother in background, by Trevor Skempton, originally appearing in "Red

Riding Hood," by the Merseyside Women's Liberation Movement, *Spare Rib* #51, 1972. Image reproduced with the kind permission of Mr. Trevor Skempton.

"The Waiting Wolf," from *Trail of Stones* by Gwen Strauss, copyright © 1990 by Gwen Strauss. Used by permission of Alfred A. Knopf Children's Books, a division of Random House, Inc.

"Daughter," by Kiki Smith, 1999. Collection of Kiki Smith, Courtesy of PaceWildenstein, New York.

Still image of Kim Cattrall as Red Riding Hood from Pepsi One television commercial, 2000. BBDO, New York for Pepsi-Cola Company. Reproduced by permission of Pepsi-Cola Company and with kind permission of Kim Cattrall.

"Little Red Riding Hood" verse and accompanying image of girl in wolf fur coat, from *Roald Dahl's Revolting Rhymes* by Roald Dahl, illustrated by Quentin Blake. Text copyright © 1982 by Roald Dahl. Illustrations copyright © 1982 by Quentin Blake. Used by permission of Alfred A. Knopf Children's Books, a division of Random House, Inc.

Illustration of girl in fur stole and hat, from *Into the Woods* by Stephen Sondheim and James Lapine, adapted and illustrated by Hudson Talbott, copyright © 1988 by Hudson Talbott. Used by permission of Crown Publishers, a division of Random House, Inc.

"Red Riding Hood," from *Transformations* by Anne Sexton. Copyright © 1971 by Anne Sexton. Reprinted by permission of Houghton Mifflin Company. All Rights Reserved.

Drawing of "expecting" wolf by Barbara Swann, also from *Transformations* by Anne Sexton. Reprinted by permission of Houghton Mifflin Company.

Illustration of Red Riding Hood in wolf's belly, from *Little Red Riding Hood* by Beni Montresor, copyright © 1989 by Beni Montresor. Used by permission of Doubleday, a division of Random House, Inc.

Advertisement for Heinz salad cream, reproduced with permission of H. J. Heinz Company Limited.

Still from *The Wolf Man*. Copyright © 2002 by Universal Studios. Courtesy of Universal Studios Publishing Rights, a Division of Universal Studios Licensing, Inc. All rights reserved. Chaney™ likeness reproduced with permission by Chaney Entertainment Inc. All rights reserved.

Photo of leather-clad motorcyclist and girl in red dress, by Ellen von Unwerth. Courtesy of eLUXURY.com. Reproduced with permission by Ellen von Unwerth. Likeness of female model used with permission by Devon Ayoki.

The Punishment of Red Riding Hood video box cover. Reproduced with permission by L.B.O. Entertainment Group, Los Angeles, California. www.lbodirect.com.

"Little Red Riding Crop" postcard. Artist: Carlos Aponte © Steve Mackes/S.O.M.E Graphics.

Photo of Reese Witherspoon and Bokeem Woodbine standing in front of Red Riding Hood mural, for the movie *Freeway*, written and directed by Matthew Bright, 1996. Reproduced with permission by Evelyn O'Neill for Reese Witherspoon and Michael Garnett for Bokeem Woodbine. Image of Reese Witherspoon and Kiefer Sutherland in car approved publicity photo from Kushner-Locke Company. All images from *Freeway* reproduced with permission of Freeway Productions, L.L.C.

Epilogue photo of janus-faced doll by Adriana Miranda, Copyright © Adriana Miranda, 2002.

ACKNOWLEDGMENTS

This book began as my college thesis just over a decade ago. If I had ever imagined that I would still be scouring the notes from my senior tutorials today, I would have written more legibly.

I am grateful for the mentors and friends who guided me through my thesis and through this book. Deborah Foster, head tutor of Harvard's Folk and Myth Department, read my senior thesis back when, and her criticisms then, I hope, made this book much better. It was a thrill to reconnect with her. My adviser, Bill Cole, became a dear friend and, despite his perfect recall of some of my most embarrassing stories, he remains a source of laughs and sound (but often disregarded) advice. I am grateful to Maria Tatar in Harvard's German department for her generous support and encouragement. Jack Zipes, at the University of Minnesota, provided me with my initial exposure to Little Red Riding Hood's many lives. His excellent anthology, *The Trials and Tribulations of Little Red Riding Hood,* is a must-read for anyone obsessed, as I am, with the fairy tale. I also owe him a personal debt for reading through my manuscript with a careful eye.

Many people were crucial to the creation of this book. Jeanne

Hanson noticed a letter I'd written in the *New York Times*, which started it all. I owe my sincere thanks to her for getting me into this. And my deep gratitude goes to Jo Ann Miller, my editor at Basic Books, for getting me out of it. Jo Ann stuck by me, forced me to turn it all in, and told me that one day I'd thank her for it. Jo Ann: Thank you. Thanks also to Kathy Strekfus, a most thorough copy editor, Felicity Tucker for making it all come together, Sharon Sharp, Candace Taylor, and those at Basic Books working on my book's behalf.

Many thanks to the following people for their invaluable contributions: French scholar Allison Stedman graciously read through my early chapters, draft after draft. Susan Brownmiller allowed me to test my ideas from chapter six out on her, to my great excitement. Joby Margadant read early versions of some of my chapters. Caroline Oates gave me insight on werewolves. Kurt Tappe allowed me access to his trove of Warner Brothers cartoons. Phyllis Ryfeld at *Vogue* went out of her way to find and page through old issues. Mathew Bright introduced me to the twisted side of fairy tales. Dee Jones at the amazing de Grummund Library kindly sent me images from Victorian picture books.

Ghita Schwarz, a sharp reader and bright spirit, brought out the best in my writing. Michele Wucker held my hand as I went through last-minute jitters and made smart suggestions. Miriam Horn gave my manuscript an intense edit. Her knowledge of women's history and attention to detail made this book much better. I'd also like to thank Miriam's daughter, Frannie, for the loan of her Red Riding Hood doll, a photo of which appears before my epilogue.

Sharon Landau took me out for walks, listened to countless versions of the same paragraph, and has been there for me through everything. Mo Smith and her parents, Jeff Smith and Mary Olive Smith, touched me with their support. Sandro Stille read my manuscript and became my confidant. My lifelong pal Leslie Price Fager introduced me to the fairy tale fiasco known as "Sex and the City." Danny Weiss showed me what a difference a good librarian can make. Fred Phillips never tired of distracting me. Scott Granneman resolved my technical disasters, and Dana Frankfort has been an uncommonly generous neighbor. Thanks also to Silver Stanfill for, among other things, making me aware of "ladle rat rotten hut," Leslie Yarmo for her creative eye, and Katya Wesolowski and Thad Dunning for their love and enthusiasm; and to Adriana Miranda, Andrea Labis, Kate Tedesco, Rainer Braun, Brian Jendrika, Rudi Stern, Nathalie Farman-Farma, Doug Krugman, and Rob Klein — who sent me a great tip about Walt Disney's first animated short (see the first page of my introduction). I am indebted to Mara Catalan for making me look like me, only better, to Rob Weiffbach for his timely advice, and to Elaine Markson for her kind and invaluable assistance. And a huge thanks to Jim Prusky, the best research assistant I will ever have, and a truly wonderful friend. Jim: I can't possibly tell you what your help and your friendship have meant to me all these years, and especially this one. Above all, my thanks and love to Ethan Herschenfeld, who stood by me and made me laugh — the most important things. How lucky I have been to know you.

Thanks to my family: My grandmother, Dorothy Bahr Manning, is a pillar of strength. I thank her for her support, and count myself blessed to descend from her. My brother, Jeff, lent me a desk in his office, and found the hilarious ad that precedes chapter eight. My sister-in-law, Sonnet Stanfill, came up with costume references and images that only a dress historian could find. My aunt Marcia Lee was a grounding force in my life from the first moment I began this project. She has been my friend, mentor, therapist and reader, and I can't imagine this book, or indeed my life, without her.

Finally, I thank my parents, the source of the best that I am and the best things that I do. Years ago my father, Moe Orenstein, showed his unfailing support by getting up with my brother and me each morning in the dark to drive us to the swimming pool — and then jumping in with us, day after day, year after year. I love my father for many things, but especially for teaching me to persevere. My mother, Grace Manning-Orenstein, is an extraordinary woman who has forged a powerful and meaningful life that I feel honored to hold up as a model for my own. She met and married my father in the span of a few weeks, and shortly thereafter they were off for two years in Africa. During that time Betty Friedan's *The Feminine Mystique* was published, and my mother once told me that she returned to a country different from the one she had left. Sometimes I think of my mother as the bridge between a world before the women's movement and the one I live in now — someone who has fought for a richer, fuller life and a more encompassing definition of femininity. My life reflects her hard-won battles, and I hope in some way my book does, too.

INDEX

Aarne, Antti, 72–74, 231
Aarne-Thompson Tale Type Index, 9,
    73–74, 227
Abraham, 101
A Company of Wolves, 165–67
Adam and Eve, 77
Aesop, 51, 94
Afanas'ev, A. N., 227
Against Our Will (Brownmiller), 144,
    151–52
"The Age of Louis the Great"
    (Perrault), 31
Alice in Bondageland, 208
allegory, 28
America
    courtship in, 112
    family in, 123
    women in, 117
American Werewolf in London, 188
Andersen, Hans Christian, 9
Ankers, Evelyn, 187
Antichrist, 101
Arcadia, 100
Aries, Philippe, 49
Artyne, Tyse, 91, 105
Asia, 69
Augustus, 31
Austen, Jane, 59
Avery, Tex, Red Riding Hood and, 6,
    112–20, 232–33
*A Woodman Returning Home,
    Evening* (Wheatley), 58

Babylon, 77
Bad Attitude Boutique, 216
Barbie, 196–97
Baring-Gould, Sabine, 96
Barnes and Noble, 3
Basile, Giambattista, 9, 83, 211
Baume de Blanche, Louise de la, 36
The Bear's Tale (Avery), 114
"Bearskin" (Murat), 176
beast feminism, 173–75
"Beauty and the Beast," 165, 172
Beauvoir, Simone de, 140–141, 144
Besson, Luc, 127
Best in Show, 189
Bettelheim, Bruno, 193
    fairy tales and, 11–12, 236
    "Little Red Cap" and, 70–71
    Red Riding Hood and, 22, 75
    wolf and, 93
Bible, 77
"Biblioteque bleue" (Perrault), 50
Bigg, William Redmore, 57
Big Momma's House, 7
Birthway, Inc., 197
bitch. *See* she-wolf

Bitch: In Praise of Difficult Women (Wurtzel), 174
Bitch Goddess, 169
"The Bitch Manifesto" (Freeman), 174
Blake, Quentin, 164
Blitzwolf (Avery), 116
Block, Francesca Lia, 147
blood, red cloak and, 163
The Bloody Chamber (Carter), 165
Bloomer, Amelia, 119
Bluebeard, 27, 34, 74–75
"Bluebeard" (Perrault), 55, 142–143
Bly, Robert, 196
Boccaccio, 9, 211
Bodin, Jean, 97
Boguet, Henri, 95–97, 166
Book of Nonsense (Lear), 51
Bound and Gagged (Kipnis), 209
Boy George, 196, 243
Boy Scouts of America, 190
Briffault, Louis and François, 68
Bright, Matthew, 221, 224, 234
Brochard, Jean, 151
Broumas, Olga, 162
Brown, Helen Gurley, 126, 127
Brownmiller, Susan, 144–47
   rape and, 150
Brun, Ferdinande-Henriette-Gabrielle de, 151
Bruyere, Jean de la, 32
Buddha, 79
bzou, 5

C.O.Y.O.T.E. (Call Off Your Old Tired Ethics), 173
Calvino, Italo, 69
Campbell, Joseph, 79, 80–81, 203
Canis lupus, 190
cannibalism, 69, 81–82, 102
Carter, Angela, 143, 165

fairy tales and pornography and, 214–215
she-wolf and, 165–70
Cattrall, Kim, 7, 169–70
Chace, H. L., 14
Chambre bleu, 29
Chanel, 127–28
Chaney, Lon, Jr., 106, 186, 187, 197
Charming, Sperm, 11
children
   fairy tales and, 7, 49
   literature for, 49–55, 92–93
   "Little Red Riding Hood" and, 3–4, 7
   in Victorian era, 48–49, 55–56
Children's and Household Tales (Grimm), 10, 46–47, 72, 122
China, 78
Choisy, abbe de, 199–201
Choo, Jimmy, 11
Cinderella, 15, 27, 34–35, 55
   fairy Godmother in, 235
   as heroine, 121, 122
   marriage and domesticity and, 123
   pornography and, 212
   science of folklore and, 75
   Sexton and, 136
   trials of, 141
Cinderella in Chains, 208, 210
class, 8
Clinton, Hillary, 209
clothing. *See* fashion
Colbert, Jean Baptiste, 30–31, 36
Communion, 4
contes de fees, 8, 28
Coontz, Stephanie, 123
Cosmo Girl, 127
costume. *See* fashion
Coulanges, Philippe-Emmanuel de, 35
Court of Dôle, 95
Crane, Walter, 5, 46, 51, 56, 232–33
Crawford, Joan, 119, 123

Cronos, 79
cross-dressing. *See* fashion
Cruise, Tom, 189
The Curse of the Queerwolf, 197
Curtis, Tony, 198

D'armencourt, Pierre, 30
D'Aulnoy, Marie-Catherine, 29, 48,
    176
d'Orleans, Le Duc, 24
Dahl, Roald, 163–64
Darnton, Robert, 12, 75–76
Daughter (Smith), 171–72
David, 79
Davis, Betty, 119
defecation, 69
DeJean, Joan, 200
Delarue, Paul
    cannibalism and, 81
    "The Grandmother's Tale" of,
        68–69
    science of folklore and, 74–75
"Delian Little Red Riding Hood"
    (Lake), 161
De praestigiis daemonum (Weyer), 97
de Soubise, Princess, 24
Devil
    of "Little Red Cap," 56
    werewolf and, 92, 103
    wolf and, 5, 95, 186
Dickens, Charles, 3
Dinah, 149–50
Dior, 126
Discours des Sorciers (Boguet), 97
Disney, Walt, 116, 117, 122
Divine, 196, 243
domesticity
    cult of, 123
    fairy tales and, 122
    femininity and, 165
"Donkey Skin,"
Doré, Gustave, 23
Dreger, Alice Domurat, 243

Dundes, Alan, 79
Dworkin, Andrea, 144
    fairy tales and pornography and,
        212–13

Earhart, Amelia, 119
Eberhard, Wolfram, 69
Edgar the Peaceful, 201
Egbert of Lieges, 71
Ego, 4
Emma (Austen), 59
Empathy Belly, 197–98
Encyclopedia Britannica, 15
Endangered Species Act of 1973,
    201
Enkidu, 172
Epic of Gilgamesh, 77
Estés, Clarissa Pinkola, 173, 175
The Eustace Diamonds (Trollope),
    60
Evans, Edmund, 51

*Fables for Our Time and Famous
    Poems* (Thurber), 118
The Fairies, 27
fairy tales
    allegory and, 28
    archetypal motifs and, 71–72
    in Asia, 69
    change and, 12–13
    children and, 7, 26–28
    culture and, 31
    definition of, 8–9
    domesticity and, 122
    fashion and, 160–62
    feminism and, 144–46
    in France, 28–35, 175–76
    goals of, 10
    heroines in, 121–24, 141–42
    history and, 9
    Hollywood and, 10
    marriage and, 33–34, 78, 122, 141

myths vs., 80–81
  patterns of, 78
  pornography and, 208–18
  rape and, 147–52
  salons and, 8, 31
  seventeenth century and, 8
  simplicity of, 8
  sources of, 9
  structure of, 227–32
"The False Grandmother" (Calvino), 69
family, 8
  in America, 123
  idealization of, 122–23
  Victorian, 50, 55
fashion
  fairy tales and, 160–62
  heroine and, 160–61, 162–67
  "Little Red Riding Hood" and, 162–67
  Red Riding Hood and, 56–58
  wolf and, 192–203
"Father Tuck's Little Folk Series," 55
Fecunda ratis (Egbert), 71
The Feminine Mystique (Friedan), 140
feminism
  beast, 173–75
  fairy tales and, 144–46
  "Little Red Riding Hood" and, 144–46
  salons and, 32
  Transformations (Sexton) and, 140
Fenelon, Abbe, 32–33
Flatter, 193
folklore, 9, 12
  oral, 75–78
  science of, 71–75
  women in, 70
"Fowler's Fowl" (Grimm), 55, 142–43
France
  fairy tales in, 28–35
  "Little Red Riding Hood" in, 5
  marriage and, 33–36

Frauen, 83
Freeman, Joreen, 174
Freeway, 5
  "Little Red Riding Hood" and, 224–37
  synopsis of, 221–22
  wolf in, 148
Freud, Sigmund, 242
Friedan, Betty, 140
"The Frog Prince," 172
Fromm, Erich, 70, 75–76, 213
From the Beast to the Blonde (Warner), 175
Fuseli, John Henry, 187

Gaffer, 105
Garber, Marjorie, 194
Garner, James, 161–62
Garnier, Gilles, 96, 103
Gauguin, Paul, 187
gender
  questioning of, 137, 145–46
  in seventeenth century, 200–201
  wolf and, 145–46
gender bending, 200–201
Gennep, Arnold van, 78
Germany, 10
GI Joe, 196–97
Gilgamesh, 172
"The Glutton," 73
Gmelin, Otto, 172–73
godsibb, 105
Goethe, 52
Gold, Tami, 171
Goldilocks, 114
Goldilocks and the 3 Bares, 208
Goliath, 79
Good, 4
grandmother
  dominance of, 160–62
  of Red Hot Riding Hood (Avery), 117

"The Grandmother's Tale" (Delarue), 65–67
  Aarne-Thompson Tale Type Index and, 74
  ending of, 77, 83, 166-67
  heroine of, 77, 82–83
  mythic hero and, 81
  sexuality and, 77
  themes of, 68–70
The Great Cat Massacre (Darnton), 76
Grenier, Jean, 96, 103
Gretel, 142
Grimm, Wilhelm and Jacob
  children's literature and, 51–55
  fairy tales of, 9–10, 135–36
  female heroines and, 82–83, 122
  female sources of, 83
  heroines of, 56–59, 135–36
  "Little Red Cap" and, 46–47
  original transcriptions of, 48
  popularity of, 53
  sources of, 47, 72
Guy, Susanne, 151

Hades, 80
"The Handless Maiden" (Grimm), 142
Hanley, Sarah, 150–51
Hansel, 142
Hassenpflug, Marie, 48
Hayworth, Rita, 119
"Her Kind" (Sexton), 139
hermaphrodites, 243–45
Hermaphrodites and the Medical Invention of Sex (Dreger), 243
hero, myth of, 79
Hero Cycle, 79–82
Herodotus, 100
heroines
  Cinderella, 114, 122, 141
  dominance of, 161
  escape of, 69–70

in fairy tales, 119–23
  fairy tales and, 141–43
  fashion and, 56, 160, 162–67
  plot and, 160–61
  Rapunzel, 141–42
  Red Riding Hood, 112–29
  rites of passage and, 78–79
  single, 119–27
  Sleeping Beauty, 143
  Snow White, 122, 142
  transformation of, 163–75
Hill, Anita, 152
History of Hippolite, Count of Douglas (D'Aulnoy), 29–30
History of the Marquis-Marquise of Bannerville, 198–99
Hitler, Adolph, 116
Hollywood, 10, 112
Holy Grail, 77
Hood, Wendy, 7
"Household of the Witch," 73
Hughes, Ted, 138
Huguenots, 48
hunter-woodsman, 60, 92, 136–37

"I Am Woman, Hear Me Roar," 173
The Ice Storm, 7
Id, 4
independence, 81
Industrial Revolution, 50
Ingres, Jean-August Dominique, 173
innocence, 3, 112
Innocent III, 101
Inquisition, 101
International Olympic Committee, 243
International Wolf Center, 202
Into the Woods (Sondheim), 121, 164
Iron John (Bly), 196
Isaac, 101
"The Island of Happiness" (D'Aulnoy), 29

Italian Folktales (Calvino), 69
Italy, 78, 93
It Could Have Happened Once Upon a
    Time, 216

Jacob, 79, 149–50
James and the Giant Peach (Dahl), 163
Japan, 78
Jesus Christ, 79, 95
Joan of Arc, 198
Johnny Walker red label, 126
Jordan, Neil, 165
Juggling Gender (Miller), 171
Jung, Carl, 77–78, 79
Jungle Book (Kipling), 94
Junior, 197
"The Juniper Tree" (Grimm), 54

Ken doll, 196
Kenobi, Obi Wan, 80, 235
Khan, Ghengis, 94
Kipling, Rudyard, 94
Kipnis, Laura, 209–10
Korea, 78
Kramer, Heinrich, 97
Kumin, Maxine, 138, 140

Ladies' Home Journal, 140
"Ladle Rat Rotten Hut" (Chace), 14
La Fayette, Comtesse de, 29
La Fontaine, Jean de, 94, 115
Lake, Rosemary, 161
la loba, 175
Lambeth Palace Library, 95
Lang, Arthur, 70
Larson, Gary, 193
Lawrence, Martin, 7
Leah, 149
Lear, Edward, 51
Le Conte populaire français (Tenéze
    and Delarue), 74
Lee, Tanith, 165, 168–69
legend, fairy tale vs., 8, 9

Lemmon, Jack, 198
"Le petit chaperon rouge" (Perrault),
    19–21, 23–28, 36–38
Les précieuses ridicules (Molière), 32
les ruelles, 29
lettre de cachet, 151
Levi, 150
Levi-Strauss, Claude, 242
Lhéritier de Villandon, Marie-Jean,
    30, 48
"Lil' Red Riding Hood" (Sam the
    Sham and the Pharaohs),
    109–11, 126–27
"Linnaeus of folklore." See Aarne,
    Antti
Lisel, 168, 169
"Little Red Cap" (Grimm), 41–45
    as allegory of obedience, 55–56
    ending of, 60–61
    epilogue of, 61
    heroine of, 56–59
    lesson of, 61
    plot of, 228, 229
    rites of passage and, 78–79
    sexuality and, 55–56, 70–71
"Little Red Riding Crop,9 215–18
"Little Red Riding Hood"
    Aarne-Thompson Tale Type Index
        and, 73
    adaptability of, 6–7
    adults and, 3
    archetypes of, 242
    change and, 13
    characters of, 5–6
    children's literature and, 3-4, 7,
        92–93
    as courtship story, 119–20
    English variants of, 105
    familiarity with, 3
    fashion and, 162–67
    femininity and, 144–46
    heroine of, 6, 92–93
    history of, 4, 25–27, 75–78

ideas behind, 7-8
innocence and, 3
lesbian retelling of, 162
lessons of, 4-5, 241
meaning of, 3–6, 26
Meyerside version of, 160, 162–63
as morality tale, 3
moral of, 37–38
mythic hero and, 80–82
oral cognates of, 75–78
paradox of, 237
plot of, 6-7
popularity of, 6-8, 13-15
power of, 4, 242
rape and, 146–52
sexual ethics and, 4
as sexual parable, 23–28, 36
symbolism in, 4, 36–37
themes of, 8
variations of, 3-4
Victorian versions of, 5-6
villain of, 103–105
violence and, 92–93
wolf of, 92–93
See also Red Riding Hood
"Little Red Riding Hood" (Perrault), 98–100, 150
"Little Red Riding Hood" (Sexton), 136–37, 179–85
"Little Red Riding Hood and the Wolf" (Dahl), 157–59
"Little Red Riding Hood—the Real Version" (Yap), 161
Little Red Walking Hood (Avery), 113–14, 117, 118
Little Rural Riding Hood (Avery), 114, 115
Lo cunto de li (Basile), 9
"Lon Po Po," 69
Lopez, Barry Holsten, 98, 201
Los Lobos, 186
The Loss of Virginity (Gauguin), 187

Louis XIV, 23, 28, 30, 31, 35, 48, 198, 199
loup-garou, 96
Lucas, George, 80
lupus in fabula, 93–94
lycanthrope, 101
lycanthropy, 97
Lycaon, King, 100, 101

Mackey, Frank T. J., 189–90
Madonna, 198
Magnolia, 189–90
Maiden Without Hands, 136
Maintenon, Madame de, 33
Making Gender (Ortner), 142
Malleus maleficarum (Kramer and Sprenger), 97, 102
manhood. *See* men
Märchenfrau of Niederzwehren, 48
mariage de raison, 35–36
Marie of France, 100
marriage
    clandestine, 35
    fairy tales and, 33–34, 78, 122–23, 141
    France and, 33–36
    seventeenth century and, 35, 150
    Victorian, 59–60
Mars, 94
masculinity, 195
Max Factor, 126, 127, 128
men
    in seventeenth century, 198
    in twentieth century, 196
    wolf and, 186, 194
    women vs., 4, 8, 242–45
menstrual blood, 4
menstruation, 70
Mercure Galant, 198
Merseyside Women's Liberation Movement, 160
Miller, Jennifer, 171
Millien, Achille, 68

misogyny, 195
mistaken identity, 69
mitonner, 28–29
Molière, 32
Mona Lisa, 24
Monsieur, 198, 200
Montespan, Marquise de, 34–35
Montressor, Beni, 194
morality, 8
Morland, George, 57
The Morning After (Roiphe), 147
Morphology of the Folktale (Propp), 227
Moses, 79
Mother Goose, 27–28, 83
Mother Goose Tales. *See* Tales of Times Past with Morals
Mowgli, 94
Mr. Mom, 194
Mrs. Doubtfire, 197
Ms. magazine, 152
Murat, Henriette-Julie de, 176
Musso, Paul, 161–62
myth
   fairy tale vs., 8, 9
   of hero, 79
mythology, 9, 80–81

Napoleon, 52
The Nation, 195
Neurians, 100
Newman, Charles, 138
The New Yorker, 126, 138
New York Radical Feminist Organization, 152
New York Times, 192
Nicholson, Jack, 188–89
Nightmare (Fuseli), 187
nineteenth century
   children's literature and, 51
   heroine of, 56
"Not So Little Red Riding Hood" (Sharpe), 148, 161

Nourry, Emile, 70
nursery rhyme, fairy tale vs., 9
Nyctimus, 100–101

obedience, 56, 60
Odalisque (Ingres), 173
Odysseus, 79, 80
Old Lobo of Currumpaw, 190–91
Old Regime, 5
Once Upon a Time When the Princess Rescued the Prince (Lake), 161
oral folktales, 75–78
Ortner, Sherry, 142
Ovid, 100, 101
Ozzie and Harriet, 123

Panchatantra, 77
The Parallel of the Ancients and Modernes (Perrault), 33
Parisian salons. *See* salons
Parker, Sarah Jessica, 11
Patterson, Haywood, 145–46
Peck, Gregory, 126
Peeter, Stubbe
   crimes of, 91–92, 101–102, 105
   story of, 95–96
   trial of, 91–92, 101
People magazine, 10
Perrault, Charles, 49, 50
   cross-dressing and, 198
   fairy tales and, 8-9, 29–31
   female protagonists of, 82–83
   female sources of, 83
   Grimm and, 48
   "Le petit chaperon rouge" of, 23–28, 36–38
   "Little Red Cap" and, 71
   marriage and, 123
   rape and, 149, 150–51
   violence and, 93
   wolf and, 187, 188
Pfeiffer, Michelle, 189
The Pharaohs, 6, 109, 126, 169

Piacevola notti (Straparola), 9
Pioche de la Vergne, Marie-
    Madeleine, 29
Plath, Sylvia, 138, 144
Pliny, 100
polygenesis, 77–78
Porky's, 170
pornography, fairy tales and, 207–18
Pretty Woman, 10
Pride and Prejudice (Austen), 58–60
Prince Charming, 121, 122, 143, 236
Prokofiev, 93–94
Promiscuities (Wolf), 147
Propp, Vladimir, structure of fairy
    tales and, 227–32
Prosser, D. W., 162
The Punishment of Red Riding Hood,
    208, 210–11, 212, 215–16
Puss 'n Boots, 27

"Quarrel of the Ancients and the
    Moderns," 31

Rabutin-Chantal, Marie de, 25
Raglan, Lord, 79
Raleigh Ensemble Players, 216
Rambouillet, Madame de, 29
Randall, Will, 189
Rank, Otto, 79, 81
rape, 4
    date, 147, 152
    fairy tales and, 146–52
    honor and, 149–50
    "Little Red Riding Hood" and,
        146–52
    pornography and, 213
rapt. *See* rape
Rapunzel, 54, 74, 121, 141–42
Ratjen, Hermann, 243
"Red Cap" (Gmelin), 172–73
red cape
    historical associations of, 162–63
    meanings of, 4

motif of, 75
sexuality and, 71
See also fashion
Reddy, Helen, 173
Red Hot Riding Hood (Avery), 112,
    114
    characters of, 115, 116–17
    grandmother of, 117
    heroine of, 115, 117–18, 119–20
    plot of, 116–17
    wolf of, 115, 117, 127
Red Riding Hood
    archetype of, 242
    availability of, 126
    Avery and, 112–20
    costume of, 56–59, 160–61
    as femme fatale, 123, 126
    as heroine, 111–29, 142
    as Hollywood stripper, 112–20
    illustrations of, 6, 22–23, 57 58
    innocence and, 112
    meanings of, 4, 15
    sex appeal of, 127–28
    twentieth century and, 112
    Victorian versions of, 46
    See also "Little Red Riding Hood"
"Red Riding Hood Redux" (Prosser),
    162
Remus, 94
Ricci, Christina, 7
Rice, Anne, 208
Ricky of the Tuft, 27
rite de passage, 78
Roald Dahl's Revolting Rhymes
    (Blake), 164
"The Robber Bridegroom" (Grimm),
    55
Roberts, Julia, 10
Roiphe, Katie, 147
Romulus, 94
Roquelaure, A. N. *See* Rice, Anne
Rosalee, 166–67
The Rose and the Beast (Block), 147

Rosie the Riveter, 116, 119, 122
Rotkappchen. *See* Little Red Cap
Rumplestiltskin, 82
RuPaul, 196, 243
Russell, Diana, 152

Saintyves, P. *See* Nourry, Emile
salons, 8, 30–33
Sam the Sham, 6, 109, 126–27, 169
Sand, George, 198
Saulx de Tavannes, Louis-Henri de, 151
"Scarlet," 148
Schiller, 52
Schwarzenegger, Arnold, 197
science, of folklore, 71–75
Scottsboro Boy (Patterson), 145
Scudery, Madeleine de, 29, 30
The Second Sex (Beauvoir), 140–41
Seinfeld, Jerry, 196
Sense and Sensibility (Austen), 59
sensitive new age guy (SNAG), 196
Seton, Ernest Thompson, 190
seventeenth century
  children's literature and, 50
  fairy tale and, 8
  gender in, 200–201
  marriage and, 35, 150
  men in, 198
  women and, 31
Sévigné, Madame de, 28, 29, 32, 35
Sévigné, Marquise de, 25
sewing, 82–83
"Sex and the City," 11, 170
Sex and the Single Girl (Brown), 126, 127
Sexton, Anne
  background of, 137–39
  feminism and, 139–40
  Grimms' fairy tales and, 135–36
  "Little Red Riding Hood" and, 136–37, 143–44
  poetry of, 139–40
  wolf and, 193, 194
Sexton, Linda, 135, 139
sexual harassment, 152
sexuality, 69
  Avery and, 117
  freedom and, 123
  "The Grandmother's Tale" (Delarue) and, 77
  "Little Red Cap" and, 70–71
  oral folktales and, 77
  questioning of, 137
  red cape and, 71, 163
Shakespeare, William, 198
Sharpe, Anne, 148, 161
Shechem, 149–50
she-wolf, transformation into, 163–70
Shields, Brooke, 221, 222
The Shooting of Dan McGoo (Avery), 115
Siddhartha, 79
Simeon, 150
sin, 163
Skywalker, Luke, 79, 80, 235
"Sleeping Beauty," 27, 34
  death spell of, 143
  heroine of, 121, 136, 143
  pornography and, 208–209, 211, 213, 215
  rites of passage and, 78
  science of folklore and, 75
  sewing and, 82
Sleeping Egg, 11
Smith, Kiki, 170–72
SNAG (sensitive new age guy), 196
Snow White
  death spell of, 143
  as heroine, 121, 136
  pornography and, 212
  rites of passage and, 78
  trials of, 142
Snow White and the Seven Dwarfs (Disney)

Disney and, 116
  heroine of, 117, 122
Some Like It Hot, 198
Sondheim, Stephen, 121, 164
Sprenger, Jacob, 97
Spy magazine, 209
Stars Wars, 80
sterility, 70
"The Story of O," 213, 215
Straparola, Giovanni Francesco, 9
Strauss, Gwen, 148
Suffragettes, 119
Sun King. *See* Louis XIV
Superman, 79
Sutherland, Kiefer, 221, 222, 234
Swan, Barbara, 194
Swing Shift Cinderella (Avery),
  114–16

Talbott, Hudson, 165
The Tale of Tales (Basile), 211
Tales of Terror, 103
Taylor, Edgar, 53
Tenèze, Marie-Louise, 74
"The Patience of Griselda" (Perrault),
  31, 33
Theseus, 79
"The Treacherous Cat," 73
Thomas, Clarence, 152
Thomason, Caroline Wasson, 93
Thompson, Stith, 73
Three Men and a Baby, 197
Thurber, James, 118, 119

"The Tiger's Bride" (Carter), 165
Timoléon, François, 200
Tom Thumb, 27
Tootsie, 198
Transformations (Sexton), 135
  contradictions and, 137
  femininism and, 140–41
  Sexton in, 138–39
The Trial of Stubbe Peeter, Werewolf,
  97–90
*The Trials and Tribulations of Little
  Red Riding Hood* (Zipes), 149
TriQuarterly, 138
Trollope, Anthony, 60
twentieth century
  men in, 196
  pop culture in, 119–20
  Red Riding Hood and, 112
  types, tale, 77–78
Types of the Folktale (Aarne), 73, 231

Uncle Remus, 94
Uncle Tom's Cabana (Avery), 115
universalism, 71
ur-plot, 227–29
The Uses of Enchantment
  (Bettleheim), 12, 22

Valliere, Duchess de la, 36
Verjuz, Jacques, 96
Versailles, 5, 23–25, 29

Witherspoon, Reese, 221, 234